RISE

RISE

SIYA
KOLISI

His truth
His story
In his words

WITH BORIS STARLING

HarperCollins*Publishers*

HarperCollins*Publishers*
1 London Bridge Street
London SE1 9GF

www.harpercollins.co.uk

HarperCollins*Publishers*
Macken House, 39/40 Mayor Street Upper
Dublin 1, D01 C9W8, Ireland

First published by HarperCollins*Publishers* 2021
This edition published 2023

5 7 9 10 8 6 4

All plate-section images courtesy of the author, with the following exceptions:
pp1, 2 Grey High School; p3 (top left and top right) Shaun Roy/Gallo Images/
Getty Images; p3 (bottom left) Carl Fourie/Gallo Images/Getty Images; p3 (bottom
right) Teaukura Moetaua/Getty Images; p6 (top) Colorsport/Craig Mercer;
p6 (middle and bottom) David Ramos/World Rugby/Getty Images; p13 (top left)
iSchoolAfrica; p15 (top) Ashley Vlotman/Sportsfile/Getty Images; p15 (bottom),
p16 (top left and top right) David Rogers/Getty Images; p16 (bottom)
EJ Langner/Gallo Images/Getty Images

A catalogue record of this book is
available from the British Library

ISBN 978-0-00-843137-2

Printed and bound in the UK using 100%
renewable electricity at CPI Group (UK) Ltd

To my wife Rachel. I dedicate this book to you! Without you my story wouldn't be complete because you helped and keep helping me to be the man that I'm striving to be every day. Your kindness, love, care, honesty and support have helped me to push through everything life has thrown at me. Thank you for your unconditional love and for loving my perfect imperfections.

To Nick and Keziah. Thank you for the gift of being your father. I hope one day you will look and see a father who was not perfect, but who loved you with the energy of a million suns and tried his best to set you up well for your own stories.

To Liyema and Liphelo. Thank you for giving me more to live for. Your strength and resilience encourage me to keep going despite any challenges and obstacles in my journey.

To my gran, aunt and mama. Honestly, I don't know where I would be without you all. You taught me the definition of the word 'sacrifice'. I will forever be living to make you all proud in everything that I do.

A NOTE ON THE TITLE

There are several reasons why this book is called *Rise*. The title refers to my journey from a township childhood to captain of a World Cup-winning Springbok team, and also to the progress that I am working to bring about in my beloved South Africa. Most of all, however, 'rise' is the English meaning of my mother's name Phakama. She is no longer here, but I hope she would be proud of me.

CONTENTS

PROLOGUE

YOKOHAMA, JAPAN, 2 NOVEMBER 2019

It's not every day that the President himself addresses us before a match. Then again, it's not every day that we're playing in a World Cup Final.

'Many people did not believe that you would come to this hour of destiny,' says Tata. Most people know him as Cyril Ramaphosa, President of South Africa, but to me he's just Tata. The room we are in is usually a place of noise and energy; it's where team meetings are held, where last night the coaching staff handed out our jerseys one by one with hugs and words of encouragement. Now it's so quiet I could hear a pin drop. 'But you *are* at that moment of destiny: for yourselves, as individual players, and for the country. Go out there on that pitch and play your hearts out. Play the best game that you have ever played.'

Play the best game that you have ever played.

His words stay with me as we file out of the room, through the hotel lobby and onto the bus. I smile at the fans held back behind roped barriers, cheering and clapping as we come past. Their presence, and Tata's, remind me that back home the entire country will be watching. People of every race, colour and creed will for a few hours, all come together to will us on with every fibre of their beings.

The bus wends its way through the traffic. Everyone's got their headphones on, lost in whatever music they use to help get themselves in the right frame of mind for such a momentous occasion. The stadium appears to our left, a hulking stone monolith swarming with green and white: our fans and England's, spectators buzzing with the excitement of being at the match of a lifetime, people who've dropped everything and spent small fortunes to fly halfway round the world.

In through a side entrance, down to an underground area, off the bus and through the corridors to our dressing room, immaculately prepared by the logistics guys. We each have our own personal cubicle in which our kit is laid out, and on the big tables in the middle are trays of food: last-minute energy for anyone who wants it. A whiteboard in the corner has the warm-up times written on it, each one down to the minute: 17.09 kickers out, 17.14 hookers out, 17.21 props out.

The physios strap us up: ankles, knees, wrists, shoulders, heads, wherever we need it. Our coach Rassie Erasmus – in the lucky white shirt that he's been wearing ever since we played Namibia in the pool stage, five straight wins ago and counting – gives us one last team talk.

'To be in a World Cup Final is a big thing. You might have been in the Currie Cup final: that's good. You might have been in a Super Rugby final: that's great. But a World Cup Final

– this is the one place where you can't have a regret. If you don't leave everything out there, you've wasted your whole lives leading up to this point.' Coach Rassie pauses, careful as always to get his words exactly right. 'If you lose a lineout, jump up and go and make the next tackle. If you miss a tackle, jump up and go and do the next cleanout. If you miss a high ball, go up for the next one. You don't have the right to worry about your mistakes. If you worry about your mistakes, you're cocky, you've got an ego problem. Because you're not representing yourselves today. It's not about you.'

He looks at me, coach to captain. 'You are fighting, Siya, for the next *lightie* in Zwide to not suffer like you suffered.' A flash in my mind, no more, of a childhood during which leading my country in a World Cup Final seemed as remote and unlikely as walking on the moon. Coach Rassie turns to our outside centre Lukhanyo Am. 'Lukhanyo, you are tackling for the boy who didn't get the opportunities that you eventually got.'

There are nods, murmurs of assent. Everyone agrees 100 per cent with what he's saying. I've been playing rugby for 20 years – schoolboy, age-group, provincial, franchise, international – and I've never played for a team as united in its desire to win as this one. From the moment Coach Rassie took over 18 months ago, he looked not just for good players but ones who have a bit of 'dog' in them: men who refuse to give up, who go to the well for each other time and again, who always have each other's backs. I trust each of them absolutely and completely.

There are the forwards. Beast, the veteran campaigner with more than 100 caps: the sweetest guy off the pitch and a rampaging monster on it. Bongi, a coiled cannonball of spiky aggression who always brings the noise. Frans, the anchor at tighthead who puts in a huge amount of work without fuss. Eben, one of my closest mates: the enforcer, the dominator, the giant with biceps like bowling balls. Lood, so skilful for such a tall and rangy guy. Pieter-Steph, the silent assassin who plays at full tilt for 80 minutes without flagging or tiring in any way. Duane, a rock at the base of the scrum: mammoth in defence, and in attack the kind of guy who'd run through a brick wall if the wall didn't step aside first through sheer terror.

There are the backs. Faf, the heartbeat at scrum-half with his Eighties rocker hair and willingness to take on guys twice his size. Handre, the kingpin at 10: ice cool, never gets flustered, keeps us going forward with his pinpoint kicking. Damian, who's hammered his way through the 12-channel in every match we've played, the hard-carrying bludgeon to the rapier outside him that is Lukhanyo with his lightning-quick rugby brain, a man who sees gaps and opportunities before they even unfold. Mapimpi, whose journey here has been even further and more arduous than mine, and who's absolutely lethal, given a sniff of the tryline. Cheslin, the magic man with the dancing feet, the hotstepper who can conjure space from nothing. Willie, the glue at full-back who pulls it all together and helps keep the energy high.

There's the Bomb Squad: Malcolm, Kitsie, Vincent, RG, Franco, Flo, Herschel and Francois. Every other team has replacements, but we've got the Bomb Squad: a gang within a gang, the guys who come onto the field like an explosion, who fix things if they need fixing or just keep on smashing through if we're on top. Every other team wishes they had the Bomb Squad; every other team fears them and what they can do.

There are the guys who aren't in the matchday 23: Schalk, Thomas, Kwagga, Cobus, Elton, Damian, S'bu and Warrick. They sit in the stands today, but they're just as vital as any of us on the pitch. They're the ones who've been playing the opposition roles in training, they're the ones who've been studying the guys we're going to come up against, and they're the ones who've helped keep the squad morale high.

And then there are Trevor and Jesse, who were injured in our first match and needed to be replaced, but who've been flown back out here so they can be with us for this, the biggest match of our lives. They walked into the hotel dining room when we were having breakfast this morning, and it gave everyone such a boost.

We 33, we band of brothers: we hold each other's hopes and dreams in our hands, and we will not let them go.

Play the best game that you have ever played.

An official appears at the door. Five minutes to go.

Our cubicles are in strict order according to our shirt numbers. Five is Lood, sitting with his elbows on his knees and his head in a towel, blotting it all out so he can concentrate on what he needs to do. Seven is Pieter-Steph, leaning back against the wall and staring into space as he breathes deeply.

I am six, and in Springbok folklore six is more than just another number. Six was the number Francois Pienaar wore when he became the first South African captain to win the World Cup in 1995; six was also the number on the back of Nelson Mandela's jersey when he took to the field before and after that historic final. Mr Mandela is one of my heroes – I have his face tattooed on my back – so wearing this number is special to me, and I never forget that. I turn to the wall and begin to pray: thanking God for my talent and for the opportunity, letting Him take over my body and do His work through me, and asking not that we win but simply that we do ourselves and our people proud.

These are the moments which make lives; the moments which years or decades down the road will burn as brightly as they do right now. It's an inestimable privilege to be here. This is our Everest, a match just like any other and yet a match unlike every other, a match which every player fears and relishes in equal measure. I feel at peace.

Two minutes.

Studs clattering on the floor. We hug each other, moving from man to man, a quick embrace and on to the next one; small recognitions of how far we've come, how near we are to the ultimate prize, and how we would rather die than let each other down. Some of these guys I've known for a decade or more, others have only made it into the squad in the past year or so. No matter. Today of all days, we are brothers.

Time to look each other in the eye. Time to believe. Time to go.

I lead the team out of the changing room. An official with a clipboard ushers me along a corridor, with a cameraman filming as he walks backwards ahead of me. My studs are silent on the blue carpet. Behind me, the boys follow in a single file of single purpose; game faces on, minds and bodies primed.

The official holds us at the mouth of the tunnel, the two teams alongside each other. The crowd noise is like thunder, rolling in great waves down from the stands. We're given the signal and out of the tunnel we come. The trophy sits on a plinth ahead of us, and I don't look at it, not for a second, not now. I clasp the hand of the young boy acting as our mascot, look up to the sky and give a quick final prayer. Vast sections of the stands are swathed in green: our fans, all on their feet hollering their support.

We line up for the anthems. England go first, and then it's our turn. 'Nkosi Sikelel'iAfrika' is one of the most beautiful pieces of music I know, but it's more than that. With its words in five languages – isiXhosa, isiZulu, Sesotho, Afrikaans and English, one after the other – it's so perfectly resonant for a team that has come together from all corners of our country. I close my eyes and sing as loud as I can, so loud that I want the stadium to shudder with the force of containing me.

Nkosi Sikelel'iAfrika
Maluphakanyisw' uphondo lwayo.

Our country in all its beauty. The blood orange of dawn in the Karoo and the long shadows over the desert scrub; the sudden green of fruit farms and vineyards in the lee of the Hex River Pass; the great slab of Table Mountain rising over Cape Town.

Yizwa imithandazo yethu,
Nkosi sikelela, thina lusapho lwayo.

Our country with all its problems. Scores of murders and rapes every week, and for every one that's reported there are many more which remain hidden. An epidemic of violence which never seems to stop, no matter the women all across the land who marched in protest a few months ago because they'd just had enough.

> Morena boloka setjhaba sa heso,
> O fedise dintwa le matshwenyeho,
> O se boloke, O se boloke setjhaba sa heso,
> Setjhaba sa South Afrika – South Afrika.

The millions of unemployed, some not just without jobs but without hope too. Entire generations lost to themselves and each other. Twenty-five years after apartheid, and still so much inequality remains. Gleaming towers of glass and steel squeezed next to shantytowns; tycoons in their limos and windscreen washers who pitch for pennies at traffic lights.

> Uit die blou van onse hemel,
> Uit die diepte van ons see,
> Oor ons ewige gebergtes,
> Waar die kranse antwoord gee.

And despite all this we are a great people, we South Africans. We are a great people, and we are good people: kind, generous, passionate, fun-loving, open, talented, creative, driven, resilient, people who work hard in the week and on the weekends love nothing more than to meet with our friends and enjoy their company. History has battered our country time and time again, and still we endure.

> Sounds the call to come together,
> And united we shall stand,
> Let us live and strive for freedom,
> In South Africa our land.

Many people see England as favourites. They walloped the All Blacks in their semi-final; we beat Wales in a tight match. The English press think their team's got one hand on the trophy already. But this just gives us even more motivation. We are playing for more than they are. We are playing for more than they can possibly imagine. Last night, my wife Rachel and I wrote down all the things we'd like to do to help our country if we win today.

Flames fire as the anthem ends. We break and take up our positions for the kick-off. Lives poured into funnels: all the training and matches, all the injuries and pressure, all the sacrifices and rewards, all the triumphs and disasters narrowed down to the next couple of hours. After that we will know, and there will only be the match that was played rather than the infinite number of possible ones that weren't. The same equation, binary and ruthless, for each man: win and be immortal, lose and be just another of the nearly men.

Play the best game that you have ever played.

Jérôme Garcès, the referee, calls out. 'White, ready? Green, ready?'

Beast's face is sheened with sweat. Mapimpi is hopping from foot to foot. Handre's geeing everyone up. Oh, we're ready. We've been ready a long time.

A hush. A moment, so brief as to be almost undetectable, when the world slows its spinning and is held in suspension. Then the whistle, and the roar, and every pair of eyes on the pitch and in the stadium and around the world is watching the ball as Handre sends it tumbling end over end into the night sky.

Showtime.

1

SCHOOLBOY

I was born on the last day of apartheid.

It was June 1991. On the 17th, the day after I was born, parliament repealed the laws underpinning the system which had for so long discriminated against black people and made us second-class citizens in our own country, confined to separate areas, separate public transport and separate schools. My birthday is also Youth Day, when we celebrate our young people in memory of the hundreds of children killed during the Soweto uprising of 1976. It's pure coincidence that my birth date has such connections, of course, but every South African can find similar things in their own lives if they look hard enough: for our country is one where history is not buried in the past but being made anew every day, and each one of us is a link between the past and the future.

I was born and brought up in a township called Zwide, just outside the Eastern Cape city of Port Elizabeth (usually abbreviated to PE or, as we called it in isiXhosa, iBhayi, but now officially named Gqeberha). It is a beautiful city full of colonial-era buildings in several different architectural styles: Victorian

Gothic, Art Deco and Cape Dutch. Its people are friendly, the weather is great, and if you like tourism and sports you can't go far wrong. But for us in Zwide, only 15 minutes away from the city centre, it may as well have been on another planet. We had no reason to go there, and even if we did, we usually didn't have enough money for the journey, short though it was. For the first decade of my life, Zwide was all I knew: it was literally my entire world.

It was a typical township, the kind of place that looks permanently half-finished. Traffic would weave around potholes deep enough to break axles, pavements were often compacted earth rather than tarmac. Some houses were made of stone or concrete and others from tin, which is a terrible material for building: in the summer it keeps none of the heat out and in the winter it keeps none of the warmth in. Some houses had walls or railings outside them, others made do with a few planks nailed together. Toilets were usually outside and often shared between several houses: sometimes the sewers ran in the open alongside the roads, and planks of wood would act as makeshift pontoons. Streetlights might sprout cables from the wiring box where people had tapped into it and were running the electricity off to their own homes. Shops weren't always proper buildings with amenities and windows: often they were shacks or kiosks, and they'd sell things like cigarettes or sweets as individual items, rather than in their packets, as that's all most people could afford. Cars often had one door a different colour than the rest: a quick cut-and-shut job with a welding torch. On garbage collection days the streets would be busy from dawn, with people going through the sacks for anything they could use or sell before the municipal workers came along.

Our house had four rooms: a kitchen, a living room and two bedrooms. The kitchen floor was made from black and white blocks which didn't stop the water rising through them when it had been raining heavily, the roof was always leaking, and the curtains were so thin that the house was light as soon as dawn broke. Four rooms might sound spacious enough, but not when you consider all the people who were living there. There were usually six or seven, sometimes more. It was cramped and we were always on top of each other. My bed was a pile of cushions on the floor, and most nights I could hear the rats running around and feel them as they scampered over me. If I got up in the night, I'd have to tiptoe round various sleeping bodies just to get to the door.

My parents were both teenagers. My mother Phakama was 18 – for a long time I thought she was only 16 when she had me, but recently I've discovered otherwise – and my father Fezakele was 15. They weren't much more than kids themselves. My mother was beautiful, bubbly and vivacious. She was the life and soul of things; she used to light up every room she went into, and she'd light up whenever she saw *me*, taking me round to all her friends. She lived with her own family, including two old men I used to call 'grandpa'. They both loved me and would give me whatever money they had spare when I went round. I would visit whenever I could. She used to wash me at an outside tap in the yard when I was a small child, and sometimes my uncle would sneak up with a rubber snake and scare me. I'd scream and run stark naked at top speed all the way to my father's house. My mother thought this was the funniest thing ever.

It was decided very early on in my life that my father's mother would look after me as my father was away working so much. He was a housepainter and he went where the work took him, often as far away as Cape Town, where he'd stay for weeks or even months until the job was done. This was a very common arrangement in Zwide, and many children were raised by their grandparents.

There have been many important people in my life over the years, people who have guided and shaped me, but none more so than my grandmother. I called her 'auntie', and without her I wouldn't be here. That's not a figure of speech. She was always there for me, no matter what else was going on: always positive, loving, supportive and protective. She carried herself well and always made sure she looked good no matter the circumstances, not because she was vain but because she wanted people to know that the Kolisi family had standards. For a while she worked at the Shatterprufe glass factory in PE, which gave us a steady income, and she'd help out other people when she got paid. Like most of Zwide's residents, she did the best she could for as many people as she could. For such a poor place, there were very few beggars in Zwide: people looked out for each other and gave what they could, even if it wasn't very much. There's a lot less inequality when no-one's got a lot to start with. When someone had a job and was earning steady money, they'd often help other people out, knowing that one day the tables might be turned. The help came by way of food as much as it did money: there'd be large communal pots of meat and vegetables with a side of *mielie pap* (maize porridge), and whoever was hungry could take their share. Jobs were hard to come by and easy to lose: for those who worked at a factory and didn't make it into work a few times because the bus service had broken down or they needed to look after a sick family member, good luck persuading their boss to keep the position safe for them.

My grandmother eventually lost her job at Shatterprufe, though it may just have been that they were reorganising rather than anything she had or hadn't done. She started cleaning other people's houses, but the money was neither as good nor as regular as it had been before. I did what I could to help: I was selling alcohol and vegetables on the street, and sometimes making bricks too. I can't have been more than eight or nine. Sometimes we didn't have enough money for my school fees, even though they were only R50 – three dollars – each year. Once, when we didn't have enough money to buy me a new pair of shoes, I wore my aunt's shoes to school, and the other kids teased me about it for months. We were certainly too poor to afford toys. I used to use a brick and pretend it was a car. It was the best thing ever. And I spent as much time with my grandmother as I could when both of us were at home. No matter what the week had brought, Sunday was our day together. She'd take me to church and Sunday school, and I loved those times so much: not just because I was with her, but also because the singing was so beautifully joyous and because everyone dressed in their best clothes and made a real effort.

But she was also getting older, and so she could work less and less, which of course meant that sometimes we didn't have enough money for food. When she went to visit friends, she'd bring back whatever food they'd given her, whether it was biscuits or bread or anything like that, and give it to me. When times were hard, she'd go without food for days on end in order to ensure that I ate. Even if it was just a teaspoon of sugar, that was better than nothing, and she would make sure I had it rather than her. I used to see her struggling, but she never cried and she never took anything for herself unless there was enough for me too.

Even so, hunger was a big part of my childhood. During term time, I knew I'd get at least one meal each day at school. Sometimes it wasn't much – powdered milk and a thick slice of white bread smeared with peanut butter, perhaps a plate of chicken with rice or *samp* (dried maize kernels) – but it was better than nothing. Outside of term time, I didn't even have that safety net. When there was no food in our house, I would hang out at the neighbours' places and ask for food. They'd give whatever they could, sometimes allowing me to keep my pride – and more importantly my family's – by getting me to fetch something from the store and then giving me food as a reward.

But there were many times when even this wasn't enough. It's hard to explain hunger, proper hunger, to people who've never experienced it. Hunger is not just being hungry, the brief sensation of discomfort which lasts only a few hours until the next meal. Being hungry is easy and commonplace. Hunger is different. It's all-consuming. It was all I could feel and all I could think about. My stomach seemed to twist in on itself, and the more I tried to ignore the pain there the worse it got. My lips felt dry, and licking them made a difference only for a second or two: then they were parched and cracked again. I had no energy so sleep sometimes came easily, but that only hid the hunger rather than cured it, and in the small hours I'd jerk awake involuntarily and the agony was worse than ever. I'd drink lots of water to fill my stomach and trick my body into feeling full. If there was any sugar around, I'd spoon that in to make the water taste sweeter and to give me some calories, but if there wasn't then I'd just go without. I'd feel light-headed and dizzy, as though my thoughts would fly clean away, but those thoughts were simply replaced by more of the same: where can I find food, what can I see that's even vaguely edible, what would I do if only I could get to eat, when will this pain stop? It wasn't always as bad as this, of course, but nor was this uncommon, and once I'd experienced it, I'd never forget it.

Eventually, my grandmother couldn't work at all. She would forget stuff: I'd walk into the kitchen and she'd be just staring into space as if she didn't know where she was. Sometimes she'd vanish and not come back for hours or even days. It wasn't uncommon for older people to disappear suddenly, and for some of them that was the last time they were ever seen. To this day, I don't know what happened to them: whether they just got confused, wandered off and couldn't get back home, maybe got hit by a car or something. When my grandmother got really bad, I'd have to wash, feed and sit with her the whole time, so much so that I couldn't go to school for a while. She'd say things that didn't make sense and there was nothing I could do: just be with her and hope she understood that I loved her as much as she did me.

One day she walked into the kitchen, smiled, gave me an affectionate slap on the cheek, and fell over. It happened almost in slow motion, and I caught her as she fell. I put her down on the floor and she just lay there, totally still. I didn't know what to do. There was a pastor living next door, so I ran to get him and practically dragged him back to the house. He knelt by her body and felt for a pulse, just like people do in the movies, and he told me she had passed. There was no doctor, no ambulance. She'd had a hard life, like pretty much everyone in Zwide, and so her death came as no surprise to any of the adults there. There was a lot of death. 'Weekends are for funerals': that's how the saying went. There was a funeral every weekend, often more than one. Everyone was welcome at a funeral, and you didn't have to dress nicely. The number of people at your funeral was a measure of how much you were loved in the community.

The choir from my grandmother's church sang at her funeral, which reminded me of her and all the happy Sundays we'd spent together. My aunt, uncle and cousins were all there, but my dad wasn't: he was working in Cape Town, eight hours' drive away, and since he didn't have a cellphone, no-one could get hold of him and tell him what had happened. No-one really paid me much attention, even though everyone knew I'd been her favourite. It was one of those times when as a child the adult world seems a total mystery to you, a different planet with its own laws and language and way of doing things.

After my grandmother died my aunt raised me, and she did a great job. She didn't take any attitude from me: if I didn't do chores then I didn't get fed, simple as that. But I still felt that the one person who'd loved me unconditionally had gone, and without her, Zwide could seem an even scarier place than before. Neighbourhoods like this are always plagued by crime and violence, and Zwide was no exception. Along with the hunger, the violence is one of my strongest and most visceral memories of my childhood.

People fought, all the time. Men fought with men, men beat women – my mother and other women in my family were subjected to violence – and men and women beat children. People were angry, sometimes they were drunk, and when everyone is prepared to resort to violence at the drop of a hat then it becomes totally normal, that was just how it was. Often I'd be woken in the night by screams and shouts outside, and when I went to the window I'd see brutal beatings happening in the street. Sometimes it was my dad, and the sounds of him crying and screaming used to go straight through me and chill me to the bone. When a man screams it's a very specific sound, a very animal sound: it's not just pain, but shame and humiliation too. I heard that sound from my dad time and again in my childhood, and there was never anything I could do to stop it or help him.

The police never got involved, of course. Crime, punishment, retribution, justice … they were all done by Zwide people inside Zwide's boundaries. That's where it started, and that's where it ended. There was an occasion in the Oom Cola Tavern – the place where I ended up watching the Springboks win the 2007 World Cup Final – when a man beat up his girlfriend for going out without him. He kicked her, smashed her face against the wall and then dragged her out of the bar by her hair, and no-one intervened. There were hundreds of people there, and not one of them did or said a thing.

Only when something was seen as affecting the whole community did people take action. There was one guy who'd been in a gang but had got out of it and got his life together. He was working, he had a job, he was doing well for himself. Then someone saw him wearing a new pair of shoes and just presumed he'd stolen them or bought them with gang money. It was at a time when the community had had enough of gangsters, and all they knew was that this guy had a reputation and a flash pair of shoes. They didn't know he'd gone straight, and even if they had known they probably wouldn't have cared. They set on him with rocks and stoned him to death. His mother was watching, and even that didn't stop them. I saw a girl of about 11 or 12, not much older than I was at the time, pick up a rock and throw it at his head, just like everyone else had done. I watched this man as the life went out of him: I saw him pass from life to death, I saw the moment the last breath went out of him.

It was at a time when I was starting to hang out with some kids who were a bit older than me, and doing what they were doing: drinking, smoking weed, sniffing petrol. We'd squeeze five rands' worth out of the pump, shake it up in a plastic bottle and inhale the fumes. I was only eight or nine, thinking I was tough and just wanting to fit in. If I'd gone much further down that path, I could have ended up a *tsotsi*, a young criminal, and from there you only have two real options: jail or death. Or both.

* * *

It was rugby that saved me. Sport was part of my life for as long as I can remember. I started out playing soccer: like every kid I wanted to be a striker, but soon enough I was moved back to defender and then to goalkeeper. I loved playing goalie, especially in street soccer when I'd dive all over the place and not care that it was hard, compacted earth I was landing on. We'd play tournaments – well, that's what we called them, though they weren't exactly the World Cup – against the kids from another street. The prize money was five rand (thirty cents), and for that we'd buy a whole heap of *vetkoeks*, pieces of dough bread filled with sausage, cheese and polony. We used bricks for goalposts and could get quite a crowd. Nine times out of ten the tournaments ended the same way: someone would break a window, we'd all scarper, the adults who'd been watching us would run after us, and we'd all get smacked.

But it wasn't long before rugby was my thing. In fact, my very first exposure to rugby had been during the 1995 World Cup, when I was just four. It wasn't the game itself that caught my eye, but rather the *haka*, the traditional Maori war dance performed by the All Blacks before their matches. To me, it was just another cool dance with lots of chanting, thigh-slapping and eye-rolling, and I'd practise it with my friends in the day and perform it for my dad when he came home from work every evening.

For obvious historical reasons, lots of people think that rugby is very much a white sport in my country, but that's not the case: there are thriving black rugby clubs all over South Africa, and especially in the Eastern Cape where I lived. There was Spring Rose, which boasted both Solly Tyibilika and

Mzwandile Stick: Solly ended up playing eight times for the Springboks, and Mzwandile would be a brilliant sevens player before becoming the Springboks backline coach and helping us win the 2019 World Cup. There was Home Defenders, where my dad had been a pretty decent centre. But Spring Rose and Home Defenders were both too far away for me to get to when I also had to go to school every day, so instead I went to the African Bombers, who were based at Dan Qeqe stadium only a few streets from our house.

The African Bombers had been going more than 40 years, almost since the start of apartheid, even though of course there'd never been any prospect of any players going on to play for South Africa. Ironically, their colours were green and gold, same as the Springboks, though that was where the similarity ended. The Bombers were run on a shoestring, and it showed. There were places where the pitches were more stone and thorns than grass, the scrum machine looked as though it was a long-dead carcass picked clean by the birds, and loose wires dangled from the floodlights. There wasn't enough kit to go round, so on matchday when we'd finished our game we'd just peel off our sweaty jerseys and give them to whoever was playing next. It was the same at all the schools, and even as a small kid I told myself that one day when I made it, I'd buy each team their own separate kits.

The first training session was hectic. The coach was called Eric Songwiqi, and I was terrified of him. He shouted and swore a lot, and if I didn't do what he told me to then I'd know about it. But I think even then I could tell the difference between adults who yelled because they didn't care about me and adults who yelled because they did, and I knew Coach Eric fell into the latter category. He wanted us to get better and play well, and he knew that some tough love was needed to make that happen.

I finished that first session exhausted, bruised and bleeding, but I walked home on cloud nine. It was the most awesome thing I'd ever done. From that first session I never looked back, and I never smoked weed or sniffed petrol again. I'd go to the club every day after school: I even did my homework at school after class so it was all finished and I could stay at the club as long as I wanted. We'd train Monday through Thursday, and after our training was done I'd hang around and watch the older age-groups do their sessions, all the way up to the senior 1st XV. Friday was the captain's run, when teams would just do some light preparation and the coaches would stay out of it, and Saturday was matchday, when hundreds of people would come and watch.

If there was a job which needed doing around the club, I'd do it. I became the water boy for the 1st XV, crouched by the side of the pitch as these huge men – at least they seemed huge to me back then – sprinted, tackled, rucked and mauled just a few feet away. At half-time, I'd hand out the bottles and listen to how they spoke urgently about what they needed to do in the second half, hear how they panted for breath and saw how they wiped sweat off their brows with the backs of their hands. The rough concrete stands in Dan Qeqe stadium were full on matchdays, and these men I was standing with were the crowd's heroes, if only for that afternoon. I dreamed that one day I could be one of them.

For all the material things the Bombers lacked, they had everything I needed. When I was there I felt safe: there was no danger, nobody would hurt me. There were roles, there were rules, there was trust. I felt that I belonged there, with a ready-made group of friends united in their love of the game. And I felt accountable. If I missed training for some reason then people would come and look for me, not just to check that I was okay but also to remind me that a no-show was an act of disrespect to the team, to my teammates and to myself. If I wanted to play, I needed to train. I couldn't just turn up when I felt like it. Training sessions weren't just about fitness and skills, they were also about bringing the team together and fostering a sense of camaraderie and kinship. I began to realise that although I was learning my academic lessons in school, I was learning my life lessons with the Bombers.

In Grade 6 I played for my school, Ntyatyambo Primary, against Emsengeni Primary, where Coach Eric was a teacher. We lost badly, something like 50–0, but after the match Coach Eric came over and said he'd seen something special in me. I just laughed. We'd shipped 50 points without reply, I'd played in boxer shorts as we couldn't afford proper rugby shorts, and he'd seen something special in me? I certainly didn't think I'd played any better than anyone else. To this day I don't know what it was that he saw, but then again that's one of the things that makes a teacher special, that they can spot things – talent, skill, attitude, potential – in a child which neither the child nor most of the adults around them have noticed. Either way, I'm very grateful, because that match set in process a chain of events that would change my life.

Coach Eric asked if I would switch schools and come to Emsengeni, where he could help develop me and keep an eye on my progress more easily and completely than he could if he just saw me at the Bombers. He meant for me to start at the beginning of the next academic year, but I was so keen that I'd moved within a week. My favourite place at Emsengeni quickly became a small lawn running between the classroom blocks with a pair of large trees at either end, where we'd play informal games of rugby during break time: it was a lot softer underfoot than the actual pitch, that was for sure.

Coach Eric moved me around a bit to see which was my best position. He started me at prop, because at the time I was a chubby little thing with sticky-out ears: the other kids nicknamed me 'Shrek'. Then he shifted me to wing, but that didn't last long, mainly because I was the slowest wing in the history of all rugby. Eventually he put me in the back row, which I loved and which was clearly my best and most natural position.

I needed a father figure and Coach Eric fulfilled that role, no doubt. He took me everywhere I needed to go and fed me when he could. He was the first positive male role model I'd ever had: someone with a good job, a sense of responsibility, and most of all a caring nature. Now he wasn't a pushover, not by any means. If I stepped out of line he'd come down hard on me. But the crucial difference was that I actually listened to him, as I wanted to gain his approval. And even though he went out of his way for me, he never did so at the expense of anyone else. He never played favourites. He was always there for any child who needed him, whether at Emsengeni or the

Bombers. As the old saying goes: 'In 100 years' time it won't matter what car I drove, how big my house was or how much I had in the bank: but the world may be different because I was important in the life of a child.'

Under Coach Eric's tutelage, my play came on in leaps and bounds: so much so that when I was 11 I was selected for the Eastern Province Under-12 squad at a provincial tournament in Mossel Bay. We did a couple of training sessions at St Alban's Prison in PE, which even for a township boy was an eye-opener. It was – and still is – one of South Africa's most infamous prisons, a brutal and vicious place which took only the most dangerous offenders and was notorious for prisoner abuse, overcrowding and gang violence. I've no idea who thought it would be a good idea to make us run the gauntlet of these prisoners to get to the training pitch: they were behind fences, of course, but they were also shouting abuse and jeering, which to us kids was pretty intimidating. It was probably a cost-cutting exercise or something.

The trip to Mossel Bay, almost five hours' drive away, was the first time I'd ever been outside the PE area. I couldn't remember ever having been as excited before. Every mile in the bus was something new and special to me, heading west on the N2 motorway with the sea always on our left: the surf town of Jeffreys Bay, the bungee jump site at Bloukrans Bridge, the twin headlands that flanked the estuary at Knysna. There were two other guys from the Bombers with me, Phaphama Hoyi and Zolani Faku – Phaphama played in the backs and Zolani was a hooker – but most of the other kids I'd never met before, and with the white kids there was a big language barrier: they didn't speak isiXhosa, and the only English we spoke was slang we'd picked up from TV shows or elsewhere. But we were just kids goofing around, so it didn't really matter what language we used. There was a guy called Nick Holton on the bus, and he and I hit it off right from the start. He was at a school in PE called Grey Junior, but he wasn't at all snobbish or offhand. Before coming to South Africa his grandparents had run a farm in Zimbabwe and he'd spent a lot of time hanging out with the black kids whose parents worked on that farm, so he was pretty chilled about sitting with the three of us. In any case, he was in something of a minority himself, as there were only about two or three guys there with English as their first language. All the others were Afrikaners, and though there wasn't any sense of the Afrikaner kids being down on the English ones – at least not that I remember – I guess it was only natural that people instinctively stuck with those they knew and/or spoke their language.

When we got there, it was like nothing I'd ever seen before. The biggest crowd I'd played in front of up until now was probably a couple of dozen people, perhaps 50 at the outside, but there were hundreds of people here: kids in uniform who'd come along just to cheer, parents, grandparents, the works. I saw huge 4x4s with picnics on their open tailgates, and tables groaning with food beneath umbrellas and gazebos. There was a medical tent with bandages, dressing and liniments: in Zwide first aid was cold water and a sponge, and if that didn't work then tough. I even saw, for the first time in my life, a kid with blond hair. Heck, I'd rarely even played against white kids at all, just the other township schools and clubs.

I played in purple boxer shorts, as I didn't have a proper pair of shorts. Phaphama, Zolani and Nick were in the A-team, and I was in the B-team, but I didn't care. I just wanted to play, and at least the ground looked a lot softer than the fields I was used to playing on. Our opponents came from Border, Western Province, KwaZulu–Natal, South Western Districts and so on. I didn't care who they were, I just wanted the ball in my hand and to have some fun.

It was a great day. The A-team didn't fare so well, but we in the B-team won all our matches. I did what I always did – ran hard at people, offered myself in support if someone else had the ball, and kept encouraging my teammates. I wasn't especially big or quick, but I worked my socks off and understood where on the pitch I needed to be at any given time to maximise my usefulness. Towards the end of the day I was beginning to tire, which was down purely and simply to nutrition. I was used to not eating very much and I'd had several matches over the course of the day, so the last two or three were really hard: I was running out of energy, but I was also playing against kids who'd never known anything but three square meals a day.

What I didn't know until a few days later was that one of Nick's teachers at Grey Junior, Andrew Hayidakis, had been watching the matches with more than just an average spectator's passing interest. He had his eye on Phaphama, Zolani and me, and had been in touch with Coach Eric before the tournament about the possibility of offering us bursaries to Grey Junior, not just to play rugby – although that was obviously a big part of it – but also to get the kind of education we could never have dreamed of in Zwide. The bursary scheme had been going for a decade or so, helping boys from townships all around PE, but this was the first I'd heard of it. Coach Eric hadn't told us before the tournament: he hadn't wanted to pressure us any more than he needed to, and he knew that telling us we could be playing for an opportunity which would change our lives and those of our families would more likely than not terrify us and make us tense up and play badly.

I've a feeling that Grey wanted Phaphama and Zolani much more than they wanted me, but that Coach Eric had more or less said we came as a threesome or not at all. Mr Hayidakis came to see us and explained what the bursary entailed. It was a full scholarship, with everything included – education, clothing, pocket money, whatever was needed. He and the other members of staff involved in the scheme felt that we had something they could nurture and grow. The scholarship would cover one year at Grey Junior and then five more at its senior school, Grey School. Both were boarding schools, and everything there would be on a totally different level from what we were used to: not just the teaching and the facilities, but the aspirations of the boys who went there. A good job for kids from Emsengeni was being a taxi driver. For Grey boys, the sky was the limit: they could be lawyers, doctors, businessmen.

Even Springboks.

This was my life and my opportunity. My grandmother was dead, my father was often away working, and my mother had remarried and was living elsewhere. Coach Eric, who'd always had my best interests at heart, clearly thought I'd be mad to pass up the chance. He'd be losing three of his best players (though we could, and would, come back for matches whenever we had the opportunity) but he knew it was far more important for us to fly the nest than for him to try and keep us. So I jumped at the chance.

I was determined that it wouldn't change me or somehow dilute my essence. Being a Grey boy wouldn't mean I was no longer a Zwide boy, not if I could help it. I wouldn't prioritise one identity over the other: I'd make sure they'd live alongside each other, equal and indivisible, points on the same spectrum. We're all nothing without our past: it's what helps us make sense of our present and future. It's one of the oldest clichés in the book, and like all clichés it's one because it's true: you could take the boy out of Zwide, but you couldn't take Zwide out of the boy. Even then I knew something which still holds true today: I will always be a child of this dust.

Worlds flitted past the windows of the taxi. Apartment blocks and rows of shops, proper buildings rather than shacks, and from there to the lush green of the Mill Park suburb: large houses half-hidden by imposing gates, rows of shiny cars gleaming in the sunshine outside the Mercedes dealership. Then the taxi turned into the grounds of Grey itself, with the great clock tower rising high above the whitewashed buildings into a deep blue sky, and it was all I could do to get my head round the fact that this would be my home – or at least half my home – for the next few years.

The facilities were like nothing I'd ever seen before. There were cricket nets, tennis courts, a swimming pool, grass and

AstroTurf pitches, and squash courts; a music block, an art room and two computer rooms. Compared to Emsengeni, it may as well have been on a different planet. It was hard to believe – no, it was pretty much *impossible* to believe – that all this was only 15 minutes from Zwide.

Maybe I should have been scared, but I wasn't. I was just excited. My grandmother had always told me that Jesus had treated everyone the same, so whoever I connected with I connected with, simple as that, and the colour of their skin didn't matter. So I just went there with an open heart and an open mind, and resolved that anybody who did good by me, I'd do the same by them.

It wasn't easy to start with. I pretty much couldn't speak a word of English, and that put me very much on the back foot. It excluded me from all the little things every other pupil took for granted – being able to read and listen to instructions, knowing what was going on in lessons, being part of conversations between mates. But it also made me feel stupid when I wasn't. At Emsengeni, I'd been one of the top two or three in the class. Now I was at the bottom; I struggled with my academic work. I was scared to speak. I would say one or two words in English and complete a sentence in isiXhosa. Nick and some other guys rallied round. They taught me English – rude words first, of course, though we were still too young for them to be really rude – and helped me with my work. The two things fed off each other: the better I got at English, the less I needed help with work. It took me most of my first year to become fluent in English, but after that I never looked back.

Since we were going to take isiXhosa as a second language, Phaphama, Zolani and I were allowed to skip Afrikaans classes and do remedial English lessons instead. Our teacher, Mrs Mukheibir, helped us by centring some of the learning around rugby, expanding our vocabulary by making us talk about the game in English. She took us under her wing out of the classroom too, letting us spend weekends at her house and taking us to game parks and so on. Lots of the kids had been on safari and seen wild animals, so for them it wouldn't have been that exciting, but we were rapt.

Even the most basic things were new to me. I had a bed for the first time, as part of a dormitory with six boys in it. I had a locker for the first time. I wore socks for the first time. Most of all, perhaps, I had enough food for the first time. I would just eat and eat; at mealtimes I'd have finished my first helping by the time my mates were just sitting down, and I was going up for thirds by the time they'd cleared their plates. The staff had to slow me down and stop me from eating too much, but none of them really understood what an abundance of food felt like to someone who'd known proper hunger. How could they? I was small for my year, which made people wonder even more how I could eat so much, but of course the two things were connected; and it would only be some time later, after years of the kind of nutrition the other kids had had all their lives, that I'd grow properly.

I began to dream differently. I believed I could become anything in life because I had good teachers, good facilities around me, and people saying, 'You can be whatever you want.' I wanted to be a doctor all of a sudden, whereas in the township you just wanted to do what the next guy was doing. And this confidence made me fearless. My attitude was always just to throw myself headfirst into things. Every test, every obstacle, every experience was something to be relished. What was the worst that could happen? I'd fail, but I'd have learned a lesson and next time I'd be better. In my first year we did a PE exercise, and part of it involved jumping in the swimming pool. I'd never swum before, but really, how hard could it be? A stone wouldn't have sunk any quicker than I did. My friends fished me out, laughing as hard as I was coughing and spluttering. Obviously, this whole swimming thing wasn't as easy as it looked. But I also knew it couldn't get any worse, and six months later I was playing for the water polo team.

I had a year in Grey Junior before moving on to Grey proper. Grey Junior ran on a house system, with every boy assigned to one of four houses: Draycott (yellow), School (red), Edwards (purple) and Faure (green). The houses weren't actual buildings; instead, they were groupings in which you competed for academic, sporting and cultural points, and the competition was fierce. We hadn't had the facilities for art, music and drama in Zwide, but Grey Junior took them as seriously as what happened in the classroom and on the sports pitch. *Tria Juncta in Uno*, ran the school motto: three joined in one, a balanced development of mind, body and spirit.

The discipline at Grey was very different from what I was used to. At home, I was disciplined harshly for anything and everything. Many adults beat me, including my grandmother, though at least she did so with love. Everyone else did it because that's the way it was. Grey policy was 'to discipline with dignity' and was aimed at the group as much as the individual. There was a sliding scale of a dozen possible punishments, graded in order of severity: reprimand, written work, detention, parent interview, counselling, parent letter, special report, specific tasks, service to the school and/or community, suspension of privileges, suspension and expulsion. In other words, thought had gone into it, and some of the stages actually involved trying to help the boy who was in trouble rather than just smacking him.

Grey was also big on the kind of sportsmanship values that Coach Eric had been instilling in us. Schools rugby in South Africa is a serious business – some would say too serious – but Grey tried to keep things in perspective. 'When we play our games we try our best to beat our opponents,' the school policy said. 'To do any less would be to rob them and ourselves of some of the enjoyment that we gain from playing sport. However, we do not subscribe to the policy of winning at all costs. Such costs include cheating, displays of temper, over-robust play, disputing the referee's decision, fighting, gamesmanship, and so on. Give of your best. Practise hard and take pride in your fitness. Never give in during a match as this spoils the game for your opponents and your teammates. Keep a sense of proportion. Remember it is only a game and not a war. It is not a major tragedy for the school if we lose. Get to know the rules and abide by them. Don't try to gain unfair advantage by breaking the rules deliberately in the hope that you will get away with it. This is cheating. Accept the referee's decision without question or hesitation. Never show irritation, disagreement or disgust. Remember that even the best referees make mistakes and bear in mind that they are often doing the job out of the goodness of their heart. A good sportsman exercises self-control. He plays the ball and not the man. Leave it to the referee to sort out over-robust play. It is unsporting to look for excuses for your defeats: for example, blaming the pitch, the referee, the wind or the absence of one of your players. Show courtesy and friendliness towards visiting players. Take pride in being neat and properly dressed for your sport. Treat all equipment and facilities with the utmost care.'

The training programme was also much more than I was used to. In Zwide, we basically turned up and played. We did skills sessions and some basic fitness, but that was pretty much it. Here, every day was structured. Monday was a 5k run (plus push-ups and planks if you'd been punished for something); Tuesday was burpees, lunges, squats and crunches; Thursday was press-ups, pull-ups, Spiderman crawl and bicycle crunches; and Friday was bounding, sprints and jumps.

There was a house system at Grey just as there had been in the junior school, though obviously there were more of them as there were more pupils. Where Grey Junior had four, now there were seven: Noaks (green), Johnson (yellow), Thurlow (blue), Lang (white), Vipan (purple) and Meriway (black and red). Meriway was the only boarding house, so that was the one I was in. The houses all had a motto, but we had two because Meriway had originally been two separate houses, Meredith and Way. Fittingly enough, both mottos would in their own way come to apply very strongly to my own life. The Meredith motto was *Heb Dduw Heb Ddib, A Dum A Digon*, which was old Welsh for 'Without God you have nothing: with

God you have everything'; and Way's was *Fit Via Fi*, Latin for 'The way is achieved by force'. I would later have cause to reflect on the first when it came to my faith and putting my life in Jesus' hands, and the latter is of course true of any rugby team and especially the Springboks with their historic emphasis on physicality.

In the township there was one rule – I had to be home at a certain time – and even that was pretty flexible. At Grey, there was a time and a rule for everything: a time to eat, a time to study, a time to brush our teeth. The routine was brutal. Every morning there were six bells, timed to the minute. The Rising Bell went at 6.10 and did what it said on the tin: got us out of bed, with no snooze button or lie-in allowed. The 6.30 was the Out of Showers Bell. From there we had nine minutes on the dot to be dressed and by our beds before the Warning Bell at 6.39 and the Inspection Bell at 6.40, when we had to stand at the end of our beds and be inspected by a prefect and a master. The fifth bell was for breakfast at 6.50, and the sixth at 7.40 was for us to be out of the boarding house and on our way to assembly and lessons. And that's how it went on all day, until the procedure was reversed in the evening: dinner bells, prep bells, silence bells and lights out bells. Compared to Zwide, when I could be out on the streets until late, this was something totally different. And the change even extended to after lights out, as I would never be woken by drunken beatings in the street. Things like that didn't happen on Grey's manicured lawns.

* * *

There were plenty of sports on offer at Grey – cricket, hockey, rowing, swimming, water polo, golf, squash, athletics, basketball, tennis and so on – but rugby was, of course, by far the most popular and most prestigious. The school hadn't always been so keen on the game – it was almost 40 years from the founding of Grey in 1856 to the first match against Muir Academy in 1893, and even that was played in black coats and straw hats – but gradually rugby had gained popularity, and by the time I arrived there the school had eight open teams for the top two years and at least four each at U14, U15 and U16 levels. At the height of the season it could sometimes feel, in the nicest possible way, that Grey was a rugby club with a school attached rather than vice versa.

As I went up the years, the training became more intense. It wasn't long before I came across Suzie, a massive tractor tyre which I had to flip or pull on a rope behind me as I sprinted up and down the pitch. Suzie wasn't just there to make me stronger and faster; she also mimicked pretty accurately what it felt like to be holding someone up in the tackle or bursting through a couple of defenders trying to cling onto me. Soon the workload was dwarfing what I'd been used to in the junior school, let alone back in Zwide. Mondays were light sessions designed to run out the stiffness from the game two days previously: we might play a game of touch or do some sprints. Tuesdays were the hardest, when we really got put through the mill: full contact games plus defensive drills and bag work. Wednesdays were video and gym, Thursdays were specific tactics for the upcoming match dependent on the opposition, and Fridays were always light: it was too easy to effectively play the match in our heads or against each other ahead of time, and only find out on Saturday afternoon that we'd left our best efforts on the training pitch and hadn't shown up when it counted.

This may only have been schoolboy rugby, but we tried to be as professional as possible in our approach, particularly on game day. We couldn't play our best if we were just doing normal stuff all morning and then wolfed down some lunch before going to play. We'd have a final team meeting to go over the game plan one more time, then smaller meetings – forwards, backs, lineout jumpers, even one-on-one with the coaching staff – if need be. We had a biokineticist and a physio. We'd get changed, the coach would say a few words, we'd pray and huddle, and out we'd go. I would get bigger, and better, and do it for a living as an adult, but in many ways playing for Grey was little different to playing for the Stormers or the Springboks.

Being small for my age proved far from being a disadvantage. It actually helped me, as it meant I had to be street smart and think my way around the field as opposed to physically dominating everyone. I worked hard on reading the game – not just seeing what was happening as it unfolded in front of me but also trying to anticipate where the play would be five or ten seconds down the line, so I could put myself in the right place at the right time. Part of this was using my teammates as best I could rather than trying to do everything myself. I got as much satisfaction from a well-timed, well-aimed pass as I did from a good run or a sidestep. The team aspect of rugby was one that I'd always valued, right from the first time I'd stepped onto the field at the Dan Qeqe stadium, and the game was just much better when everyone was playing well and having a good time. Until I grew I wasn't necessarily the star player of the team, the one who caught the eye of the casual spectator; but I always tried to make myself the backbone, the one whose workrate, ball skills and rugby brain meant that I was constantly in the thick of the action.

One day in June 2005, when I was in Grade 8, the Springbok team came to practise at our school fields. They were playing France in PE, and we had the best facilities in the area. We all went down to watch, and my heart was pumping so much that it felt ready to burst. These were men I had only ever seen on TV, and now here they were. Even the smaller guys looked huge, and the bigger ones might as well have been actual giants. They all had such presence, too: they moved with purpose, they didn't waste energy, they looked totally focused even when walking from one side of the pitch to the other. I wasn't aware of anything around me, just the Springboks. I watched these guys, totally transfixed, and wanted nothing more than to one day be like them.

There were lots of famous names in that team – Percy Montgomery, Jean de Villiers, Bryan Habana, John Smit – but my favourite of all was Schalk Burger. He was my hero not just because I was in the back row like him, but because I loved the way he played. He was everywhere, dirty blond hair flying as he threw himself into tackles, cleaned out racks and ran the hard yards in the tight channels. I wanted to get his autograph, but I was too shy and overawed. When I went back into the boarding house I saw one of my teachers and told him what was going on. He pushed a sheet of paper and a pen into my hand and told me not to come back until I had Schalk's autograph. So I took a deep breath, joined the scrum of boys around Schalk, and asked him if he'd sign his name for me. That piece of paper was one of my most prized possessions. If you'd told me that one day Schalk would be not just my teammate but also my friend, I'd have thought you'd lost your mind.

Sometimes my friends would invite me to stay with them for the weekend. I'd seen the kind of cars these boys' parents drove when they came to watch rugby at school, so neither the size of the houses nor the beauty of their gardens surprised me. What *did* surprise me was the way they talked back to their parents. It wasn't even that they were cheeky or insolent (though sometimes they were), but that they could discuss, debate and even argue things without getting seven bells beaten out of them. 'Sheesh,' I thought, 'don't try this at home.' And of course, I saw that these kids' parents loved them, were proud of them, were interested in their lives and achievements, and wanted the best for them. Their mums would make sure their tuck boxes were full and kiss them goodbye when dropping them off back at school. I'd get a taxi home to Zwide, and before I got home and had a conversation with my dad it would be just 'Howzit?' from anyone who was around, like I'd never been away. No fuss, no fanfare.

It put township life into even starker perspective. Part of the conditions of my bursary was that I was only allowed to play rugby for Grey or provincial teams, not for anybody else, in case I got injured. But I continued to turn out for the African Bombers whenever I was back in Zwide. It wasn't just that they were still my club or that Coach Eric was still the man to whom I owed my start. It was also that I simply loved playing rugby, and as far as I was concerned the more games the merrier. Sometimes, if Grey didn't have a match on, I'd bunk out of school and go back to Zwide where I'd play for the Bombers' 3rds, 2nds and 1sts, back to back. If the Bombers weren't playing I'd go and find another club and guest for them. I was playing against adults when I was 15, and that didn't faze me – even when Solly Tyibilika, who'd played a few Tests for the Springboks on the flank, was one of them. They'd hit me hard and late just to test me out, and I knew the only way to deal with it was to get up and act as if nothing had happened – and then, when I next got the chance, to run round them. The guy who owned the Bombers had a butchery, and he'd give me free meat to help build me up, as he could see that I had a future.

Grey liked to say that 'education begins in the home and should be considered a partnership between the home and school'. That was easy enough for most of the kids there, with parents who were fully involved with and supportive of what they were doing at Grey, but for me it was different. There was no partnership between my home and the school, at least not any meaningful one. No-one in Zwide could understand what my school life was like now.

It wasn't easy, the switch from poverty to privilege and back again. When we'd go back to Zwide, I wouldn't change out of my uniform. I was proud of that uniform and what it represented. Some people would have a go at me, and the easiest thing to do would have been to change outfits, but I knew that if I took the easy path rather than the right one, I'd regret it.

It wasn't just that I was proud of it. It was also that I wanted to show people that if I could do it then so could they. I wanted to change their perception of what was possible.

Equally, I was determined that I wouldn't change, not deep down where it counted. I was still the same Siya I'd ever been; I still had time for my friends and family, and I still liked to have fun. I may have had two lives, but there was only one me. I didn't become a different person on that taxi ride up and down the R75 from Zwide and Mill Park and back again. I certainly didn't think I was too good for the township now I had rich white friends too. If other people thought that I was getting above myself, well, there was nothing I could do about that.

One day when I was 15, I came back to Zwide from Grey and, rather than go and hang out with my friends as I usually did, I just went to sleep. It was funny. I didn't know that anything had happened but I must have sensed it, just because my behaviour was so out of character. My dad came into the room.

'Your mum has died,' he said. 'She just went to sleep and never woke up.'

I didn't reply. I felt so helpless. 'What can I do?' I thought. 'She's gone.' My favourite memory of her was one Mother's Day when I'd bought her a card. It was something she'd never thought she'd get, and she'd told me then how much she bragged about me to her friends.

Now she was gone. My dad put a blanket over me, and I went back to sleep. I think he thought I was going to kill myself or do something stupid – go to sleep and not wake up, just like she had – but I wasn't. I was just numb. My mother had had two other children, a boy called Liyema and a girl called Liphelo, and I wondered who'd look after them now she was gone. They were my half-siblings, but I hardly knew them.

I thought I might feel closer to my dad once my mum had gone but I didn't, not really. Sometimes he was around, sometimes he wasn't, but whenever he was, it felt like he was always drinking and fighting. And of course I fought too, because that was all I knew. There was just so much anger in me, and the only way I could get it out was through alcohol and violence. Sometimes my dad would have to come and get me off the streets at night. Pretty much every weekend I went back to Zwide I'd get in a fight, usually because I'd been drinking. Once I was stabbed in the neck with a glass. The guy fled and I chased him until my friends stopped me and he got away. The next day I found him, said I was sorry and that was it.

Another time I ended up with my ear hanging off. Someone had stolen my jacket, and when I found the guy wearing it I set upon him. Then another guy came along and we started going at it. He took out a knife and began stabbing me. I managed to prise his fingers from the handle, and he dropped the knife and started running. I chased him, but when I rounded a corner he was waiting for me and kicked me hard. I hit the side of that wall running full tilt and tore my ear half off my head. I had to have my ear stitched and bandaged before going back to school and sitting exams with my head wrapped in gauze.

Fights weren't usually personal; they were just whoever happened to be standing nearby, probably looking for a fight too. Any excuse would do. Someone might taunt me for not being up with the newest township slang, or accuse me of thinking I was all that, or of looking at him threateningly, or of being soft now I was at a white school, anything. It didn't matter, as long as it led to a scrap. This was what we all thought it took to be a man, what we all thought was the way to solve problems. This was the way I had to prove myself, each and every time. I couldn't duck a fight or walk away; I had to stand my ground and smash the other oke up. Weekends during term time, and every day during the holidays, I'd be fighting. It was as natural a part of my life as eating, sleeping or playing rugby.

My township mentality was all about survival. Keep alive, that's what it was. But there was also so much I loved about Zwide: hooting taxis, kids playing soccer and skipping rope, guys doing BMX tricks, the excitement when people were celebrating something, the way that guys would go and wait by the robots (traffic lights) early every morning in an attempt to find work for that day, even though there might not be enough to go round, because that was the spirit they had, that was their desire to provide for their families.

Most kids at Grey had no idea what it was like to live where I did and how I did. That's not a criticism; they'd never been exposed to it. I didn't find it hard to deal with the fact that they were so ignorant of my life and the lives of millions like me. What I *did* find hard was how few of them were interested in rectifying that, in stepping out of their bubble, their comfort zone, and seeing a different side to the country. One of the reasons Nick is such a good friend is that he was one of those few. He'd learn isiXhosa, he'd come to Zwide. For him, I wasn't just a guy he saw during term time and not in the holidays. I was Siya, and my life mattered to him. It's hard to get across how important that is when you're not used to it.

In contrast, Grey was a haven, and sometimes I'd go home on a weekend but then ring the school and ask if I could be picked up and brought back as there was too much fighting going on even for me and it was too hectic. The bursary scheme I was on had been going around a decade, so there were already quite a few black kids at Grey: probably 50 or so out of around 800 in total. I wasn't bullied, and I don't know of anyone who was, at least not seriously. There was one kid who took a dislike to me, which I think was equal parts hand-me-down racism and jealousy at the attention I was getting for my rugby, but that was pretty much it, and in any case most people saw it for what it was and took my side against his. People in general were quite cool, and I think pretty much every kid there realised how lucky they were to be having that kind of education.

Like most private schools, Grey had its fair share of unique traditions and practices, all helping to reinforce the fact that this was its own little world with its own microclimate. There was an annual quad race round the cloisters inspired by the movie *Chariots of Fire*, where the two fastest matric students tried to make it all the way round before the chimes of the clock at midday finished. Very few managed to make it, and I certainly wasn't one of them: I'd been the slowest wing in all rugby back in Zwide, and not much had changed on that front.

You weren't allowed to walk through a door before some-one older than you. In your last year, any boy younger than you had to greet you when you walked past a certain section of benches where they were sitting. Those with full colours, which were awarded not just for sport but achievements in academia and music too, got to wear white blazers with azure piping, which were the bomb. In matric year, Grade 12, you were called an 'Old Pot' and assigned a 'New Pot', a Grade 8 student, who would do chores for you – laundry, waking you up, and so on. Mine was a guy called Nick Beswick, and when one night I wanted to go out with a couple of friends – strictly against school rules, of course – I asked him to sleep in my bed and pretend to be me. As chance would have it, one of the hostel masters was doing his rounds in the small hours with a torch, and Nick put on his deepest voice and said from beneath the duvet: 'We're all here. Please leave!'

But respect and care didn't just go from younger to older. If the New Pot had a problem, it was up to the Old Pot to try and help sort it out in the first instance, and only involve the housemaster if that didn't work. Nick was a good guy and I liked to help him whenever and however I could. In that matric year, I had a lot of provincial teams keen to sign me, and they'd often send me kit and equipment – boots, scrum-caps, training tops, supplements and so on. I had all I needed already, so I'd just give most of it to him.

I also learned how to be smart and play the system. We were allowed to fail one subject and still pass matric, so I figured that I should just find the subject I was worst at, do no work in it whatsoever, and use the time I'd saved for extra rugby training and practice. It wasn't hard to find the subject in question: accountancy, which I found boring and difficult in equal measures. So I went to my accountancy teacher and said: 'Listen, can I please not do this subject? I'm going to fail it anyway, so there's no point me wasting your time and mine.'

'Accountancy's a useful skill,' he replied. 'You'll need it in later life.'

'Not in the career I'm going to have.'

'What's that, then?'

'I'm going to be a Springbok.'

He gave me a hard stare. 'Siya Kolisi,' he said eventually, 'you are a very arrogant young man.'

But being a Springbok was exactly what I intended, and with reason. Partly, it was the effect of the 2007 World Cup, the first I'd really paid attention to. I'd been too young in 1995 and 1999, and the Springboks had been so bad in 2003, losing to England in the pool stage before going out to New Zealand in the quarters, that it had been hard to get too excited. But now I was on the age-group fast track, and the Boks had a good chance, so I watched transfixed along with every other rugby fan in the country. Again the Boks were drawn in the same pool as England, but this time the boot was on the other foot and they won 36–0: a shutout against a Tier One nation, pretty much unheard of.

I was also beginning to watch games as a player rather than simply a supporter, seeing who was doing what, why they were doing it and how effectively they were managing it. In particular, of course, I concentrated on the back-row players, watching their work at the breakdown and the way they linked between forwards and backs. The final was a rerun of the England pool game, and though the margin was tighter – only 15–9 this time – the result was the same. The Boks were world champions.

The celebrations went on for a long time. Most people were just happy that we had become world champions again, even if in wider social terms it didn't feel as seismic as 1995 had done. But for me, it was a bit more than that. Those men who'd come home with the golden trophy were the same men I'd seen training on our pitches at Grey two years previously, the same men who'd gone through the schools and age-group system I was going through. If they could do it, then why couldn't I?

But mostly it was because, and there's no modest way of saying this, that as a schoolboy player I was flipping good. Grade 10 was a breakout year for me. It was the first year that I appeared on the national rugby radar, not because I was so good but simply because the selectors didn't monitor our progress before that, and that in turn was because until that age boys are still growing and changing too dramatically for realistic assessments to be made. Early starters and late bloomers can both give misleading impressions. A kid who's started puberty at 12 might be much bigger than his peers and look like a good player because of that, but when the others catch up physically he'll recede into the ranks; a kid who only begins puberty at 14 may not look all that, but give him a few years and he'll be a different proposition.

That year I captained Eastern Province at Grant Khomo Week, the U16 provincial tournament. For me, even the name of the tournament was resonant. Mr Khomo had been captain of the Bantu Springboks, an all-black national team, back in 1950 when sport had been strictly segregated by race, and later became an administrator who helped advance the cause of black players in rugby. He was one of the first people who showed that rugby wasn't just a white game.

One of the things I've always loved about rugby is the way that friendships can be made not only with your teammates but your opponents too. In my first term at Grey Junior I'd been playing eighthman (as we call the number eight position in South Africa), and my opposite number for Dale College had been a boy called Scarra Ntubeni. It was the start of a friendship which endures to this day, and which went from schoolboy rivalry to teammates for Western Province, the Stormers and the Springboks. Now at Grant Khomo he was captaining Border, one of our rivals. Both sides went unbeaten, but we never got to play each other. We were declared champions, which really upset Scarra; he said it was only because we had played the more fashionable provinces, and that they were the better team! It was a proper Eastern Cape rivalry, fiercely contested but full of respect. In the end, we did get to face off at the Boet Erasmus stadium in a curtain-raiser to a Currie Cup match, and rather annoyingly – no, *very* annoyingly – Border won and declared themselves South Africa's real U16 champions. Not that Scarra ever reminds me of it or anything …

I played well enough in that week to be called up for the national schoolboy elite squad, which lasted another week, this time at a training camp. They assessed our skills, gave us a medical, checked our diet and conditioning, and generally started to build a picture of who might really make it. But my game went to another level not long after Grant Khomo Week, once I'd had a growth spurt. It happened pretty much over the course of the vacation between Grades 10 and 11, when I grew 10 cm taller and put on 5 kg. When I'd been small and pretty fast, I'd had to box clever in my play; now I had the power to go with it. Just like Coach Rassie, Nick likened me to a dog: I'd been a puppy, still quite small but with enormous feet and hands, and now I was a *boerboel* mastiff.

When I got the ball I'd just run, bouncing guys off me and brushing through players like they weren't even there. The attention on schools rugby, and the small world we operated in, meant that news of my playing spread far and wide, and sometimes we'd have people from other schools coming to watch our games instead of their own teams just so they could see me. It was flattering and marked me out as someone who everyone was aware of on campus, but I tried to never let it go to my head. I was always aware how fortunate I was not just to have been given that talent but also the opportunity to express it fully, and neither my friends nor the staff would have allowed me to get too big for my boots. Being a good rugby player was important; being a good person was imperative.

I'd been in the A-team all the way through the age groups, and made the 1st XV in Grade 11, my second last year. Playing for the firsts was the most special thing you could do at Grey. The buzz around our matches started long before kick-off. It was in the air for the whole week: people talking about it, wishing us luck, the hushed hopes and expectations. Even some of the teachers were a little more indulgent of late work and the like. At Friday assembly the team was announced, the captain made a short speech, and then everyone did the 'G', the school war cry. Sometimes a Friday afternoon lesson was cancelled so that everyone could go to the stands and practise the chants for the following day.

Then on matchday it was as if all PE had come to watch. There could be 20,000 people there: pupils, old boys ranging from those who'd just left and had come with their sisters and girlfriends to those in their seventies who looked a bit misty-eyed at being back for such an occasion, and the thousands of spectators who had no real connection to the school other than that they lived nearby.

For some boys, matches like these would be the highlight of their career. But even for people like me who went on to play pro, there was something special and unique about it. When I became a Stormer and later a Springbok, I knew that millions of people would be watching me on a weekend: but that didn't bring the sense of closeness that a school community did. This wasn't our living and we weren't adults: we were still school-boys and on Monday there would be lessons again, but for a few hours we felt like a mixture of ancient warriors and modern superheroes. Our kit would be immaculate: azure jerseys, white shorts, navy socks. We'd walk up the 1st XV steps behind the pitch, a privilege reserved only for the team: the steps were normally cordoned off and only opened just before kick-off. The sounds of our studs on the steps would let the supporters' stand know we were coming, and an enormous roar would swell as we ran onto Philip Field.

There were always a few Grade 11 guys in the 1sts, but this year, 2008, almost half the team were in my year. We had the first black captain in Grey's history, Bonakele 'Bones' Bethe; Phaphama had developed into an unbelievable centre who scored tries for fun (he'd scored 60 one year at age-group level); Zolani was one of the best schoolboy props around; and overall we were one hell of a team, among the top three schools in the whole country. It was 30 years since Grey had gone through a whole season unbeaten, and we were desperate to emulate that team, to carve our name in Grey history as the Invincibles.

There was only one team who could stop us going the whole season unbeaten: our biggest rival and sister school, Grey College in Bloemfontein. The two schools had been founded a year apart by the same man, Sir George Grey, who had been Governor of the Cape Colony. Grey Bloem were older than us – 1855 against 1856 – but much more importantly they were much better at rugby than we were. This was the 40th match between the two schools, and we had won only seven. There was a thin line between arch-rival and nemesis, and Grey Bloem tended to the latter more often than any of us at Grey wanted to admit.

I'd beaten them at U13 level in my first year, the same year that the 1st XV had beaten them, and I remembered the celebrations afterwards: the whole school was on a high for days. The venue alternated each year, with us hosting in odd-numbered years and them in even-numbered ones, so this year it was our turn to go to them. It's a long way to Bloemfontein, seven hours in a coach heading more or less due north, and for once our reputation preceded us. They'd enjoyed some easy victories over us in the years beforehand, but both sides knew that this one would be different. Beating them on home turf would have been great, but doing it away would be arguably an even greater achievement.

It didn't quite happen. In the final minutes, we were five points down. A try would have drawn us level and a conversion would have won it, and maybe if we'd been at home it would have been different, when the crowd roared us on until they were hoarse and the noise and support gave us a lift when we were exhausted and didn't think we could go to the well even one more time. Try as we might, we just couldn't make it happen. It finished 22–17 to them.

It was the only match we lost all season, and my disappointment was somewhat tempered by the fact that I was going to Craven Week. What Grant Khomo Week was for U16s, Craven Week was for U18s: the pinnacle of schoolboy rugby, the most important part of the season. It was named after Dr Danie Craven, one of the most legendary names in Springbok rugby. As ever we played for our provinces, and at the end of the week the organisers picked an overall SA Schools team.

By the end of the week I'd made it into that Schools team, as a sub. I was disappointed not to make the starting XV, but I knew I had another year left to do that. And in any case, being in the team at all is a huge honour, and the buzz around a player once they have that honour is subtle but unmistakeable. The provincial academies' scouts are out in force, taking notes and seeing who they might want to sign. As a calling card and opportunity for any would-be pro player, Craven Week is critical.

I wanted to play for Western Province. That was where Schalk Burger played, and the lifestyle in Cape Town seemed ideal for me: big student population, lots of parties and a laid-back vibe. But it was the Cheetahs who came in hard for me with a firm offer and a decent contract. The Free State has always been a hotbed of rugby, and I knew they had good structures in place for me to rise through the ranks from the academy, and so I signed. Maybe I should have held out for other offers, but there was no guarantee that any of them would have come in. Sure, I was now an SA Schools player, but that wasn't by itself a golden ticket. It was flattering that the Cheetahs had really gone after me, and they seemed to have my best interests at heart. This wasn't Premiership soccer, where I could sit on the bench and make millions each year. I had to get it right, and if a union wanted me to sign with them and held out the realistic prospect of Currie Cup rugby, Super Rugby and then the Springboks, that seemed a good deal. At 17, I found it hard to gauge my worth accurately: it was too easy to do myself up or down unrealistically, to be too arrogant or overly self-critical. And since I was only 17, the contract was post-dated to my 18th birthday.

My final year at Grey should, at least in rugby terms, have been the best. I was well known throughout the entire Eastern Cape rugby community, especially among the AmaXhosa people for whom my success was really important. When we played Dale College, which was a mainly black school, most of their kids were supporting us just because I was playing. It was crazy. I'd get parents wanting to take pictures with me and all that.

We should have been unstoppable, since we had half the previous year's team, but as so often life doesn't work that way. Part of our problem was injuries, which meant we were always swapping players in and out and rarely had a settled matchday 23. Another was that we lacked depth: although we had a very good nucleus of players, there was quite a drop-off from them to the next guys in line. But to be totally honest, we were also a bit complacent. We thought it would come easily, and it didn't. We had some good results, most notably an 84–0 drubbing of Clifton, but on the flipside Grey Bloem shut us out 16–0 in front of our home crowd, and we were also losing games we should have won.

One of those games was at least partly my fault. All the time I'd been playing for the Bombers on the side, I'd been risking the whole thing coming apart, and eventually it did. I injured my ankle playing for the Bombers one Saturday, and it was so swollen that I couldn't walk. To hide it I had to stay in bed on the Monday. I eventually said that I'd injured it playing soccer in the street, and was told I'd be out for three months. That didn't stop me trying to play the following weekend. Paul Roos Gymnasium were in town, looking to avenge the 41–16 stuffing we'd given them the previous year. I did intensive rehab that week, but the doctor said no, I was nowhere ready to play. I stood on the sidelines watching the match with the other spectators, and believe me that was no place to be when I should have been playing. I was still living every tackle, run, pass and scrum, but I had no outlet for that energy.

I was so desperate to play that I actually went back to the hostel and got changed into my rugby kit. When I came back and the spectators saw me, they let out a huge cheer and began to chant: '*Si-ya, Si-ya, Si-ya!*' There were ten minutes to go and the scores were tied. Even on a crocked ankle, I knew I could manage ten minutes – the crowd and the adrenalin would have got me through – and I could probably have made enough of a difference for us to have won.

The coach said no. I tried to remonstrate with him, but he was adamant. Then Paul Roos scored and I knew there was no way back for the team. I was so mad that I wouldn't even look at him; I just stalked off back to the boarding house.

He'd been right, of course, though that was something I wouldn't realise until later. I was 17 and thought the next game was the most important thing in the world, so missing it felt like a disaster beyond reckoning. I didn't see the bigger picture. He did. He knew that letting me play would have risked serious damage to my ankle, which could in turn have had enormous ramifications for my future career. It wasn't worth the risk, not remotely.

It also helped me understand something that I think many people forget, and even more so now than back then: that schoolboy rugby is, and always should be, just a game. What made the 2008 Grey team so special was not that we won so many matches but how tight and talented a unit we were, with the kind of trust in each other that not only makes good teams but also ensures lifelong friendships. The winning came as a result of all that. Unfortunately, this win-at-all-costs attitude not only instils bad values in people, but puts pressure – too much pressure – on the kids who play the game. They can either burn out or give up altogether if they don't get a professional contract. Rugby shouldn't feel like a job to those who play it for fun. When it comes to seeking an edge, it's a short step from training hard to taking steroids, or to developing mental problems when things go awry. Being a well-rounded person is more important than being a good rugby player: that applies at any age, but even more so at 16 or 18. If we keep on with systems that measure people only by their results in a narrow field, we risk creating individuals who fit that famous definition of a cynic: those who know the price of everything and the value of nothing. Especially as a kid, if enough people tell you you're wonderful then you start to believe the hype, and you find it hard to handle when you realise – as you inevitably will – that where it matters you're no better than anyone else.

I was back in time for my second stab at Craven Week, where once more Scarra and I hung out a lot when we weren't playing. He'd switched to hooker by then, and he was really worried that he wouldn't make the SA Schools side. We (Eastern Province) played Western Province in the unofficial final, and the WP hooker Gary Topkin ran right over the top of me. Scarra was watching, and the look of horror on his face was a picture. He came to me after the match and said, 'Of all the players to run over you, why did it have to be the hooker? You're so lazy in defence you might as well have been standing at full-back!' He thought my missed tackle would cost him a place in the SA Schools side. I told him not to worry, because he'd played well enough to make it; and I was right. He was selected on the bench alongside Zolani, with the starting hooker a certain Bongi Mbonambi who, exactly ten years later, would take that role in the World Cup Final itself. And if you ever wanted to see the difference between Grey High and Grey College laid bare, here it was: we had only Zolani and me in the squad, but they had six, all starters and evenly distributed throughout the team (full-back, centre, scrum-half, prop, lock and flanker).

I made the team as eighthman, which was a relief: anything less than a starting position would have been a disappointment. It was matric year: schoolboy rugby would soon be over, and in its place would come the professional game. I already had a contract with the Cheetahs, of course, but the more people paid attention to me during Craven Week the more I regretted signing with them. There were other provinces interested in me – including the one I most wanted to play for, Western Province – but there was nothing I could do about that.

Perhaps if I'd stuck with my accountancy classes I'd have been more business savvy, because it transpired that there was a way out of the situation. Scarra had just signed with an agent called Hilton Houghton, who was negotiating him a deal with Western Province. Western Province were keen on me too, not just for my own play but also because they knew that Scarra and I were mates and would be sources of support for each other as we moved through the ranks. Hilton offered to represent me as well. He said he would talk to the Cheetahs and sort it all out, and that's just what he did.

I felt bad, because I didn't like breaking an agreement already made. I'm a loyal person, and that kind of stuff doesn't sit well with me. But this was what was best for me, and the Cheetahs understood that.

I went a bit off the rails in my last days at Grey. For most people, it was the usual whirlwind when you leave any place you've been for a long time: a mixture of nostalgia, gratitude, regret and the knowledge that this can't last forever. There were parties, exchanges of contact details, promises to stay in touch, all the usual. But for me there was also a self-destructive element which even at this distance freaks me out a bit.

For six years Grey had been the rock in my life, the place where I knew everyone had my back and where I could always count on love and support. Now that was gone, and I felt like my life was in flux again: arguments with my dad and uncle back in Zwide, and the knowledge that if professional rugby didn't work out then I wasn't sure what I was going to do. I was scared of failing, but I was also scared of moving on. I got really drunk, which for me was already a common thing and more than just teenage bravado; it was my way of dealing with things I found too hard to cope with any other way, because when I drank I could obliterate the world just as my dad could when he drank. I ran in front of cars, trying to get hit. I called Hilton, still drunk, and said I didn't want to do this anymore, I'd changed my mind and didn't want to be a professional rugby player. He arranged for me and Scarra to come and live with him in Cape Town straight away: we literally got on the bus after school ended for the final time and went to his house in the suburb of Kommetjie.

He was a good man, which was more than could be said for some of his neighbours. One day I was walking back from the taxi rank a few blocks away when suddenly I was surrounded by armed patrol officers; not the police, but the private security company which helped keep the area safe. There were motorbikes, cars, vans, bakkies, the whole works, like this was something out of a movie. One guy put a gun to my head. They were yelling that someone had been robbed and I fitted the description of the suspect.

In other words, I was the first young black guy they'd found.

'I'm staying with Mr Houghton, right there.' I pointed to Hilton's house, which was no more than 100 metres away.

'Prove it.'

I then saw a man who lived in the neighbourhood walking past. He'd seen me and Scarra coming and going plenty of times over the past few weeks, and he knew exactly who I was. I called out to him.

'Excuse me! Can you please tell these men that I'm staying with Mr Houghton?'

He looked at me, and looked at the armed response men, and then he looked down and away.

It was the simplicity of the gesture that really stuck somewhere deep in me. It would have been the easiest thing in the world for him to tell them that I was who I was. He just chose not to. That was worse than anything he could have said.

I don't know how long they kept me there. I was crying. I thought they might shoot me on the spot; if the neighbour was anything to go by, they may well have thought they could get away with it. Eventually, they realised that I wasn't who they were looking for – maybe they got a call saying the actual culprit had been found, I don't know – and they all just got back in their vehicles and left. Not a word of apology, nothing.

It was a reminder – not that I needed it – of two things. First, that some people would always choose not to look beyond the colour of my skin when they saw me; and second, that I would need to rely on myself, because in the end that might be all I had.

2

STORMER

Newlands: the grand old dame of South African rugby and my favourite stadium of them all, nestled in the lee of Devil's Peak with the sky turning purple at sunset. This is the place where Pieter Hendriks shook his fist in triumph as he scored against Australia in the opening match of the 1995 World Cup, the game which sent the Springboks on the high road to a trophy whose impact still resonates today; this is the place where I would take so many steps on the way to helping the Springboks repeat that feat almost a quarter of a century later.

It's not like other stadiums, Newlands. I felt all that history whenever I stepped out onto the pitch; the first game here was played back in the nineteenth century, and of all major stadiums in the world only Lansdowne Road in Dublin is older. The wind can swirl madly and change direction mid-match. The stands rise high on all four sides, creating a cauldron effect. The crowd sits much closer than in other stadia, at times feeling as though they're practically on the field with the players, and they make so much noise that sometimes we can't hear the calls.

And that crowd comes in all colours, shapes and sizes. Go to Loftus Versveld or Nelspruit and the spectators are predominantly Afrikaners, emblematic of Springbok rugby as it was for so long, but at Newlands different groups of people have always mixed together much more freely. Indeed, there are still pockets of fans who support the All Blacks even against the Springboks because that's what they did all the way through apartheid. And though the spectators are fiercely partisan – it does feel like having an extra man sometimes – they also appreciate good rugby no matter who plays it. A dazzling try will bring them to their feet irrespective of which side has scored.

Every time I played at Newlands I gave 100 per cent, be it for Province, Stormers or the Springboks. Some players don't go all out for their franchise sides, saving their best for the national team. They might not even mean to, but they do. For me, every match there was like my first one, and I was always determined to do all I could to help the team and have that awesome crowd keep cheering us.

If that makes me sound like the ultimate model professional – well, I wish. To start with, I was very keen on keeping on with the things I was good at, such as ball-carrying, but much less keen on defence. Schoolboy rugby was much more about attack, rightly so, as that's what's fun at that age. Schoolboys don't want to spend hours learning the intricacies of defensive systems.

I was one of 40 or 50 school leavers who joined the Western Province Academy that year. We all knew there wouldn't be nearly that many by the end of the year. It was a winnowing period. At each stage numbers got cut, and if I wanted to be a success I had to make sure I was still standing after that cut. That in turn wasn't down to just talent, as everyone who made it even that far was talented. As much as talent – probably more so, in truth – it was down to character, work ethic and the desire to keep on improving. People got weeded out, either because the coaching staff didn't think they were up to it or because the players themselves realised that this life wasn't for them.

We had a special group of players that year. Some years work out better than others, that's just the nature of these things, but ours was pretty standout. There was Nizaam Carr, a brilliant loosie and all-round athlete; Frans Malherbe, a tighthead who was already being earmarked as a future Springbok; and Eben Etzebeth, a giant lock. Like me, Nizaam and Frans had been to powerhouse rugby schools (Bishops and Paarl Boys' High respectively), but Eben had come through Tygerberg High School, which didn't have the same kind of reputation.

Early on in my time at the Institute, I found out that I'd been playing for the past two years with what was basically a broken shoulder, and I'd need an operation. It was scheduled for a couple of months' time, and there were two of us in the same boat. The other guy decided not to train until the operation was done, but I wanted to keep going. Trials for the U19 team were coming up, and my reputation was probably good enough to have been picked whatever happened, but I didn't want to be chosen purely on the grounds of what I'd done before. I didn't want to be that guy who was seen, fairly or unfairly, as coasting along. So for those two months I did all the training, including full contact every time that was on the schedule. Even the day before the op I was smashing into people at full pace. Maybe medically it wasn't the smartest thing to be doing, but it won me respect not just among my teammates but also the coaching staff and the senior squad too, and that was just as important. When I was selected as eighthman, I knew I'd done it not just the hard way but also the right way.

Being unable to play after the op was frustrating, not just in itself but because it was easy to feel that everyone else was forging ahead and leaving me behind. I couldn't let myself succumb to that kind of negative thinking, so instead I made a real effort to look at the situation from the other way round. Injury was inevitable sooner or later, not just for me but for everybody. Today it was my turn; tomorrow it would be some-one else's. So there was no point stressing about it. Moreover, injury time wasn't wasted time, quite the opposite. I could use it to get really fit in the gym – a shoulder injury didn't stop me getting on the exercise bike, for example – to learn the game better by spending time on video analysis, and so on.

I treated the recovery from injury itself as a test to be completed as quickly and well as possible. The standard recovery time from the procedure I'd undergone was between four and six months. The surgeon and physio reckoned that the four-month window should be a maximum rather than a mini-mum, and that I should shoot for three months. In the end I was back in two months, while the other guy who'd had the op at the same time was still in a sling and ended up being out for twice as long.

The Institute was based in Stellenbosch, and the main Province facilities were in Cape Town, so I divided my time between the two. Stellenbosch is South Africa's premier wine-growing region, the heart of the famous wine route, so there are always lots of tourists around, lots of cafes, bars and restaurants: a happy, prosperous, vibrant and relaxed place. Most of all, Stellenbosch and Cape Town both have huge student populations. Students mean partying, and wherever there was a party that's where I'd be. I was a real party animal, a joker and a drinker, and I was young enough and talented enough to do all that and play good rugby.

In fact, my first game back after the op was a good example of this. I wasn't supposed to play at all and had had a few drinks to celebrate the operation's success, but then someone got injured and I was in. Nick was playing 10, and I went to him before the start.

'Brother,' I said, 'whatever you do, don't give me the ball today.'

'Sure thing,' he replied.

First breakdown, he popped the ball to me, and I got klapped by their entire back row. Not ideal with a hangover. Nick thought this was wildly funny, and for the next 80 minutes whenever he had the ball he'd look around for me and pass me that thing as though it was laser-guided. After a while, I figured that I might as well accept this was the way it was going to be, and in the end I played pretty well.

That was the only criterion: you could do what you liked off the pitch as long as it didn't affect your ability to train or play. Missing a training session without a proper reason was the biggest sin of all, and there was a strict three-strike policy for those who did: first a warning, then sent home for a fort-night, and finally thrown out of the Institute for good.

They started us early, with sessions beginning at 6 a.m. This was a deliberate choice, not just because it helped ensure that we could get a full day's training in with breaks for rest, meet-ings and rehab, but also because at that time in the morning you see who really wants to be there and who can still put in the effort when they're tired.

Gradually, though, I worked out that I only had one half of the equation right. It wasn't enough just to not affect my play; it was actually about doing things to ensure that play improved. Sure, I could play with a hangover and get away with it, but wasn't it more desirable not to have that hangover and play even better? Getting away with it was a baseline, but it wasn't maximising improvement. There were no classes offered in self-control and discipline, yet those were two of the most vital skills a young rugby player needs to develop. After all, there were plenty of opportunities to indulge in the good life and celebrate my successes, both real and imagined.

We also had to adjust to a massively skewed ratio of train-ing to game time. At school there had been matches every weekend, which forced a specific weekly rhythm: preparation, game, recovery, preparation, game, recovery. Improvements in skills and fitness came largely through playing, and we'd work out specific tactics for each opponent, but the rigours of the calendar meant there was little time for systematic long-term coaching. In the first few months at the Institute, we didn't play more than a handful of matches. Instead, we focused on 'chasing the load', or being able to handle the much greater physical and psychological demands of professional rugby. We had to rate everything we did on and off the field on a scale of one to ten, and if those numbers were too low we had to find ways of getting them up.

The two men in charge of the whole set-up were Rassie Erasmus and Allister Coetzee. Coach Rassie was overall director of rugby for the entire region, while Coach Allister was in charge of the senior team. In years to come, these men would be instrumental in progressing my Springbok career – Coach Allister would make me a regular member of the starting line-up, and of course Coach Rassie would make me captain – but at the time they were the head honchos who we were all desperate to impress. We didn't see that much of them, but now and then they'd come down to watch us play, and we were all well aware that even when they weren't there our performances were being fed back to them. They had expectations of us, and even if they rated someone very highly they still didn't play favourites.

Some of the older players took me under their wing and looked after me, but none more so than Bryan Habana. He was the fines master too – which shows you the esteem in which he was held, since that post is almost always the preserve of the front rowers – and fined me a few times when I'd done something wrong, but never in an unfriendly way. He'd take time out before a match to see if I was okay, or afterwards if things hadn't gone well; not making a big deal of things, but always there. He was and remains an awesome human being, and I tried to follow his example when I became a senior team member and looked out for the younger players coming through.

Most guys there had options if this whole rugby thing didn't work out. I felt that I didn't. I'd had a great education at Grey, of course, but my family weren't any richer or better connected because of that. Grey had given me the chance to express my talent for rugby and it had the resources to help me improve. My grades there meant I wasn't going to go off and become a lawyer or an accountant if this didn't happen for me; there was no family farm for me to help run. I *had* to make it; I had no alternative. Every day my mindset was the same: 'You have nothing, this is all you have, you'd better make this work, this is where you're at, how much do you want it?'

I compared my situation to that of a teammate of mine. We weren't exactly at the same stage – he was at university while I was at the Institute – but he was a hell of a good rugby player too, at least until he did his anterior cruciate ligament and needed an entire knee reconstruction. That forced him to assess how much he really wanted to be a rugby player. He could definitely have played franchise rugby, perhaps even found himself on the edges of the Springbok set-up, but he knew he was unlikely to go further than that: and that would have been a big commitment for a smart guy with lots of career options who'd always regarded rugby as a fun thing to do with his mates rather than the be-all and end-all. So he gave it up. His situation was different from mine.

There were still lots of small reminders of where I'd come from. Audi offered me sponsorship and a loan vehicle, which was great, except for one thing: I didn't know how to drive.

And since I'd always had someone to give me a lift to training, or the team bus to take us to matches, I'd never really bothered. I felt a bit embarrassed telling Audi that though I'd love a car it wasn't quite as simple as that, but they were great, paying for me to have lessons and get my licence. And perhaps because of these reminders, I felt very evangelical about the game. I wanted to get as many people watching rugby as possible. Every player received an allocation of tickets, and sometimes I'd take mine – and any spare ones that were going – and hand them out in the street to people who wanted to come and watch. I'd done a similar thing back in Zwide when playing for Grey, organising for buses to go and pick people up to come and watch us.

I was called up for the 'Baby Boks', the Under-20 Springbok side. It was another stepping stone on the way to full international status, and there were a few guys who I'd known through Craven Week and the SA Schools sides like Pat Lambie, Elton Jantjies and CJ Stander. We went to Argentina for the Junior World Championship, which wasn't my first time abroad – I'd been on overseas holidays with schoolfriends at Grey and their families – but was the first time I'd travelled outside South Africa as part of a rugby team, wearing our blazers proudly and clocking the looks from the public as we attended functions, posed for photoshoots or just did some sightseeing. I scored two tries – my first points for my country – in a rout of Scotland in the pool stages. But we came unstuck in the semis against – who else? – the All Blacks. South Africa against New Zealand is the most storied and fiercest rivalry in international rugby, and even at junior level you feel it. It doesn't matter what age group you're playing in; there's nothing quite like running out to face 15 guys dressed all in black, and you never forget any matches you play against them, no matter the result.

I made my debut for Province in February 2011. It wasn't an especially big game – it was against the Golden Lions in the Vodacom Cup, which is one down from the Currie Cup, and there were only 7,000 spectators in Newlands – but it was still a thrill pulling on the famous blue and white striped shirt with the red disa above the heart for the first time as a 1st XV player. People had warned me that the game would be a lot quicker than what I'd been used to so far, but I didn't find that to be the case. We snatched a draw with pretty much the last kick of the match, and then went on a winning spree for the rest of the group stage before losing to the Sharks in the quarter-finals.

From then on, it all happened pretty fast. In June, I played my second Junior World Championship, this time in Italy, and while I was out there I was called up for the Stormers. They were scheduled to face the Crusaders in the Super Rugby semi-final at Newlands in early July, and since both Duane Vermeulen and Pieter Louw were out with injury I was next in line. I headed back after the England game in our pool, the only one we lost, having beaten Scotland and Ireland.

I was going to be on the bench. The Crusaders were pretty much as good as it got: their pack formed the nucleus of the All Blacks' pack who in a few months' time would be world champions, and they also had Dan Carter at fly-half, the best 10 in the world. They'd beaten us eight out of the last ten times we'd met, and even our home advantage wasn't all that it could be given the size and passion of the New Zealand fanbase in Cape Town.

This was a massive step up for me, and I had to be absolutely sure not to mess it up. My instructions were simple: get an early night and plenty of rest. So what did I do? I went out with one of my teammates, but then we were mugged and I was beaten up so badly that my tongue was too swollen to speak.

I was taken for scans, where the doctors confirmed there was no way I could play. I was only 20 years old and had just messed up the chance to play a Super Rugby semi-final against the likes of Richie McCaw, Dan Carter, Kieran Read, Sam Whitelock and Sonny Bill Williams. Coach Rassie was furious with me, and rightly so. I shouldn't have gone out in the first place. I could tell myself that my presence wouldn't have made much difference to the result – we lost 29–10 and, an early penalty apart, never even had the lead – but again that wasn't the point.

We lost the Currie Cup semi-final too later that year to the Lions. On a personal level I'd had a decent season – I'd played Vodacom and Currie Cups, and would have had a Super Rugby runout too if I hadn't been such a jerk. I'd taken the leap to pro rugby in my stride, and I was still only 20. But semi-final losses are the hardest of all to bear, and as a franchise we'd had two of them.

* * *

We needed to do better in 2012. People were down on us, especially as Coach Rassie had left to take up a job with the Springboks, but we felt good about the season.

I made my Super Rugby debut in the first game of that new season, against the Hurricanes at Newlands. I was on the bench, but after just 15 minutes Schalk got injured. The crowd fell silent when they saw that he was hurt. He was the guy who'd given me an autograph back at Grey and someone I looked up to so much – I never thought a moment like this would come along. He couldn't continue, so he was carted from the pitch in a motorised buggy and I was on. It was earlier than I'd expected – I reckoned I'd get maybe 20 minutes at the end, if that – but that didn't matter. It could be difficult as a sub, when I was mentally primed to have a certain amount of warm-up time before going on, but I'd also have to adjust on the hoof when things didn't happen as planned. It was 7–3 to us at the time, and over the next ten minutes or so two penalties to us and one to them took the score out to 13–6.

Then we had a lineout on their five-metre line. Tiaan Liebenberg's throw found Andries Bekker, we formed a maul and drove for the line. I was the guy at the back with the ball in hand, so all I had to do was dive for the ground when I saw the tryline. Thirteen minutes as a Stormers player, and I was already a try scorer! Jean de Villiers lifted me off my feet in a massive bear hug.

We were never headed again. There was a moment early in the second half when Beauden Barrett brought the scores back level to 23–23 by converting his own try, but we soon stretched away again and won 39–26.

Dressing rooms are usually happy places after wins like that – an exciting game, good opponents and a capacity crowd – but our joy was tempered by news that Schalk had torn his medial ligaments and would be out for at least six weeks. It was a bitter blow – he was our captain, an inspirational figure on and off the field – and we would miss him, but for me at least there was no denying the uncomfortable truth: that his misfortune was my opportunity.

Any professional sportsman or woman who says that these kind of calculations don't enter their head is lying. When it's your living, you want to play as often as you can. If you're the one in possession of the jersey, you don't want to give someone else the chance to take it off you; if you're the one warming the bench, you want to get the chance to show what you can do on the pitch, and as often as not that comes about because the guy ahead of you gets injured. It's not right or wrong, fair or unfair; it's just the way it is. Schalk was my hero, and had been for a long time: seven years earlier it had been his autograph I'd sought ahead of all the other Springboks when they'd come to train at Grey, and now I'd got to know him I knew that he was every bit as awesome an oke as he was a player. He was the guy who dominated all the fitness and conditioning charts at Province, and I'd set myself to push and challenge him on that front; if you want to be the best you have to beat the best, and he was that guy.

But right now, none of that mattered. This was my chance to stake a claim for that six jersey and make it mine.

I did just that. The 2012 season was a step up from anything I'd done before. Nine months previously I'd been playing

Junior World Championships against the stars of the future; now I was up against the best players in the world. We won our first seven games on the bounce and only lost two out of the total 16 to top not just the South African Conference but the entire table (there were 15 sides, five each from South Africa, New Zealand and Australia). We were never lower than fourth at any stage in the season, and ended up two points clear of the Chiefs and eight points ahead of the Reds.

Schalk's knee didn't clear up in the six weeks predicted, or even the six weeks after that. In fact, he ended up missing the entire season. I like to think that I was playing well enough to have made it a fight for the jersey if he'd made it back, or at the very least to have looked at switching around some back-row positions, but in the end it didn't come to that. And the experience was invaluable. Each one of those games was a learning curve, not just the matches themselves but everything around them too: the training, the tactics, the way guys prepared, how to deal with jet lag and travel, and so on.

But winning the regular season championship wasn't enough; there were play-offs to go through in order to determine who was going to be Super Rugby champion. Our semi-final was against the Sharks at Newlands, and it wasn't just the fact we were playing at home which would help us. We'd also had a week off as automatic semi-final qualifiers, while the Sharks had had to go to Brisbane the previous week to beat the Reds. They'd come into form at just the right time – they'd played superbly in that victory over the Reds – but our defence was resolute and our ability to conjure tries from broken play was second to none.

It didn't quite happen. Louis Ludik scored late in the first half to give them an 11–3 lead, and we were still a score adrift at 16–9 near the hour mark when JP Pietersen ran hard at our defence, stepped inside and scored. With 15 minutes left Jean de Villiers took a sweet angle to send Gio Aplon through and bring us back to 23–16. The comeback looked on, and the crowd were in full voice. A penalty with eight minutes left put us only four points down: a try would be enough. But three minutes later, the Sharks were camped on our 22 and gave their fly-half Frédéric Michalak the chance to drop for goal. It wasn't the prettiest kick ever seen – flat, wobbling and staying low in flight – but it went through the sticks, and that was all that counted. In the red zone, with 80 minutes gone and the next dead ball signalling the end of the match, I ran hard at the defence but was wrapped up, and a couple of phases later the Sharks got a turnover, kicked the ball out, and that was it. Another semi-final, another loss.

From a personal point of view, the campaign had been a success. First seasons come in all shapes and sizes, and I'd had a good one. I was new on the block and getting spoken about more with each game that passed. I put in enough big hits and made enough metres with ball in hand to have caught the eye of the casual fan, but also – more importantly – impressed my teammates and coaches with the less flashy, vital stuff: positioning, workrate, support play, and so on. Anyone can look a hero out in the wide open spaces, but it's the hard yards at the breakdown and the bottom of the ruck which make the biggest difference.

If things were happening for me on the pitch in 2012, though, that was nothing compared to what was happening off the pitch.

There's a restaurant in Stellenbosch called Gino's, an Italian place which started out in Joburg in the Eighties and became so popular – queues on Friday and Saturday nights could be five hours long – that they soon opened a second branch in Stellenbosch. Gino's is a perfect university town restaurant – fun, bouncing, affordable and informal (it was originally called 'Paesa', which is how Italians address someone from the same village as themselves, but they changed the name as too many people couldn't pronounce it). Most of all, Gino's is a family restaurant, family-run and family-orientated, which made it the perfect place to meet the woman who would become my wife.

It was 19 May 2012. We'd just beaten the Waratahs in a pretty dull Super Rugby game at Newlands, and I went to Gino's with my girlfriend at the time, some of the Waratahs boys, and the cousin of a woman called Rachel Smith. We'd been there a while when Rachel arrived with her brother and sister. She didn't think I was anything special: in fact, she thought I was quite rude because when they arrived I was sitting in a corner and didn't get up or say hi to them. Then she sat down on the other side of the table, so I didn't really speak to her too much all evening.

But there was something about her which really got to me. It wasn't just that she was beautiful, though she was: it was the way she carried herself, the sense that here was someone special and not like other women. I sent her a Facebook message not long after that, and we began chatting. At first it was just as friends; I was in a relationship at the time, even though it was on and off and not particularly serious. I was young, still 20, and full of it. I loved rugby, I loved drinking, I loved girls. I wasn't much of a long-term bet for anyone looking for a relationship.

I really liked Rachel and I told her so, but my actions were bad: I just wasn't mature enough to deal with it. I knew she felt the same way and that she found it hard to totally let herself go. It took her a long time to allow herself to love me. Gradually I realised that, whoever else I was with, I always wanted to be with Rachel. We were good for each other. We had qualities and strengths that the other didn't have. She brought a lot of calmness to my crazy. I could get caught up in this world with a lot of money and the extreme stuff that sportsmen get up to, but she'd never been about either of those. In turn, I helped soften some of her harder edges. She was really driven, this tough fighter woman, and she found it a challenge to have someone come to her and say, 'No, you have to be nicer to people, you have to be kinder,' when she was used to fighting in everything she did. To be challenged like that by me brought her to a much better place.

Of all the things I loved about her, one of the biggest was the fact that she didn't need me. There were girls who would be all over you because you were a pro rugby player in a rugby-mad city, but Rachel wasn't one of them. She couldn't have cared less. She was fiercely independent, and she'd had a tough childhood like me, though in some ways even more hectic. A year older than me and from Grahamstown (now Makhanda), about an hour and a half's drive from PE, she was born not breathing and the doctors took a while to rectify that.

I knew there was a theory that when choosing a partner you look for something you don't have yourself but which you admire in other people: well, I'd only ever really had to look after myself, and I found the side of her which nurtured other people really attractive. In turn, she said she liked the way I was around people. Some of the guys she'd been out with before were often so rude to the people who would, for example, come to their car window to ask for money or food. That was a total turn-off for her, a dealbreaker. But if someone on the street asked me for help I'd always try to help them: find them something to eat, give them money, something like that. I'd never just ignore them. I knew all too well what it was like not to have anything.

There are so many things, large and small, that I love about Rachel. I first ate Mexican food with her. I first ate sushi with her. She taught me how to use chopsticks. She taught me how to drive in a small Hyundai Atos. I once missed a junction and had to do a U-turn, but I took it too quickly and the car ended up on two wheels like in some sort of movie stunt. She was chilled, but I freaked out. I took my feet off the pedals and my hands off the wheel. Somehow I stopped the car and said, 'I'm out. You have to drive. It's the passenger seat for me.'

There are few places in the world where absolutely everyone is cool with mixed-race relationships, and South Africa isn't one of them. When our relationship became public we took our fair share of flak, especially on social media. There were

I did a photoshoot for the *Herald* newspaper when I was in the 1st XV at Grey High School.

Playing 1st XV Grade 11 for Grey against our arch-rivals Grey College, Bloemfontein, at their ground in 2008. It was the only game we lost that season.

We played Grey Bloem at home in my final year of school and lost again, 16–0. I went to play for SA Schools after this.

Playing for Grey against Kingswood College in 2009. We won 71–13.

The only hostel boys to be elected as school prefects, we were all aged 17.

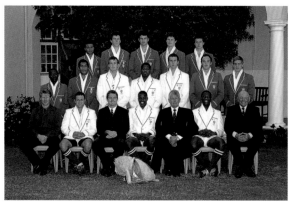

Grey High School 1st XV team photo, 2009.

Playing (and scoring!) for Western Province against GWK Griquas
in an Absa Currie Cup match in Cape Town, 16 July 2011.

Playing for the Stormers against the
Sharks in a Super Rugby match in Cape
Town, 3 March 2012.

Making a break for the Stormers in a
Super Rugby match against the Highlanders
at Forsyth Barr Stadium in Dunedin,
New Zealand, 7 April 2012.

In 2018 my old club team the African Bombers played in the
Cape Town 10s tournament for the first time – and won! Mzwandile
Stick and I were the coaches that day.

In Joburg, on the day we departed for the
2019 Rugby World Cup in Japan.

We learned how to make sushi in Japan,
which was great fun.

On one of our days off in Japan we went to see how they made swords.

I was out for dinner with the boys and was thrilled when we saw Goku from the *Dragon Ball* series.

Here we are – the infamous sushi-making squad!

Japan vs South Africa, 2019 Rugby World Cup quarter-final, tackling Amanaki Mafi with the help of Handre Pollard. We won 26–3.

The coin toss prior to the final in Yokohama, with match referee Jérôme Garcès and Owen Farrell of England.

Taking down England's Tom Curry during the match. We dominated the forward battle and ran out 32–12 winners.

This was an important moment for Eben and me, as we had been playing together since 2010, the year after we left school – from Western Province U19s to winning the World Cup with the Springboks.

My dad, Rachel and the kids got to come on to the field after the World Cup Final victory. It was special to have my family share those moments with me; it is their medal just as much as it is mine.

Prince Harry came into the changing room after the final to congratulate the team.

My wife, children, brother-in-law, father-in-law, father, best friend, mother figure and brother figure got to celebrate with me at the post-match function at our hotel – I was also presented with my 50th Test cap.

Rachel and I visited businessman and philanthropist Vincent Mai and his wife Annie in New York City. Vincent took us with some of his family to an ice-hockey game, my first ever. It was amazing. Go, Rangers!

black people asking why I couldn't have found a black wife and white people asking why Rachel couldn't have found a white husband – as though that was the way these things worked! I didn't think about any of that. I fell in love with her, that was it. The way I was brought up, my grandmother never told me not to love someone because of their skin colour. She just said if you love the person, you love the person, it doesn't matter who they are. And bring them home to your family. When I brought Rachel home to my family, they loved her and they enjoyed her company, and that was the most important thing.

Rachel and I hadn't been together very long when I went through something really important to any Xhosa male: the initiation ritual, where boys go into the bush as *abakwetha* and make the transition to manhood. Most boys do it straight after they leave school, but I had been too caught up in my rugby career, and every time I'd thought about doing it after that there'd always been a reason not to – a move from the academy to the senior Province team, a training bloc for the Super Rugby season, things like that. I knew that if and when I became a Springbok, the opportunities would narrow still further. To the outside world the process may seem weird, archaic, even brutal, but within Xhosa culture it's very much valued, and I knew of at least one successful rugby player who'd never undergone it and was viewed in certain quarters as not a proper man as a result.

There's an old rugby saying – 'What goes on tour stays on tour.' It's often said half-jokingly. The same thing applies to initiation, but in this case it's said deadly seriously. It's a sacred thing done with the guys and we pledge never to share what happened with those who weren't there, though the basics are well enough known: you temporarily surrender your name, your clothes are shredded, you carry a short stick with a white cloth tied to one end, you eat and drink very little, and you build up to the ceremonial circumcision and the period of recovery that follows it. You go through so much there. There's often bullying and fighting, and some people really can't hack it. You're alone, you can't sleep, you're sore and there's nothing you can do about it. You listen to the pain. And you think.

Rachel was waiting for me when I came back from the bush. My dad wasn't there as he was in prison. It was tough for me as I wanted him there to experience that with me; he hadn't been around for many, if any, of my special moments, and this in particular was something I wanted him to see.

I was called up for the squad for the first Rugby Championship (it had previously been the Tri Nations, involving South Africa, New Zealand and Australia, but now Argentina had joined so it had been renamed). But I was one of the 'young guns', not expected to play but just to gain experience being inside the camp, blend me in slowly and give me the necessary exposure. So I was released back to Province before the internationals began, and on the same day that the Springboks were playing Argentina I broke my left thumb in a Currie Cup game against the Golden Lions. I knew it was broken the moment it happened – a fracture has a kind of deep-seated pain which I knew wouldn't easily pass, even if a sprain could be more sharply painful – and the x-ray showed that I'd need surgery.

That was the rest of the season gone, so we decided to kill two birds with one stone and do a shoulder operation at the same time: the same operation as I'd had a couple of years previously, only this time on the other shoulder.

In my absence, and after three successive semi-finals in major club competitions, Province beat the Sharks to win the Currie Cup. Now I encountered the flipside of that feeling I'd had earlier when Schalk was out, wanting to be involved at all costs: that when I wasn't involved, I didn't feel that a team's success belonged to me in any way. I'd played in a couple of the Currie Cup pool matches, but not at the sharp end of the competition, and certainly not in the final. Technically I was part of a Currie Cup-winning squad, but I didn't feel it, and to this day when people ask me how many trophies I've won I say, 'Just the one' ...

At the end of the year, I was awarded Newcomer of the Year in the South African Sports Awards. It was a huge honour, because the awards covered all sports rather than just rugby, and I was in some pretty serious company: Olympic gold medal swimmer Chad le Clos won Sports Star of the Year, cricketer Vernon Philander was Sportsman of the Year, and athlete Caster Semenya was Sportswoman of the Year.

On the pitch, the 2013 Super Rugby season wasn't nearly as successful as the previous year had been. We finished mid-table both overall and of the South African teams, which was a big comedown from the previous year. We never really got any momentum going, and only five victories in our five last games elevated us even to that mid-table status; up until then we'd been hovering round about 10th or 11th rather than 7th.

For me, however, the season would be memorable in another way. There was a break before the final three rounds so that international matches could be played, and the Springboks were playing a quadrangular tournament with Italy, Samoa and Scotland. I wasn't in the squad for the first match against Italy, which we won 44–10: Francois Louw started at six, with Marcell Coetzee on the bench. But Francois had been given permission to miss the next match, against Scotland in Nelspruit, so he could get married. Marcell took his place and I was named among the replacements. There was no absolute guarantee I'd get on, of course, but rugby was by now so clearly a 23-man game that I would almost certainly take the field at some stage.

It was the week before my 22nd birthday, and I was going to be a Springbok.

3

SPRINGBOK

In most countries, the national jersey is a fairly uncomplicated symbol that the wearer has ascended to the top of the game. In South Africa, it's much more than that. For so long, the Springbok emblem of a leaping antelope represented only a small part of the country and reflected how that part felt about themselves: that rugby was a sport for real men, white Afrikaner men, while soccer was a game for black men. For the Afrikaner in apartheid South Africa, the Springbok jersey was part of a holy trinity along with the old flag, striped in blue, white and orange as a nod to their Dutch forebears, and 'Die Stem', the anthem which sang of the trekkers' glories. Both the flag and the anthem went soon after apartheid ended, but the jersey endured, thanks in no small part to Mr Mandela himself, who wanted to use it to unite the nation.

And now I was going to be a Bok.

In the build-up to my debut Test, the Springbok captain Jean de Villiers made sure that he was sharing a room with me. He could have had his own room, both as captain and as someone with more than 50 caps, but he gave that privilege up so he could be there for me: to calm me down if I needed, talk me through what I could expect and what was expected of me, and reassure me that I belonged at this level. There was a lot to remember in terms of calls and moves, and he helped me with those too.

The match took place on my last day of being 21. My dad was in the stands. It was only the second time he'd seen me play, and the first time he'd been on a plane. His leg was in plaster – he'd broken it falling off a wall – so getting him all the way there had been a bit of a kerfuffle, but he'd made it. I knew he'd be more emotional than me; he'd been a good rugby player himself, and even though we'd missed so much time together during my youth, I was incredibly proud that he was here.

I was well aware that I was only in the 23 because Francois Louw was away, but I also figured that selection issues were firmly in the camp of 'things I could do nothing about'. All I could do was play my best and see what happened from there.

The game was only four minutes old when Arno Botha was injured. For some reason I always had the same instinctive reaction to an injury that early in a match: no, it can't be that serious. It's totally irrational, obviously – how serious an injury is has nothing to do with how long the game's been going on for – but still. Either way, it was obvious pretty quickly that Arno's injury was bad enough for him to have to come off. I was the only designated back-row cover on the bench. I was coming on.

I had only a few seconds to get myself ready: training top off, gumshield in, frantically trying to remember the lineout calls I'd been struggling with all week. My mind was suddenly going at a million miles an hour. I'd waited all my life for this moment, and now it had finally come I suddenly didn't feel quite ready.

Our forwards coach Johann van Graan put his arm round my shoulder. He was an interesting guy: not only was he very young for a coach – only in his early thirties, so he was a less remote figure for me than some of his colleagues – but he hadn't played rugby himself at any really high level. He had just always been big into analysis and had turned himself into a respected coach, which is easier said than done when some players can still be a bit 'show us your medals' in their attitude.

'Siya,' Johann said.

'Yes?'

'Don't worry about the lineout calls. Just play. Just be you.'

I'll never forget those words. They were the best thing anyone could have said to me. Then the official tapped me on the shoulder and on I ran.

I was Springbok number 851. The number is a small thing but an important one; the moment you take the field you're a Springbok, whether that's your only cap or whether you go on to win 100, and they can never take it away from you.

Eben was the first person to give me a hug, then Jean, then Bryan: my Stormers teammates, letting me know they had my back and that I was good enough to mix it at this level.

Just play. Just be you.

So that's just what I did. I ran well, I put in good tackles, I secured a turnover, and I almost scored a try – what a feat that would have been, to go with the try on my Super Rugby debut the previous year. Lots of people say their Test debut goes by in a flash, but I can remember all of it.

Scotland were a decent side. They were 10–6 up at half-time, and in the shed during the break Jean emphasised one thing above all to us: that when the second half started, we had to score first, absolutely had to. Scotland were playing well, and we couldn't let them get more than a converted try ahead.

We came sprinting out for the second half, fired up by Jean's words – and within two minutes the Scottish lock Tim Swinson came barrelling up the middle and the centre Alex Dunbar was out wide to finish off the move on the overlap.

We huddled under the posts as Greig Laidlaw lined up the conversion. I was panicking. I thought, 'No, we're the Springboks, this can't be happening.' I looked to Jean for words of defiance and encouragement ... and saw that he was laughing!

'Don't worry, boys,' he said. 'We'll get 'em. Just keep playing.'

We did keep playing, and we did get them. Laidlaw's conversion to make it 17–6 were their last points. We found another gear, and scored three tries – a penalty try when Scotland collapsed a maul near their line, a try from my old Grey school-mate JJ Engelbrecht, and one right at the end from Jan Serfontein which put a slightly undeserved gloss on the score at 30–17. I was named man of the match – on my debut! It was the kind of thing I'd dreamt about, and pretty much every match report mentioned me and praised the way I'd played. I knew that Test rugby wouldn't – couldn't – always be so easy, but I'd enjoy it while it was.

After the game, I asked Jean why he'd been laughing. He just said that he couldn't show us how much he was panicking for fear that the panic would spread and inhibit our play. It was a lesson I'd remember both as a player and later as a captain: not necessarily that every reversal needs to be laughed off, but that a bit of kidology is needed now and then.

Not long afterwards, I got a call from a number I didn't recognise. It was my old accountancy teacher from Grey, the one who'd told me I was arrogant for ditching his subject and proclaiming that one day I'd be a Springbok. He congratulated me wholeheartedly and laughed that, ironically for a discipline where balancing the books was always essential, there was no zero sum here: rugby's gain was definitely not accountancy's loss.

I retained my place on the bench for the next match against Samoa. The match wasn't nearly as close – we were 32–9 up at half-time and ended up winning 56–23 – but the Pacific Islands sides are always physical, they always smash their opponents around, and this was no exception. I came on for Pierre Spies at half-time as he was feeling a knock, but only seven minutes later I tried to tackle one of their props and got smacked in the head as he ran over me. I went off for an HIA (head injury assessment), but in those days they were still pretty basic – a few questions for which I'd have had to have been more or less comatose not to answer correctly – and five minutes later I was back on. I don't remember much about the rest of the match. It wasn't anything extraordinary, playing with concussion like that. All I needed to remember was which side I was on, who was wearing the same jerseys as me, and which way I was going. Muscle memory and instinct did the rest.

I played the Rugby Championship in 2013, but always as a sub: 16 minutes against Argentina in Johannesburg, 12 against the same opponents in Mendoza, 10 against Australia in Brisbane, six against New Zealand in Auckland, 21 against Australia in Cape Town and 42 against the All Blacks in Johannesburg when Willem Alberts had to come off injured just before half-time. Twenty minutes is the minimum I felt I needed to really have an impact, and it was hard to make an impression with relatively little game time. The same applied in the autumn internationals in Europe, where I had 14 minutes against Wales and six against France. Clearly it was good that I was in the team at all, and I knew that every player felt that they should start, but it was still frustrating. It was no accident that my best performance, the man of the match outing against Scotland, should have come when I played pretty much the whole game, albeit by accident rather than design. That debut might have been the start of great things, with me kicking on and establishing myself in the side. Now I felt that I was treading water, not really getting a chance to show what I could do but at least in the mix rather than out of the national set-up altogether.

If 2013 would end up feeling frustrating, it was nothing compared to 2014. For the Stormers, the heady days of topping the Super Rugby table only a couple of years beforehand seemed as though they'd happened in a different era altogether. The team was playing badly right from the start, a 34–10 defeat to the Lions, and on a personal note I was seriously out of form. We lost five matches in a row in the early part of the season, we were either last or second last for nine consecutive rounds, and only a good run towards the end lifted us up to 11th.

Playing in a struggling team is hard on both an individual and collective level. The collective level is obvious – the team is losing, after all, and try as the players might it can be hard to snap out of negativity – but as an individual whatever I did didn't seem to make a difference. Occasionally, I had games when I made lots of good tackles, but in attack I seemed to be just that little bit too slow to the ball or the breakdown. I tried too hard to make things happen and forgot the basics, which made things worse. I took it seriously, as I should, but too seriously, so I tensed up.

The Currie Cup offered a chance to salvage something from the year. We as a squad, and certainly me personally, decided to try and enjoy ourselves, not least because we'd play better that way. Whatever had been lacking in Super Rugby had been rectified, at least partly. As Western Province we won our first five games, and I was playing a big part in that: running, stealing and defending well. But then, early on against the Golden Lions, I tore the medial collateral ligaments in both knees. Always the Lions, always the Currie Cup: it had been in this fixture two years ago that I'd broken my thumb and been obliged to sit out the remainder of the competition, including the fact that Province won it. And so history repeated itself this time, up to and including a Province triumph (against the Lions, ironically). Twice now Province had won the Currie Cup during my time there, and twice I'd been denied the chance to play my part. This one didn't feel any more 'mine' than the previous one had done.

There were lighter moments, reminders of what rugby should be about. In 2014, Grey invited me back to hand out the shirts to the boys before the match against Grey Bloem. I told the boys that even though I was now a Springbok, they had the chance to do something I'd never managed and beat our school's nemesis. If they pulled it off, it would be a triumph which would live with them forever; it happened so rarely, so the ones who did it had a special place in Grey folklore. And they did it! They won 27–20, the first time in a decade we'd beaten them – and, at the time of writing, the last time too. Victories over Grey Bloem come around only a little more often than Springbok World Cups do …

With the form I was in, there was no way I should have been selected for the Springboks that year, and I wasn't. It was, by a long way, the darkest period in my career. Twelve months ago I had been man of the match on my debut and the hottest new thing in Springbok rugby. Now I felt worthless. The drop had been dizzying and disorientating, and I didn't know how to turn it round.

If 2014 was a bust on the field, off the field things were much better.

Early in the year we found out that Rachel was pregnant and due to give birth in November. We were going to be parents. I was going to be a father. The idea thrilled and terrified me all at once. I wanted to be the kind of father I'd never had myself, but at the same time I wondered whether I'd be able to. I still had a lot of growing up to do, even though I didn't realise it at the time. I thought – hoped – life would go on as normal once the baby arrived, and it would be a while before I realised that things didn't work that way.

Then in June the Springboks played a Test against Scotland in PE. I was in the wider squad but not required for the match itself, so I went back to Zwide to see my old friends. There I met my cousin, who said he'd seen my brother and sister, Liyema and Liphelo. Technically they're my half-brother and half-sister, but that's a distinction I've always ignored. They're my brother and sister in heart and soul. I hadn't seen them since my mum died, and when their own father also died and left them orphaned I'd started looking for them. I'd ask around, but sooner or later I'd always come up against a dead end: 'Oh, they were here a few months ago, but now they've been moved on and we don't have details for them.' They went from one family member to the next, but no-one was really in a position to help them long-term, or at least that's what they said.

So they were sent to social workers and sucked into the system: sometimes with foster parents and other times in orphanages, sometimes together and other times apart, sometimes in Zwide and other times in Motherwell or New Brighton. I went looking for them for so long, but it was hard. It wasn't like there was one place I could go to find out for sure where they were; even if I could have located the right government department, they wouldn't have been allowed to pass on the information to me. I lost the plot more than once with members of my extended family. Liyema and Liphelo were just kids, young and poor and defenceless, and every adult around should have been moving heaven and earth to help them, not just passing them on to an overburdened state system and washing their hands of them. And I knew that I'd be able to do what people in Zwide couldn't: put them through school and make sure they got proper opportunities.

But now my cousin was saying he'd found them. I put him in the car and he took me to the place they were staying, with a nice old grandmother. They were at school at the time, but I came back later and met them. It was very emotional, so emotional that I don't really have the words for it. It was amazing. My sister, who was six, didn't know who I was; she'd been crawling when I last saw her, and she was wary and backing away from me. But my brother was 12 and remembered me, and when my sister saw this she was reassured and came to sit on my lap. I went to a shop and filled the boot with chocolate – I just wanted to buy them as many sweets as I could. It filled my heart with so much joy to have found them again, and leaving them was so hard I almost had to be dragged away; but I told them I'd be back, and I meant it. They'd been let down by too many people, and I wasn't going to be another of them.

Back home, the baby who was due to arrive in November had other ideas. Nicholas – we named him after Nick Holton – decided he couldn't wait and came two months prematurely via emergency caesarean. Here was this tiny baby, the most beautiful thing I'd ever seen: the start of our family together, Rachel and me. No matter how many children you have, the first one is the only time you go from not being parents to being parents; the moment you're first responsible for someone else's entire existence, the threshold you can only cross one time and in one direction. Perhaps it had been written in the stars: Rachel realised that Father's Day had fallen on my birthday the previous year, the day after I'd made my debut for the Springboks.

But my family was more than just the three of us. So just before Christmas, I went back to Zwide to pick up Liyema and Liphelo and take them to Cape Town for the holidays.

'Thank you for all you've done for them,' I said to the grandmother. 'Truly.'

'You're never going to bring them back, are you?' she said.

I smiled and shook my head. 'Not if I can help it.'

And I didn't. Once they came into our home, I couldn't let them go back. We had to go through a legal process, which we started after that holiday. It would take about 18 months until we finally became their legal guardians, and I say 'we' as it was very much a joint decision with Rachel. She could easily have said, 'Listen here, we've got a small baby of our own now, we're not responsible for Liyema and Liphelo too, not in this way; let's support them from a distance, but we can't take on the responsibility of looking after them, not when we've been together for such a short time.' But she said yes from the word go. She knew what it meant to me, she knew what it meant to have a fractured family and how both she and I had suffered from our own family dramas when we were growing up. She thought, 'These are Siya's siblings, he has never had a relationship with them, he wants them: of course they're going to come and live with us. Where else would they go? It made sense then, it makes sense now and it will always make sense.'

It never even occurred to her to say no. Her view was simple: she was committed not just to me but everything and everyone I came with too.

The guardian process was long and complex. It wasn't just as simple as me saying that I was their brother and I could offer them a better life than they'd have in Zwide. There was a lot of red tape to deal with, because the rules were the rules whoever the applicant was, and this was children's futures we were talking about. It couldn't just be signed off and forgotten. They needed to be sure that Rachel and I were the best possible option for Liyema and Liphelo – they were adamant that the process is about families for children and not children for families – and that involved orientation meetings, background checks, lifestyle evaluations, interviews with social workers, income and expenditure assessments, medicals, psychological evaluations, looking at the stability of mine and Rachel's relationship, home visits, police clearance and references. There were also cultural considerations because we were a mixed-race couple, which brought questions of how much we valued Xhosa traditions like clan names and Liyema going to the mountain in order to be circumcised and become a man. It frustrated the hell out of me at times, but Rachel was much more chilled. She dealt with the majority of the paperwork and was always like, 'This is how it is, just go with it, it'll happen, and if it takes a few months longer than we thought then so what? This is the rest of all our lives.'

Nothing I'd ever done on the pitch remotely compared to being able to do this for these two children. But I'd be lying if I said the adjustment was always easy. Liyema and Liphelo had been round the houses so often – literally – that they had never been used to a permanent home. They'd never lived in any place for more than a few months at a time. And now here they were, hundreds of miles away in Cape Town, with a brother they hardly knew and his girlfriend they knew even less. There were arguments and tears, of course there were – any family has those, let alone one that has been thrown together in extreme circumstances like this one. But they knew that we loved them, and gradually they realised and accepted that this was their permanent home, that no-one was going to come and cart them off or separate them from each other. There'd be no more foster homes, no more orphanages. They were safe here.

I was often away travelling and playing, so half the time they were on their own with Rachel. For a while she carried that, and lots of other things, alone in our relationship. Hell, I was hard to be around sometimes. There were times in the early days when Rachel would have to pay for our dates because I'd spent all my money on alcohol, and this was when I was getting paid good money as a pro player, not when I was earning much less in the academy. I was a bad drunk – not violent, but prone to getting so wasted that I'd pass out in the street. I'd get arrested and then wake up in a police cell with no idea of how I'd got there or even which police station I was in. I had too much fame and money before I had the character to handle them.

* * *

Every four years the World Cup hangs over everything. If you're even vaguely in contention to be a part of your country's squad, you're desperate to make the final cut; it's the highlight of any player's career. You want to play well enough to be chosen so you push yourself harder than ever before, but that increases the risk of injury which could scupper everything. It's a fine line, and every player has to tread it.

I knew that if my 2015 Super Rugby season was anywhere near as bad as 2014 had been, I'd be nowhere near the squad. The work I'd done in the gym while injured had paid off: I felt appreciably stronger, and if ever it was going to happen it had to be this year. I also knew it would be difficult to shine if the Stormers were as woeful as we'd been. On paper we were a good side shot through with internationals, and we had the best support base in the country.

It wasn't a perfect season, but it was a good one. A brief mid-season blip apart, we were always there or thereabouts, and ended up as the best South African franchise and third overall behind the Hurricanes and the Waratahs. I played in every game and my body held up well. We had high hopes that we could go a long way in the knockout stages, but it wasn't to be. The Brumbies came to Newlands and handed us our asses. Joe Tomane had a hat-trick within 24 minutes, they were 24–6 up at half-time, and even when they were down to 13 men in the last few minutes with Henry Speight red carded and Scott Fardy in the sin bin we still couldn't find a way through. They ended up beating us 39–19, with six tries to our sole effort, a wonderful intercept from Cheslin Kolbe.

I didn't play for the Boks that entire year until the final game before World Cup selection was made. It was against Argentina in Durban, and marked my first international for 21 months. I still thought I hadn't done enough to make the World Cup squad, but when the names were announced mine was among them, somewhat to my surprise.

The World Cup would take place in England, with a few matches in Wales too. There were several obvious stand-out matches in the pool stages. Twickenham would see England take on Australia; Wembley would play host to New Zealand and Argentina; and Ireland and France would duke it out at the Millennium Stadium.

It would be fair to say that the Brighton Community Stadium, where we'd play Japan, was not among them. We were twice world champions and one of the heavyweights of the global game. Japan, in contrast, had won only one of their previous 24 World Cup matches, and were ranked 15th in the world. We were second or third favourites for the tournament: you could get 1,500–1 against the Japanese lifting the trophy.

If you had tickets to this match, the Boks against the Blossoms, you had admission to what would surely be a drubbing. The bookies backed us by 40 points.

If you had tickets to this match, what you actually had was gold dust.

It was a beautiful south coast September day, more late summer than early autumn. There was not a cloud in the sky; certainly no hint of the storm which was about to be unleashed inside the stadium.

Right from the start, Japan show that they haven't come just to make up the numbers. Outmuscled by our vast forwards, they play smart, whipping the ball away fast from set-pieces, endlessly varying the points of contact.

Determined to wrest back control, we unleash our big men at close quarters. Francois Louw and Bismarck du Plessis score before half-time: Lood de Jager just after. But the Blossoms refuse to buckle. Every time we score and threaten to put the game to bed, the Blossoms just pick themselves up, dust themselves down and come back at us.

There are 25 minutes left and only three points in it when I replace Pieter-Steph. Five minutes later the scores are level as Ayumu Goromaru kicks a penalty to make it 22–22. Jean de Villiers gathers us together and speaks urgently. We've got 20 minutes left, he says. We need to keep playing to our strengths: keep it tight, batter them up front, grind them down. If we do that then we'll win. He's not laughing now as he'd been against Scotland on my debut, and he doesn't need to hide how concerned he is. You can see the difference on the benches. Our subbed players look bemused and frustrated: theirs are energised and excited.

But I'm still convinced we'll win, and two minutes later Adriaan Strauss smashes through some dodgy tackling to put us ahead again. Handre converts to make it 29–22. Surely this is it. Rugby history is full of underdogs who live with more fancied opponents for an hour or so before finally crumbling. That's what will happen here, I feel, especially when we have a lineout on their five-metre line. If we score again that'll be it;

but no, they bundle us into touch, secure their own lineout and clear their lines.

Twelve minutes left, inside our half. Japan pluck the ball off the top of a lineout and send it fast across the pitch, ending with a dizzyingly slick three-card trick – outside pass, inside pass, outside pass – for Goromaru to glide over on a running line so perfect it has even Springbok fans applauding. The conversion's not easy but he nails it anyway, and there it is: back to all square again, 29–29.

Keep going. Keep doing the basics.

Nine minutes left. Handre slices clean through off a scrum; a show of the ball in both hands with Jean on the dummy switch as decoy, and Handre goes between two defenders before being held up five metres short. I take it on and am wrapped up in a tackle. We have the penalty advantage, so still going for the try is basically a free play. Adriaan and Eben drive on and then I have it again, right on the line, so close I can practically touch it; but Japan put their bodies on the line, I can't ground the ball, and we have to take the three. Better than nothing, but less than we need. 32–29.

Three minutes left. Japan coming at us in waves, phase after phase after phase, forcing us to constantly keep scrambling and realigning. They're like Dracula, these boys, we just can't kill them off. On the 18th phase they drive for the corner and Coenraad Oosthuizen lies on the wrong side of the ruck to stop them getting quick ball. It's the smart thing to do – what else could he do, when a Japanese try would win the game? – but it's also an inevitable yellow card, and now we'll have to play out the last minute or so with only 14 men.

Japan have a penalty. We think they'll go for poles, secure the three points and the draw. They don't. They kick for touch and the lineout. They're trying to win this thing. The crowd roar their approval.

Japan win the lineout and set up a massive maul, with even some of their backs joining in to add weight. They're over our line now, bodies everywhere as they try to force the ball down. I have my hands on it along with a Japanese player – I can't see which one – and it takes all my strength to hold man and ball up. A few minutes ago I was inches from scoring at their end; now I'm holding them out by the same margin. Small margins, tiny measurements. Referee Jérôme Garcès peers into the melee and blows his whistle.

'Scrum five, red ball.'

My teammates haul me to my feet and slap me on the back. But Trevor's injured himself in that last maul and has to limp off. Since Coenraad's in the sin bin, we'll need two new props for the scrum, and one of the other forwards will have to go off to ensure we stay at 14 men. That'll be me. I'm pulled off, with Schalk going to blindside and no-one at eighthman. The scrum sets and wheels. Garcès blows. Another penalty to Japan with literally one second to go. Surely this time they'll go for poles and the draw?

It's eminently kickable, and Goromaru has nailed seven out of his eight shots at goal so far.

Their captain Michael Leitch doesn't hesitate. He asks Garcès to set the scrum again. Now we know for sure: the

Blossoms aren't in the least bit interested in a draw, and they're not going to die wondering. All or nothing. Death or glory.

They can't do it, surely? Sitting on the sideline, sweat drying on my forehead, I'm absolutely convinced we'll hold them out and win the match, and that afterwards everyone will say what a scare it was but we've just about squeaked home.

Past 80 minutes as the two teams set themselves for the scrum. The simplest and most binary of equations. All we have to do is get the ball and kick it out. All the Blossoms have to do is score a try. All. The atmosphere in the stadium is like a living thing, crackling and vital. The scrum crabs sideways and goes past 90 degrees. Garcès blows for it to be reset.

81 minutes gone. Crouch. Bind. Set. Several tons of pressure through the shoulders of men at the very edge of their limits. The scrum collapses. Again Garcès calls for the reset.

82 minutes. Schalk, grizzled warrior of endless campaigns, picks mud from between his studs. He, like all of them, needs every bit of grip he can get. Leitch barking at his men, geeing them up for one last, supreme effort. Leitch having to shout to be heard over the waterfalls of noise cascading down from the stands.

83 minutes, and still I don't think we'll lose. Our defence is solid. We'll hold them out. Every neutral cheering for the Blossoms. Atsushi Hiwasha with the feed once more. Fourie pushing him, niggling. Us with the shove. The Blossoms going backwards, the ball coming loose, Schalk and Fourie scrabbling for it. Amanaki Mafi scooping it up from under their noses. Still Japan's possession. Hiwasha going left to the blindside. Leitch driving on. Our thin green defensive line spread

across the pitch: making their tackles, checking their numbers, dragging each other into position.

Hiwasha spinning it right, out to the open prairies. Leitch again. Makabe. Tatekawa. The Japanese forwards making the hard yards. Suck in the defenders and go again, go again, go again. Hiwasha sniping towards the corner and giving it to Leitch a third time. Leitch was just at the bottom of a ruck; how the heck has he got up again so quickly? Leitch scragged by Adriaan. The crowd yearning, their noise now a high animal keening, as though by force of will alone they can propel the Blossoms over the line. Hiwasha sending it left again, out to the waiting runners. That thin green line stretching ever thinner.

The ball with Mafi in midfield. Jesse going high on him. Too high. Not a lazy tackle but an exhausted one, the tackle of a man who's been to the well once too often and now has nothing left to give. Mafi shrugging him off. Mafi still running.

Bend and break. The thin green line finally snaps.

And now it happens almost in slow motion. Mafi with Male Sa'u and Karne Hesketh outside him. Handre and JP covering. Three on two. JP with the winger's eternal dilemma: come in or stay out? Mafi missing out Sa'u and passing straight to Hesketh. Hesketh with a little hitch-kick as he takes it. Sa'u pointing to the corner, screaming Hesketh on. JP diving for Hesketh. Hesketh diving for the line. Hesketh sliding, grounding, scoring.

Try. Victory. Earthquake.

Players and spectators leap around in a demented ecstasy, the most joyous of communal madness. In the stands, grown men shake with tears. These are the faithful in their replica shirts, the ones who've followed their team through loss after loss and never, ever dreamed of a day like this, a day when anything seems possible; a day for kings, heroes and every underdog.

We knew the kind of hammering we'd take from fans and press alike, but it was important to give Japan credit and embrace our conquerors with wide smiles. There was a lovely picture the next day of Schalk hugging Shinya Makabe, and you couldn't tell purely from the shot who'd won and who'd lost. When we were asked about the game – which we were, over and over – we said that the better team had won. It was diplomatic, but it was also the truth. They had been the better team, and we just hadn't been good enough.

The atmosphere in the dressing room was funereal. Guys just slumped there and stared into space. It wasn't that now we'd have to win every remaining game in the group just to get through: sooner or later in a World Cup it's win or go home, so in some ways it made no difference how early we started that process. It was the knowledge that we'd been on the wrong end of definitely the greatest upset in World Cup history, probably the greatest upset in all of rugby, and possibly the greatest upset in all sport.

Our next game was against Samoa a week later. For the purpose of our survival in the tournament it was vital that we won; for the purpose of our confidence it was vital that we won big. We did both. I was on the bench again, but whereas against Japan I'd got 25 minutes with the game in the balance, now I had only 13 minutes with the match already won. It was 29–6 when I came on for Schalk, who'd had a monster game, and three more tries from Schalk Brits, Bryan and JP made it 46–6 by the end. I played okay, hitting my rucks, staying on the shoulder of the ball carrier, making my tackles and having a carry in heavy traffic, but I didn't find any real opportunity to impose myself on the match.

And that was the last time I played in the tournament. For the next match, against Scotland, Willem Alberts was picked as sub with Francois, Schalk and Duane the starting back row, and that's how it stayed for the rest of the tournament: victories in that match against Scotland and the next one against the USA to ensure that we finished top of the group despite the defeat to Japan, then a hard-fought quarter-final victory over Wales before going down 20–18 to the All Blacks in the semi.

I helped out in training and did my bit, but to be brutally honest I didn't do all I could have. When I compare it to how the dirt-trackers behaved in Japan four years later, the myriad ways they helped the starting 23 prepare, it shames me, it really does. Whenever I had time off, I just drank. I was bored and feeling sorry for myself, there were other guys around in the same boat who were always happy to hang out, and it was all too easy for me to hit the bars and pubs and be a good-time guy. Rachel had come out with baby Nick, and this would have been the perfect opportunity to spend some time with them; but no, I preferred to be out with the boys. It was an awful time for her, and I was too selfish to realise. Handre's partner (now wife) Marise would hang out with her, and they became really close, but in the end Rachel got fed up with me being a jerk and flew home a week early.

A few of the boys went to Twickenham to watch the final between Australia and New Zealand, but Eben and I had tickets to watch Liverpool play Chelsea. I'd been a Liverpool fan since I was a kid. This was the first time I'd ever seen them play, and I couldn't wait. The only snag was that the seats we had were among the Chelsea fans, and we knew enough to be aware that soccer crowds in England weren't like rugby crowds. In rugby stadiums, opposing fans mingle happily and there's never any hint of trouble. English football was different. Whatever you do, we were told, don't celebrate if Liverpool score. You don't have to leap around and feign delight if Chelsea do, but don't celebrate a goal against the home team. The fans don't mind neutrals, but they do mind opponents.

Chelsea went 1–0 up early on, but just before half-time Philippe Coutinho equalised for Liverpool. Instinctively I leapt up and started screaming, just like I did every time they scored when I was watching on TV at home in Cape Town. Hundreds of heads whipped round to glare at me: Chelsea fans. Angry. *Furious*. Hurling abuse at me.

Eben stood up alongside me, all 6 ft 8 in of him, and folded his arms so his biceps looked even bigger than they are normally. The abuse faded away into mutterings as the fans gradually sat down again. We followed suit, and Eben leant over to me.

'You do that again and I'll klap you myself.'

In the second half, Coutinho scored again before Christian Benteke made it 3–1. I was as good as gold and didn't celebrate either of them, but inside I was cheering my heart out.

On the way out of the stadium, a few people came up and asked me for my autograph. For a moment or two I didn't know what was going on. I couldn't believe that an English soccer crowd would recognise any Springbok rugby players – why should they? – and they certainly wouldn't recognise me, who'd barely featured in the tournament. Then I heard a passer-by say, 'It's definitely him, it's definitely Bony,' and I realised they thought I was the Manchester City player Wilfried Bony.

So I did the only thing I could, and signed all their programmes with the most stylish Wilfried Bony autograph I could muster.

A few weeks after the World Cup had ended and we were back home, I was lying on the grass on a Sunday morning, as hungover as it's possible to imagine. My eyes were bloodshot and I stank of alcohol. 'This is how you look when you've been bad,' said Liphelo. She was six at the time, the perfect age for a child to tell you a home truth without even realising that they're doing so.

Rachel had had enough. If it had been an isolated incident that would have been one thing, but it wasn't. It could have been the week before, or the week before that, or the week before that.

'We're going to church,' she said. She always went to church on Sunday.

'See you later,' I grunted.

'*We*,' she said. 'We're going to church. That means you too.'

She was right, and I knew it. The trajectory of my life was bad. I had to stop behaving like this or else I'd lose my family. It wasn't 'Stop drinking', because drinking would have been fine if I'd just had a couple of beers and stopped there. It was 'Stop drinking until you're obliterated, each and every time'.

Because that's what I was. Whenever I opened a drink it was as though there was a message at the bottom of the bottle saying 'Drink me, keep on going.' I'd binge and not remember what had happened the night before. Picking up the pieces of the story from other people was fun for a while – 'Ag! Man, you'll never believe what you did, you were so wasted' – but I'd soon begun to tire of it and think that there must be more to life than this. And that's what my dad was like too. I'd look just like him when I was drunk, and I hated that, because he was a nightmare when drunk. But even all this couldn't stop me. I knew it was wrong, I knew it was a one-way ticket to disaster, but I still did it.

We went to Hillsong Church in Century City, Cape Town. There was a sign outside: BAPTISMS PERFORMED TODAY. I hardly knew what a baptism was or what it involved, but something in my heart said, 'Do it.' I didn't prepare for it, or study, or talk to priests or anything. I just felt that this was something I needed to do, and that it had been put in my path for a reason.

There was a tank of water with steps at either end. I got in. A crowd of around 50 people were there, little children at the front. A member of the church's clergy stood either side of me and held one wrist each as I was submerged. The pastor, Phil Dooley, began to speak. 'As the Gospel of Mark says, "And it came to pass in those days, that Jesus came from Nazareth of Galilee, and was baptised of John in Jordan. And straightway coming up out of the water, he saw the heavens opened, and the Spirit like a dove descending upon him. And there came a voice from heaven, saying, 'Thou art my beloved Son, in whom I am well pleased.'" A baptism is the outward declaration of the decision you have made in your heart to surrender to Jesus. It provides a marker in your life that anchors your faith when you face the hard times of life. It becomes a reference point that God has saved you and is faithful to continue what he has started in your life. Being baptised is a public declaration of your personal decision to make Jesus Lord and Saviour of your life. According to 2 Corinthians, chapter 5, verse 17: "Therefore if any man be in Christ, he is a new creature: old things are passed away; behold, all things are become new."'

And I did feel new after that. It wasn't that all my problems suddenly stopped or that I became an instant saint, far from it. I'd still struggle with alcohol from time to time – as a team we'd bond over a couple of beers and it was hard to say no sometimes – and my commitment to Jesus would occasionally waver. But deep down I wanted to be better – a better person, a better father, a better husband – and that path began the moment I went under the water in Century City. It was proof that you can overcome everything if you believe. I had the choice: worship God or worship alcohol. But when you consider where each path led, it wasn't really a choice at all.

I asked Rachel to marry me not long after. I popped the question during a helicopter ride over Cape Town. It was the first time either of us had been in a helicopter. Man, those things look dangerous. I was having not just second thoughts but third and fourth ones too. My hands were sweating and shaking. *We're going to crash. This thing is going to drop clean out of the sky.* But it was too late. And once we were up there the views were so spectacular that I almost forgot about my fear. I pulled out the ring and asked Rachel if she'd marry me. Luckily she said yes, as I didn't have a Plan B if she hadn't.

I was putting down roots, trying to improve not just my life but the lives of those around me too. I also knew that had it not been for a lucky bounce of the ball, almost literally, at that U12 tournament in Mossel Bay all those years ago, I would never have been in this position to start with. And I realised that I'd never found out who'd funded the bursary which had allowed me to go to Grey. I'd just gone there without thinking about that side of it too much. Sure, I'd taken full advantage of the opportunities, but still. Someone had given me that chance, and I wanted to thank them.

I asked Grey if they could put me in touch with this person. I guess they must have checked with him first, for data protection rules as well as courtesy, and then they gave me his details. He was called Vincent Mai and lived in New York, though he was South African through and through: born in the Eastern Cape, played rugby at Grey and UCT, and then went into banking, where he'd made enough money to fund his philanthropy. He'd begun the bursary scheme in the early 1990s, just after Mr Mandela had been released from prison, and sponsored around six boys a year, so I was about the 75th kid he'd helped (the number is up near 200 by now).

I wanted him to know how much his generosity had not just benefited my life but changed it, so I sat down and wrote him a letter.

Dear Mr Mai,

You don't know me, but my name is Siya Kolisi and I play rugby for the Springboks. I have a beautiful family, whose picture I enclose, and a life I could never have imagined when I was growing up in Zwide. None of this would have been possible without you. Thank you.

Best wishes

Siya Kolisi

I attached a picture of my family and one of my Springbok jerseys. A few days later Uncle Vincent rang me, and we began a friendship which I treasure to this day. For a long time it was done entirely on the phone and via email, and when we finally met in New York after the 2019 World Cup we instinctively hugged. He hugged me like a son and said how proud he was of me. We spoke for hours about what we could do to make South Africa a better place, and found that we had so much in common: the same sense of humour, the same outlook on life. We'd sit on the porch and talk about things – not rugby, but life. He does so much good for people without ever shouting about it, he works so hard to make things better in society, and that really inspired me. He made me breakfast – eggs with tomato – one morning, and oats with blueberries the next. It was amazing to see New York with him, and we pledged to do more of it; he'd take us as a family to his favourite place in the Karoo, and we'd go visit him again in the States. It felt like I'd known him forever and just been apart for a really long time, rather than two people meeting for the first time. Nowadays we speak almost every week, and my kids call him grandpa. He is an incredibly special human being, and I feel privileged not just to have him in my life but to know how much he helped change that life.

The 2016 Super Rugby season featured an expanded roster of 18 teams, including for the first time franchises from Argentina and Japan, so the teams were divided into two groups: one featuring five New Zealand and five Australian teams, the other six South African teams plus the Jaguares from Buenos Aires and the Sunwolves from Tokyo. There were some matches between the two groups, though, and as with most things like this it sounded much more complicated than it actually was.

We had a good season under our new head coach Robbie Fleck, finishing third overall across both groups with 10 wins from our 15 games and securing ourselves home advantage for the quarter-final. I played every game, starting the majority of them, and was much happier with my form than I'd been the year before.

This fed into my international career too. Allister Coetzee had taken over as Springbok coach, and first up were three Tests against Ireland. He picked me to start the first Test, my first start for the Springboks in 14 caps. Coach Allister had been my coach at the Stormers and knew what I was capable of. It was also a reminder of the non-controllables every player has to contend with: for example, that some coaches rate you and others don't. If you're a bona fide unquestioned worldie then fine, you're always going to get picked, but not many people are. It's easy to be angry and resentful when a coach picks another player over you when you think you'd be the better choice, but it's just as easy to forget that when you're the player in favour there's another guy chafing at the unfairness of it all.

Being a regular member of the starting XV made a huge difference to my play. It was a virtuous circle: being seen as a valuable team member gave me confidence, which improved my play, which further cemented my position, which increased my confidence, and so on.

We played Ireland three Saturdays in succession, and I started each match. The first game I played all 80 minutes, the next two 67 and 60 respectively. Like anyone I preferred to still be on the pitch at the end, but the modern-day game is such that at least one back-row player is going to get substituted each match, and if it was me that allowed me to empty the tank a little quicker.

It was special that the first game, my first start, was at Newlands. The crowd gave my name an extra-loud cheer when the teams were read out. They knew what a long road it had been for me – it was four days short of three years ago that I'd made my debut – and they appreciated that I gave my all every time I stepped onto this pitch, be it in blue and white or green and gold. It was less special that we lost 26–20 having been level at half-time, but we made up for that by taking the next two games 32–26 (having been down 19–3 at half-time) and 19–13 respectively.

An ankle ligament injury ruled me out of all but the first three minutes of the Super Rugby quarter-final against the Chiefs – I watched from the sidelines as they pulverised us 60–21 – and the Rugby Championship, which didn't go much better. Of the six matches we played (home and away against Argentina, Australia and New Zealand) we won only two, the home games against Argentina and Australia. Most worrying of all was the gap between us and New Zealand. Less than a year ago we'd been within two points of beating them for a place in the World Cup Final, and now they were sticking more than 40 points on us in Christchurch and more than 50 in Durban.

Rachel and I got married on 13 August 2016 at Franschhoek. I never imagined walking up the aisle on crutches wearing a moon boot (or a controlled ankle motion boot, to give it its full medical name), but that was the way it was. We had 200 people there, from every corner of my life: Zwide, Grey, Stormers, Springboks and all Rachel's friends and family too. It was also Liphelo's birthday, which made it extra special, especially when we all sang 'Happy Birthday' to her.

I got ready with my groomsmen, all laughing and joking with beers, but when the ceremony started and Rachel came down the aisle I just lost it and started crying. She looked so beautiful, and there was so much love in the air. The enormity of it all just blindsided me. Perhaps no-one ever knows what it will feel like until you're actually there. Pastor Phil conducted the ceremony, and before we made our vows he said, 'At a wedding you arrive separately but you leave together. Rachel, God has given you the keys to unlock Siya's potential; and Siya, God has given you the keys to unlock Rachel's potential.'

When it came to my speech I spoke pretty much without notes. I had some in my hand, but I didn't really use them. I thanked Andrew Hayidakis for taking a punt on me and changing my life by taking me to Grey; I spoke isiXhosa to Coach Eric and addressed him by his clan name, Mawawa; and I told Eben how much his friendship meant to me. But it was Rachel who the crux of the speech was about, of course.

'We've been through a lot,' I said. 'When I met you I put you through a lot. I know I made a lot of mistakes. I was young. I thought certain things at that time were the important things, and they weren't. I was looking everywhere else, and I wasn't concentrating on the main person. Through all my rubbish, all my mistakes, you stuck by me, you believed in me. You didn't get up and walk away. You stayed. All of that rubbish has made me what I am today. And you pushed me so much, I wanted to be a better person. I wanted to have a family but still go out and have fun. I get all the praises, but I know who keeps the family together. I don't tell you enough how much you mean to me. You might think I don't notice because I don't share a lot, but I do. Today is the proudest moment of my life. I can finally say I became a man today. I promise you here, I will give you my best every day.'

I was still recovering (from the ankle injury, not the wedding!) when the northern hemisphere autumn internationals rolled around: the Barbarians, England, Italy and Wales on successive weekends. If the Rugby Championship had been bad, these were worse. We scraped a 31–31 draw with the Barbarians, whose preparation had – as always with the Barbarians – involved a lot of drinking and not a lot of practising. Then England beat us 37–21, their first victory against us in a decade and a score which would have been worse but for a late try from Willie le Roux when the match was already long decided, and on the last weekend Wales beat us 27–13.

But it was the third match of the four, against Italy in Florence, which really plumbed the depths. The Italians were ranked 13th in the world and were comfortably the worst team in the Six Nations. They'd lost 68–10 to the All Blacks the previous week, and they'd not only never beaten us; they'd never finished a match within 15 points of us. Confidence might not quite be everything but it's a lot: they were confident and we weren't. They won 20–18 and received a deserved standing ovation from their home crowd. It wasn't quite as much of a shock as the defeat to Japan had been, but in two ways it was even worse. First, we hadn't played that badly against Japan, but we had here: dropped passes, elementary mistakes, no structure. Second, we'd put things right after the Japan match because we'd still been a good and purposeful team. We didn't look like that anymore. 'We're at an all-time low,' said Jean after the match, and he was right. 'We're not going to offer any excuses,' Coach Allister added. 'What happened today was not worthy of what we stand for as a team and as a rugby-playing country.'

By the time the 2017 Super Rugby season came around I'd been off for six months, far longer than I'd ever been since beginning to play as a kid in Zwide. I was desperate to get back into things and reclaim my place. After years of not being injured but playing badly and not being picked either, it was particularly frustrating to be injured while first choice and playing well. But though I was doing everything to speed rehab along, and working with the Province medical team I knew well, the body heals at its own pace. I could minimise the time spent in rehab, but I couldn't eliminate it altogether.

The year 2017 felt different before it started. I was now a father of one with another on the way, a husband and a first-choice Springbok. I was 25 and coming into the peak of my career. It wasn't so long ago that I'd been at my lowest ebb, and not so long before that that I'd been the next big thing, but there are always next big things. The trick is to keep the last two words while getting rid of the first: to go from boy to man while continuing to improve, both as a player and a person.

We had a good squad, the nucleus of which – Frans, Eben, Nizaam, Scarra and me – had been together since our time in the Institute, so there was plenty of experience to call on. Coach Robbie was going into his second season. 'Last year I started out on the back foot,' he said, 'but this time I know I have buy-in from the players, and they have confidence in me. I am in a far better spot than I was last year.'

Juan de Jongh was captain, but in a warm-up game against the Lions before the start of the season he tore his medial collateral ligament. Ten to twelve weeks out, the medics said. We would need another captain.

I wasn't expecting Coach Robbie to ask me. I was totally surprised when he did, and am grateful to this day for his decision. I knew that he liked how I was around the other players, always trying to be a positive force, but he was one of the first people to tell me that I was going to do more with my life than just play rugby. In fact, the seeds had been sown the year before at my wedding: he was the one who'd been perhaps most profoundly affected by my speech. 'When I heard that speech, I was blown away,' he said. 'It was so uplifting, delivered without notes, coming straight from the heart: the way you spoke about your upbringing, where you wanted to go and what you wanted to achieve. It wasn't anything to do with rugby: it was the way you connect with your peers, the values you hold and try to espouse in everyday life, the great values that any coach would want in a leader. The room was captivated, you know? If I'd ever doubted your leadership potential, that convinced me. I knew I'd found my captain.'

But Coach Robbie was also blunt. He told me I had to get my act together and switch mentality. I realised that though I was an ultimate team player and loved being around the guys, I also had to stop hiding a little bit and put my head above the parapet more: man up, show leadership. So although I was flattered that he asked, I was also unsure.

'I don't have much experience of being captain,' I said.

'And I don't have much experience of being head coach,' he replied. 'Come on. Let's do it. Let's learn together, let's move forward together, let's make mistakes together.'

As they said in *The Godfather*, that was an offer I couldn't refuse. I also knew that Coach Robbie saw a lot of himself in me. In his playing days he'd been pretty naughty sometimes, and he liked the fact that I knew how to have fun, first into and last out of every party. Pro rugby is a serious business, but there's also lots of downtime, and sometimes you need to let off some steam.

I knew too that I had a solid core of senior players around me who would help. As I'd discover with the Springboks, there's never just one leader in a team, and no successful captain does it on his own. You need a core of four or five senior okes around you who will have your back and take on some responsibilities for you when you need them to. I had Eben, Frans, Pieter-Steph and Duane, and that was just the forwards.

We hit the ground running with a decent victory over the Bulls, and at no stage in that entire season were we outside the top two in our group. It wasn't until our seventh match that we lost, and that was against a Lions team which was carrying all before it. That sparked a mini-slump, with three heavy defeats away to New Zealand franchises (57–24 against the Crusaders, 57–14 against the Highlanders and 41–22 against the Hurricanes), before finding our form again and winning four of our last five to secure a spot in the knockout rounds.

We had home advantage for our quarter-final against the Chiefs. They were 9–3 up at the break. I scored a try not long after the restart to bring it back to within a point, and – one penalty kick each later – that was still the gap with five minutes left. But then Aaron Cruden put Shaun Stevenson over in the corner and there was no way back for us: our third quarter-final defeat in three seasons.

It was disappointing, as much for the fact that we felt we should have gone further as for the defeat itself. But as Coach Robbie said, it was a learning process for all of us. On a personal level, I'd played not just well but consistently so, and the captaincy had forced me to come out of my shell a bit more in terms of dealing with the coaching and management staff. There were lots of arguments in that 2017 season; Coach Robbie and I were both learning and both making mistakes. But he always spoke to me and trusted me, and I took a lot of what he said on board. When guys would fight in training, he'd say, 'There, you missed your moment to stamp your authority.' That was my biggest weakness, and one which is a problem for lots of new captains: I wasn't hard enough on my team-mates when I needed to be. I had been part of the boys for a long time, and we were a very tight group, so it was tough to suddenly see myself as set apart from them. Every captain has to keep a certain distance once he has the armband. I wasn't just one of the boys anymore; I was set a bit apart, I had to make the decisions, I had to be the link between players and management.

I was back in the Springbok team for a three-match series against France, starting each game at six and doing my best to stake a claim to being the best openside flanker in the country. We won all three games comfortably and averaged well over

30 points per match, which was a relief after the disasters of 2016. I played probably the best matches I'd managed for my country, and was man of the match in the second Test. It was Father's Day, the day after my birthday, and for some reason I always played well around that time; I'd been man of the match on my debut four years ago on the same day. Here I scored a good try, scooping the ball off my feet, and did all the hard work for Elton Jantjies to touch down too: ripping the ball off Uini Antonio, slicing through the defence and giving him the offload. But it was my all-round game which pleased me the most, the sense that everything was clicking and that whatever I tried came off. I had the vision to see opportunities and the skill to exploit them; it was as though my brain was working quicker than usual, and I felt like I could play forever without tiring. It was a sweet vein of form I was in, and made all the sweeter by the bad times I'd been through the past few years. The lows felt terrible when I was in them, but without them the highs wouldn't have felt so sweet. It was a lesson I had to keep reminding myself of: that if I kept on going through the lows then eventually I'd find the highs.

The problem was, as I was about to find out, that it worked the other way too.

With Warren Whiteley injured, Eben was made captain for the 2017 Rugby Championship, and I was confirmed as vice-captain. Some people tried to make something of the fact that I was Eben's captain at the Stormers, but to me they were two separate issues. The teams were different, the demands were different and the coaches were different. And it wasn't like I had any great desire to captain the Boks, or any sense of entitlement that I should have the job. I was just glad to be a regular starter and core member of the team.

The 2017 Rugby Championship started well enough – deceptively so, in fact. We beat Argentina comfortably in PE and Salta on consecutive weekends; I scored one try in the first match and two in the second, where again I was man of the match. I loved playing in Argentina. The fans were so passionate wherever we went, and we were always reminded it was an away game: the crowds were hostile, partisan and committed, demanding that you play well to beat their boys.

In Perth we held the Wallabies to a 23–23 draw, and next up were the All Blacks in Albany. We'd played six matches this year and not lost one of them. We felt resurgent. They'd won all three of their Rugby Championships so far, and though New Zealand on their home turf is always a challenge – to say the least – we genuinely fancied our chances of giving them a run for their money.

And for the first 13 minutes we did. We were on top of them in the scrums and defensively solid. Then Beauden Barrett kicked a penalty, and three minutes later Rieko Ioane scored, and the floodgates opened. They came from all angles, crossing the line again and again: Nehe Milner-Skudder, Scott Barrett, Brodie Retallick, Milner-Skudder again, Ofa Tu'ungafasi, Lima Sopoaga and Codie Taylor. The streaker who appeared early in the second half was more of a threat to their momentum than we were.

Final score: 57–0. Say it again: 57–0. One Tier One nation playing another. It's rare that both sides of the scoreline are so humiliating. Sometimes you ship a lot of points but score quite a few yourselves; sometimes you don't score many but neither do they. This had all three elements of a total disaster: they put 50 on us, the margin was vast, and worst of all we were nilled. Throughout 80 minutes we couldn't manage a single score. There's a particular shame in being nilled, and this was all that and more. That match felt like it would never end. Quite often in a match you lose track of time, and when you look up at the scoreboard you're surprised that either so much time has passed or so little. This wasn't either of those. This just seemed as though the clock was perpetually running at half speed while the All Blacks came tearing through time and time again. They did it effortlessly. Sometimes the individual margins weren't that much – a split second at the breakdown, for example – but they were always the right side of those margins, and that mounts up pretty quickly. And the fact that they cracked our lineout codes really didn't help, not just in itself but also because that rippled through to the rest of our play. It was 31–0 at half-time, and no-one said much when we were in the shed. What was there to say?

It didn't matter that we'd gone six games unbeaten. This was the worst defeat in Springbok history, at least in terms of the scoreline, surpassing the 53–3 defeat against England in 2002. At least that day the Boks had had a man sent off early on and had been forced to play the majority of the match with 14 players. We had the full complement, but we'd have needed all 23 of the matchday squad on the pitch at the same time to have stopped the All Blacks. The only positive we could take was that we hadn't given up, but even that was a double-edged sword; a score of that magnitude would have been easier to accept if we had just chucked in the towel.

I took Rachel on safari after that. She was heavily pregnant with our second child Keziah, who was named after the second of the three daughters born to Job in the Bible. The reaction I got for daring to relax and unwind! My social media was full of people asking how dare I go away, as though I'd committed some kind of criminal offence and should be working round the clock in penance. I didn't go away because I didn't care about the result; I went away because there was nothing to be gained by fretting endlessly about a match which had passed, and time and space away from it all would be good for me. Not a single person in the squad did anything other than hate that experience, and to a man we were all determined to put it right, but beating ourselves up about it wouldn't accomplish anything. We would just be emotional and incapable of dispassionate assessment. We needed to approach it with clear heads and be two things: honest with each other about what had gone wrong, and smart about how to fix it.

Picking oneself up after getting smashed is one of the hardest things in rugby. Thankfully, perhaps, our next game was against Australia rather than the All Blacks, and for the second time in this championship we drew with them. Even that was bittersweet, though: this was the first time Australia had avoided defeat on our soil since the Rugby Championship had begun in 2012.

That just left the return match against the All Blacks, at my home stadium Newlands. If there's one stadium in South Africa we didn't want to play the All Blacks in, it was Newlands.

There was no altitude advantage as there was at Ellis Park or Loftus Versveld, and there was still a large support base dating back to apartheid days when black people would support the All Blacks against the Boks.

Newlands was a sell-out and the atmosphere was absolutely jumping. We were really motivated and turned up big time, determined to avenge what had happened in Albany. This was the greatest rivalry in world rugby, and we had to show ourselves worthy of it. We'd conceded 114 points against them in our past two meetings. We couldn't afford to ship another cricket score.

We scored first, Elton knocking over the penalty after Whitelock had infringed. The crowd roared their approval; we weren't going to get nilled again. That wasn't a flippant consideration. The humiliation of a zero is so great that sometimes three points feel like a lot more than three points. Ryan Crotty scored for them to make it 8–3 at the break, and the second half was nip and tuck. We'd score a try, then they would, then we would, then they would. With two minutes to go we were a man down (Damian de Allende had been sent off for a late tackle) and a single point behind, but the All Blacks held out to take the match by that, the smallest of all possible margins. It was better than the Albany match had been, but a loss was still a loss.

Weird as it might sound, in some ways it felt even worse than having been spanked 57–0. When we'd been comprehensively beaten we knew there was nothing else we could have done, but when we lost by a point we'd torture ourselves with all the what-ifs. But this reaction in itself was a positive thing. No-one thought we should be satisfied with 'nearly' or having got closer than before. We all knew that, at the end of the day, professional sport is a results business.

Just as it had been 12 months before, the northern hemisphere autumn internationals gave us a chance to end the year on a high; and just as 12 months before, we blew that chance. We had to play Italy, France, Wales and Ireland. We beat Italy easily (and mercifully too, after losing to them the previous year) and France narrowly. The Wales match was a narrow defeat, 24–22.

But the Ireland match … The Ireland match was awful. They scored four tries and four penalties: we scored one penalty. Final score 38–3. We were abysmal. Former coach Nick Mallett said, 'I don't care how positive you are as a personality: there are no positives to take out of this game,' and it was hard to argue. In some ways it was almost worse than the All Blacks one. We kept hoping it would come right: we had good players, but we weren't delivering. We got stuffed up, and after that we all knew something had to change.

Exactly what that change should be, however, was more problematic. As ever in a team that isn't totally united, players' viewpoints were pretty tied to their own status on the team. The ones who were playing regularly and getting opportunities were much less keen on change than the ones on the sidelines. That was perhaps natural, but it was also harder to justify when we were getting beaten so badly that our fans were streaming out of the stadium long before full-time.

We beat France by a point the following week, then I missed the Italy match to fly home and be with Rachel for Keziah's birth, then I came back for the Wales match which we lost by two points. Usually Springboks get to fly business class, either because the union has paid for that or because we get upgraded by the airline, but when I flew back and forth for Keziah's birth it was strictly economy; no-one was giving upgrades when we were playing like this.

Coach Allister had been in charge for 25 games and won only 11 of them, so it was decided that he should step down. I was sorry to see him go. He was a good coach and a good man; I'd worked with him since I'd started at the Stormers, and he'd often called me in for chats, asked about my dad and my family, and been a sort of father figure to me in some ways.

Coach Rassie was brought back as director of rugby, with responsibility for all national teams through the age groups. But he was also clearly the best choice for head coach as well. It must have been daunting, trying to carry off two full-time roles at once, but we were in a dire place and we needed him. So out went Coach Allister, in came Coach Rassie, and along came massive changes.

One of the first things Coach Rassie did was host alignment camps where he'd lay out what he expected of us off and on the pitch. We didn't do any training or skills work at these camps; we just listened, talked and thought about things. Coach Rassie knew how crucial it was not only that everyone was on the same page but that they were there because they wanted to be, because they'd bought into his vision, rather than because they'd felt themselves forced into it.

He came up with three areas we needed to concentrate on: results, public perception and transformation. They were all linked, of course, but equally they were distinct entities too.

First, results. We needed to win, first and foremost. 'Don't come here with stories of inspiring people, unifying the nation, being role models,' he told us. 'Don't start with that stuff. That stuff is the spin-off of winning.' So we wanted to inspire? Great. Then start winning. Winning didn't by itself inspire, but we couldn't inspire unless we were winning. Everything else stemmed from that. That famous shot of Madiba on the podium with Francois Pienaar? That shot only happened because Joel Stransky dropped a goal.

Coach Rassie came up with a phrase which would be the touchstone of his reign: 'Let the main thing be the main thing.' The main thing was rugby, and that would always be the case. 'This is how it's going to be,' he said. 'I don't give a damn for your personal goals. I don't care what your sponsorships are or how many followers you have on social media. The Springboks are more important than any of those. Everything you do, you do for the Springboks. You put the collective first. And if you do that and play well then the team will start winning things, and from that everything else will flow. Your personal goals will end up being more rewarding, not less rewarding, if you buy into this and play the long game. But that's a side-effect, not the main thing. The main thing is rugby, and we need the main thing to be the main thing.'

He said that Ireland had only 160 professional players in the whole country, which meant that every player who was there had really, really wanted to get there and was prepared to move heaven and earth to stay there. With so few professional spots available, the winnowing process at every stage was ruthless and ensured that as little complacency as possible crept into the system. The Irish players would constantly be asking their coaches for extra training, scheduling their lives so that they could perform better, and so on. He told us all this, and I just thought, 'What have I been doing with my life?'

One day, at an analysis session, the coaching team showed a video they'd prepared of me. Sometimes teams do this to big a player up, either for his own sake or to show the rest of the team what they should be doing. This was just the opposite. It was two or three minutes of how lazy I was: how slow I was to get up after a tackle, how I'd walk rather than run back to where play was, and so on. The whole squad was watching. I thought I'd been playing well, but seeing that showed me how much I'd been coasting. I felt embarrassed. That was the point. Coach Rassie wasn't doing it out of spite or because he thought I was a poor player. He did it because we all needed a kick up the backside, me more than most, and this was part of that.

For Coach Rassie, it wasn't enough just to do the things we'd been doing but better; we also had to do stuff we'd never even considered before. The analysts would send us clips of our play, ask us to rate ourselves, and if our ratings varied too far from those of the coaching staff we'd discuss why. I'd visualise the match ahead of time – not just the match but its component parts too, its scrums and breakdowns and counter-attacks – so that by the time I came to play it I felt as though it was almost done already. And I'd work on my body language, as when I was tired I'd often look it, which in turn would give other teams encouragement. I'd have my hands on my hips, my arms down, all that kind of thing. Pieter-Steph du Toit was detailed to keep an eye on it and buck me up whenever he saw it beginning to go, and he was the perfect person for the job, as he went full tilt from minute 1 to minute 80. If you were to turn on the TV in the middle of a match and just watch Pieter-Steph, you couldn't tell from his body language how long the game had been going on or what the score was; he just always looked completely up for it.

It can be tempting as a player to concentrate on not making mistakes, to play everything safe. Coach Rassie wasn't having that. He didn't want us just to chuck the ball around with no strategy or structure like we were playing sevens on the beach, but nor did he want us to be afraid of failure. He wanted us to play without fear. There was no shame in missing tackles, he'd say, only in not attempting them; no shame in messing something up, only in not doing your best to rectify it. But equally he said that we were so focused on that extra 1 or 2 per cent that we'd forgotten about the first 90 per cent or thereabouts. Innovative attacking strategies were all very well, but they needed to be underpinned by basic structure. And he wanted to build on all the good things Coach Allister had done rather than just throw the baby out with the bathwater. Under Coach Allister, margins of error had been slim and consequences serious. Coach Rassie wanted us to play smarter: forwards running from deeper in diamond formation so the scrum-half could see them individually and assess who best to pass to rather than just chucking it at the nearest guy. The chances of breaking the line and making 20 metres might decrease, but the chances of retaining the ball for the next phase would drastically increase.

He also dropped the 30-cap rule, which would make a big difference. As it stood, players who played abroad – as so many did for financial reasons, for the money was better in absolute terms, and when you factored in the weakness of the rand the difference was night and day – were only allowed to represent the Springboks if they had 30 caps. The rule had been put in place to try and stem the exodus of top players abroad, but all it had done was make the Boks weaker.

Second, public perception. Coach Rassie said that too many people saw us as overpaid and entitled. 'People put money aside all year so they can come and watch you play even one time. How *dare* you even think of not giving your best, both on and off the field? What gives you the right to shortchange them?' Lots of us were posting on social media, but to what end? To show off, as often as not, or to cover for the fact that we weren't doing the basics properly. Along with 'let the main thing be the main thing' came another adage: 'Work hard in silence and let success be your noise.' The All Blacks weren't putting pictures of their training sessions up on Instagram, were they? They were working hard for each other without shouting about it, and when it came to noise – well, was 57–0 loud enough?

We had to connect back to what the Boks meant. As Matt Proudfoot, our forwards coach, said, 'South African boys are born watching the game from a very young age. You understand it, it's tangible. What it means to you is important. That's what creates the lifeblood of the Springbok, and in return the Springbok creates that lifeblood because that's what little boys want to be.' We had to honour the ones who'd look up to us as we'd looked up to them: Willie who'd been given a rugby ball for every birthday, Pieter-Steph who said, 'When we'd *braai* at night I would lie on the grass and look at the stars. I wished, hoped and prayed that I would become an unbelievably successful Springbok.'

Those connections are very much part of how South Africans see themselves: hard-working, humble, team players, part not just of the people but of the land too. 'You get the right people,' Coach Rassie said, 'not the best people.' Often the two would align, of course, but when they didn't then he would always go with the right person over the better person. A talented player was no good if he was flaky or prone to sulks and loss of concentration. He wanted to build a squad of hard workers, scrappers, men he could trust to do the job; men in whom the fans would see reflections of themselves.

Finally, transformation. Pretty much every coach in the professional era had been given the task of ensuring that a certain percentage of players not just in the national team but in the age-group and emerging teams too were players of colour. And pretty much every coach had found themselves unwilling or unable to hit these targets. Coach Rassie took it head on. He had open conversations about everything with us, and in doing so ensured real, proper, organic transformation, because the best players would play.

Do the work harder and better than the other guy and you'd be in. It was a genuine meritocracy and true equality, because it was equality of opportunity: everyone would get a fair chance. Coach Rassie even extended this to things we hadn't even considered. We'd always been given numbers for things like hotel check-in, with the coach as number 1. He scrapped

that. Numbers would from now on be allocated in strict alpha-
betical order of surnames, which meant that Lukhanyo (Am)
would be number 1. Coach Rassie also took away the fines
system, which he thought was antiquated and sent the wrong
message. Behave like adults, he said. If you make a mistake,
learn from it rather than pay for it. He was about advancement
rather than punishment. And he'd announce matchday 23s in
front of the whole squad, explaining why people were starting,
on the bench or in the stands. That way, both he and we were
accountable, and the chances of people complaining about
things in small groups were minimised.

Coach Rassie's 2018 target, specified in his contract, was 45
per cent players of colour in all matchday squads, going up to
50 per cent by 2019. He said three things about that. First,
knowing the figure was a good thing, so we all knew where we
stood. Second, he wouldn't be handing out cheap caps or alter-
ing squads just to make those numbers. Third, there was enough
talent in the Super Rugby franchises – which he and his staff
kept a close eye on – for us to be competitive and transformed
all at once, and the new policy of honest selection would help
that. Few, if any, black players had ever been kept in the team
when they didn't deserve to; lots of white players had. No more.

Just to show how serious he was about integration, for our
first home game under his leadership, against England at Ellis
Park, he picked 11 black players in the matchday 23 and gave
three black players their first start. But his biggest decision,
and the biggest shock, he saved until last; and it came in a
normal team meeting with no warning at all.

'Siya will be captain for the England Tests,' he said.

4

SKIPPER

'Siya will be captain for the England Tests.'

The room erupted in applause.

I was there, but I wasn't there. To this day I remember everything up to the moment Coach Rassie said that I'd captain the team for the series against England. Everything that came after that sailed right past me without stopping. Physically I was in the room; mentally I was halfway to outer space.

Me, Springbok captain? It wasn't something I'd remotely considered. Sure, I was Stormers captain, but I was pretty new to that job, and I'd only started a handful of matches for the Springboks. I could think of several people who were more obvious choices.

My teammates came over and shook my hand or hugged me. I wasn't really aware of them, or of who said what. The only one I really remember is Eben, who asked how I was feeling.

'I can't answer that,' I said.

'I know just what you're talking about,' he replied.

When the meeting broke up, I called Rachel.

'Are you okay?' she said. 'Your voice sounds weird.'

'I'm Springbok captain,' I said.

The line went dead. A moment later she rang back. 'I dropped the phone,' she said. 'Just in case I heard you wrong and it shocked me. So say again what you just told me.'

I laughed. 'I'm captain of the Springboks.'

She told me to call my dad immediately and tell him, but I couldn't; it wasn't official yet, and I was still trying to make sense of it all.

People don't believe this, but it's absolutely true: the fact that I was the first black captain didn't occur to me. Coach Rassie held a press conference to announce the news. 'I've coached Siya right through the academy years, right until he played for the Stormers, so I know what he can do, I know his qualities and I know how he has grown as a man and as a captain.' He emphasised that the captaincy was only for the June Test matches, and added, 'I like Siya because he is humble, he is quiet, and the way he is playing at the moment is not flashy.' In other words, he saw that I embodied the values of the team he was trying to build.

I was asked over and over again whether I thought it was a political appointment, something token, a sop to transformation without any intention of deeper change. I remembered the period in 2014–15 when I had doubted myself. But this was different. I was a senior player now, I'd been in the starting line-up for two years, I was captain of one of the best Super Rugby teams in the country. So I replied the only way I could: with the truth. 'I'm a rugby player, not a politician. But I think it is a genuine appointment by Coach Rassie because he's not that kind of a person. And all I want to do to reward him is to make sure that I deliver on the pitch.' It was a challenge, bigger than any I'd ever faced before. I reminded myself that all my life had been about overcoming challenges one way or another, and they'd all seemed like the biggest thing in the world at the time. But I'd overcome them all, and I'd do the same here.

It soon became clear that that was easier said than done. I hadn't remotely expected my appointment as Boks captain to come with so much hype. I knew there was a lot around being a captain off the field – extra media duties, pre-match meetings with referees, management liaison, looking out for guys who were struggling – but this was next-level stuff. 'The plan was never to get the country behind us,' Coach Rassie said. 'It was a very sudden decision, there were not a lot of conversations beforehand. Myself and Siya didn't chat for four or five months about it, we didn't strategise. Siya was the best-performing Super Rugby captain. The whole emotional thing that went around in South Africa with him being the first black captain caught Siya off guard, and it caught me off guard. In retrospect, I was a bit naive in not realising it would be such a massive thing.'

It was indeed a massive thing. My appointment meant so much to so many people. To them, I wasn't just a rugby player, let alone just a skipper. I was a symbol, a totem, a talisman, and with that came an awesome responsibility not to let them down.

When you're a kid growing up and you find your heroes, more often than not they look like you. You see where they've got to and you think, *One day, that could be me*. No black kid had ever looked at a Springbok captain and seen themselves in him. Now they could. And not just kids, of course. Every black person in South Africa had one of their own as captain of what had always been a predominantly white team. For so many years, people of my skin colour and background had never had this. Now they did. I was their reference point, and the message that sent was incredibly powerful. *It Can Be Done*. Four words without which the world would never change.

Archbishop Desmond Tutu said that my appointment 'makes us walk very tall' and described his ideal South Africa as 'a special society in which the cream would rise to the top, regardless of colour and class'. I took those words very seriously, and to everyone who asked – and there were a lot who did – I said, 'I hope I get to inspire not only black people but every South African, because I don't only represent black people but everyone in this country.' Being a professional sportsman can be tough and occasionally I questioned if it was all worth it. But then I just thought about where I'd come from and about the people that looked up to me. For me to be able to help people inspired by me, I had to play every week. That was my duty. I wasn't only trying to inspire black kids, but people from all races. When I was on the field and I looked into the crowd, I saw people of all races and social classes. We as players represented the whole country. I told my teammates: 'You should never play just to represent one group. You can't play to be the best black player or to be the best white player to appeal to a community. You have to play to be the best for every South African. We represent something much bigger than we can imagine.'

It wasn't just the destination that was important, but the journey too. Being the first black captain was made immeasurably more meaningful by the journey I'd taken to get there, because that journey was one which had been denied to thousands of talented players before me purely because of the colour of their skin. I was, as far as I know, the first Springbok captain to speak in isiXhosa at a press conference, certainly for more than a few words. IsiXhosa was the language of those players of colour who had missed out until now. No longer.

There were even comparisons to Mr Mandela. It was an honour and very flattering, but it was also wrong. I played rugby, I existed in a smaller world. He spent all those years in prison and then achieved so much when he was freed. I had to do what I could as a rugby player to help people, especially those in the townships, but it was nothing compared to what Mr Mandela did.

In every team I'd played for, club or country, there had always been guys from different cultures, which in turn made for complex dynamics. Harnessed well, those dynamics could massively improve a team's performance; harnessed badly, they could cause all kinds of problems.

As Coach Robbie said, 'Tactics and relations with referees are something that can be taught and learned. But what Siya has, that can't be taught, is an innate ability to connect people and pull them together as a group. That comes naturally to him. He has the ability to pull people together and fight for a common cause with ease.'

People say to me all the time: 'You come from the township, you must have been happy when you left' and I'm like, 'No, I am the person I am because of what I learnt from when I was younger.' I wouldn't change my past for anything, but moving schools helped me to understand people from different backgrounds. I liked to spend as much time as possible with each individual, I wanted to know what they liked and what they didn't like. It was something I grew up with, getting to know people and fitting in with everybody. It was important to understand what was important to other people.

For example, I knew how much music and his family meant to Eben. That sort of stuff was really important. The more I got to know people, the more I knew what to say as captain. I stayed away from the news and so on as far as possible. I knew that a lot of people had been responding very positively and it was great to hear of the backing for the team, but I hadn't read a lot of it as I didn't want to put too much outside pressure on myself. I knew that after the series was over I'd sit down and have a moment, but not until then. There were three Test matches to be played.

I'd played at Ellis Park a lot, but the atmosphere for the first Test against England was different from anything I'd ever experienced. Beast was right behind me in the tunnel, but unknown to me he stopped and held the other guys back to let me take the field alone and give me space and time to feel the atmosphere and the moment. The roar of the crowd as I ran on ... wow! It was like a 747 at take-off, engines wide open at full throttle, pure thunder spiking energy into every part of me.

I roared too as I sprinted on: part aggression for the contest to come, part response to this outpouring. And when I looked up at the stands I could see many more black faces than I was used to at Ellis Park. There were still only pockets of black fans rather than whole stands full, but I could still see them – and I could definitely hear them. Boy, could I hear them.

The isiXhosa commentary that day was by SuperSport's Kaunda Ntunja, and that was another area where things were changing. He'd been commentating for almost a decade by the time I became captain, but my appointment really helped spike interest in what he was doing. I felt a great affinity with Kaunda, and not just because like me he'd played in the back row for South African Schools two years running (in fact, he'd been the first-ever black player to captain the side). He loved rugby and rugby people, and his commentary was so distinctive and powerful. He used the isiXhosa language too, and so beautifully, less like a traditional commentator and more like a revivalist pastor. His introduction to my first game as captain went viral on social media, and though the English translation can't get across the power of his voice or the rhythm of his words, it gives some sense of how he approached the mic.

'The day is 16 June, the year 1991. On this day in Zwide township outside Port Elizabeth, the Kolisi family welcome the birth of their son. This baby will not be raised by his father or his mother. This baby will be raised by his grandmother, and he is given the name Siyamthanda, which means "we love him". Because, despite being born into great difficulty and poverty, he was loved a lot. It is during his youth that Siya meets Eric Songwiqi. It is Mr Songwiqi who tells the 11-year-old Siya: "Young boy, you will play rugby because in the near future you are going to play for the Springboks." It's his mentor who thrusts him into rugby, and as the English saying goes, "the rest is history". And right now that time has come. Siya is the first black player in history to captain the national team, right here in our rainbow nation. Rise up Zwide! Rise up Motherwell! Rise up Walmer! Rise up Kwazakele and New Brighton! Because this boy is yours, representing all of us. Siya is our grandson, our son, our nephew, our younger brother. He is Nicholas's father, Rachel's husband. He is Gwayi, Gqwashu, Gxiya, our leader. A cement truck with no reverse gear! Let the teams battle each other!'

England were always a tough side to play against, and under Eddie Jones's coaching we knew they liked to start fast. Teams which do that get a psychological boost as well as a simple scoreboard advantage when they have points on the board early, so it's imperative to stop that happening if at all possible. The longer we could keep them scoreless or near to scoreless, the more frustrated they'd get.

'Don't let them get off to a flyer,' Coach Rassie said. 'Whatever you do, don't let them get off to a flyer.'

So what did we do? Let them get off to the mother of all flyers, of course.

Elliot Daly kicks a penalty from inside his own half to open the scoring after two minutes – we'd seen him do similar for the Lions the previous year at sea level in Auckland, so in the thin air of the highveld his howitzer boot has no problem with the distance – and then they run in three tries in quick succession: Mike Brown in the corner, Daly himself, and then their captain Owen Farrell under the posts.

As Farrell lines up the conversion and we huddle under the posts, I can hear booing in the crowd; not against England, but against us. We're being sliced to pieces, George Ford at 10 is pulling strings like he's a puppetmaster, and our fans aren't happy. I know what they were thinking: *We had to endure 57 points by the All Blacks and 38 by Ireland last year, and this is just more of the same despite all the fine words and hope around Coach Rassie's return*. I don't blame them. In their shoes I'd be thinking the same thing too.

I look round at my teammates. Half of them look shellshocked. I remember how Jean had laughed during my debut against Scotland when they'd scored first after half-time, but this feels very different. That match had still been close, and we'd always felt we had the beating of Scotland. This is another kettle of fish altogether. England are rampant – the kick sailing over our heads makes it 24–3 with an hour left still to play – and I have to say something. But what? Nothing in my career has prepared me for this. Perhaps we've all lost our focus a bit in the build-up with all the fuss around my captaincy? I just can't think of the right words, let alone the right tone to say them in. I don't want to say the wrong thing and lose their respect.

Be yourself, I think. *I'm not someone who gives* Braveheart *speeches. I'm all about my deeds. Don't try and pretend to be something you're not.*

I turn to Duane. 'Duane, you speak,' I say.

And he does. He's forceful, like he always is; that's why the guys look up to him. He emphasises that we have to get the basics right; some of our tackling's been poor. We're making England look much better than they are. It's time for us to start playing some rugby of our own. Stuff the points difference against us. We still have plenty of time to put things right.

Duane's fired up, and that transmits itself to the team. Handre drills a long kick into their 22 and yells encouragement at us as we charge after it. Moments later Faf's touching down, and then S'bu Nkosi too, following up his own grubber and taking advantage of Daly totally misjudging the bounce. When S'bu goes over again a few moments later for a brace on his debut, we've taken back all but two points of that lead and the crowd noise is through the roof. Six tries in the first half, and already England are hooking one of their players off; not an injury change but a tactical one to try and shore up their defences. Six tries soon become seven, with Willie bisecting Brown and Daly, and there's just time for an England penalty to make the score at the break 29–27. Yes, 29–27!

The second half is less hectic, perhaps inevitably. When Aphiwe Dyantyi scores to make it 39–27 it looks like we'd done enough, but two late tries from Maro Itoje and Jonny May mean the gap at the end is only three points, 42–39.

Still, we'd hung on, and that was what mattered. I'd have treasured my first match as captain even if it had been a deadly dull 3–0 win in driving rain, but to have been such a breathtaking match full of dazzling attacking was the icing on the cake.

* * *

After the match, I went over to the part of the ground where the Gwijo Squad were. The Gwijo Squad were a bunch of men and women who'd come from the Eastern Cape in taxis, picking up people along the way, and they'd sung African songs all game long. There were only 80 or so of them in the crowd, but from the noise they made you'd have put it at 500 or more. These were my people and it meant so much to me that they'd come all this way for me. It wasn't enough for transformation to take place just on the pitch; it had to be in the stands too, to show that this was a sport for everybody whether you were playing or watching. The Gwijo Squad had worried about hostile reactions from white supporters – 'The football ground's over there,' 'This isn't the place for your sort,' that kind of thing – and had braced themselves for a backlash, even going so far as to put some of their bigger guys on the outside of their seating area in case someone tried to get physical with them. But in fact the opposite had happened: the squad's energy had surged round the ground, and lots of other supporters had joined in too.

In the days after the match the Gwijo Squad had thousands of people signing up to join them, and they became part of the build-up to every home Test. They always gathered outside the team hotel the night before the match, and I always went out and sang with them. The songs they sang were called *Amagwijo*, traditional and spiritually significant African songs, songs of love and mourning, of challenge and ritual, songs which spoke to our roots and reached deep into our ancestral past, songs which have been sung for generations at coming-of-age initiation rites, weddings, funerals and at times of celebration and struggle. The Gwijo Squad felt the same as I did: a responsibility to something bigger than any one individual, to all those fans who thought they could never support the Springboks because of what the badge had represented for so long. That's why I loved the Gwijo Squad so much, as they were making sure our culture was being seen and heard.

The second match against England was in Bloemfontein, and it was Beast's 100th cap. Bloem is still very much an Afrikaner heartland, but to hear the crowd cheer Beast to the rafters as he took to the field carrying his two small kids Talumba and Wangu was another small reminder of how things were changing. 'African child, it is possible,' said Kaunda on commentary, and he was spot on. It was not so long ago that the idea of a black player gaining 100 caps for the Boks was about as unlikely as the prospect of him receiving a rapturous welcome in the heart of the Free State. But both happened, and we won that match too to take the series with one game still to play.

England won the third Test at Newlands, and afterwards we got together with the England boys at the post-match function. We had a couple of sing-songs with some of the players, including 'Shosholoza', a traditional song originally sung by miners from what was then Rhodesia on their way to work in South Africa's diamond and gold mines. It's a beautiful song, 'Shosholoza'; the miners used to sing it in time with the rhythm of swinging their axes to dig, and Mr Mandela and his cohorts on Robben Island also used to sing it as they were working. The title means 'go forward' or 'make way for the next man', which has always struck me as being particularly applicable to rugby: working through the phases, using your teammates. Hanging out with the England guys was really cool, and that for me is one of the most amazing things about rugby: we bash each other up for 80 minutes and afterwards we chat and get to know each other.

But though we'd won the series, and my appointment had been such big news, my form was suffering. I hadn't been at my best for the Stormers all season – it was a little ironic that I was Springbok captain now rather than last year, when I really had been on fire – and I needed to take stock and reset after the England series was over. I had three weeks free with nothing but conditioning in training camp, and it was just what the doctor ordered. Coach Rassie made my job so much easier. 'Just be the best you can be for as long as you're on the field,' he said. 'Focus on that, not everything else off the field.'

So I shut out all the external stuff and just worked on my fitness and strength. I hadn't been fit enough before, and that had hindered me in more ways than just playing; it had meant I'd always felt a little undercooked and overwhelmed. By the end of these three weeks I felt physically bulletproof, and that in turn gave me a ton of confidence. I felt capable of dealing with anything, on or off the field. The bigger the challenge, the more I relished it.

Which was lucky, as playing the All Blacks on their home turf is as big a challenge as rugby offers.

Coach Rassie had always been clear in his thinking. We had fewer than 15 games before the World Cup kicked off when he took over, and in that time he had to build the best squad he could and work out who his best 23 were. He was prepared to lose a few games along the way if that meant trying out combinations and seeing what worked and what didn't. Short-term results would be traded against the goal of long-term success. We could play our best team every weekend and win the majority of games, but that wouldn't allow for new talents to come through or for much by way of cover in case of injury or loss of form. For too long we'd been in reactive crisis management mode, forever responding to what was in front of us rather than looking further down the line.

The flipside of that was that there were games we had to win, and one game in particular: New Zealand in New Zealand. It wasn't simply a question of avenging the 57–0 defeat the previous year, though that was definitely a factor. Nor was it just about restoring some sort of parity to the greatest rivalry in world rugby, though that was a factor too. No: it came down to something far simpler than either of those. To win the World Cup, we'd almost certainly have to beat New Zealand away from home, and if not then we'd have to beat a team who'd beaten them. Either way, it amounted to the same thing: New Zealand were the benchmark. Beat them away from home and we could start thinking of ourselves as contenders. Fail to do that and we'd always be playing catch-up. And it wasn't just us, the team, who'd start believing if we won. Fans, coaches, opposition teams, even the referees – they'd all start to believe in us too.

We started the 2018 Rugby Championship by beating Argentina at home, but then lost to them and Australia away in consecutive matches. However, in the week before playing New Zealand we didn't feel nervous at all; far from it. We were cocooned in our bubble, we were training well and we felt super-confident. Everything was above board, as it always was. The team sheet went up on Monday morning, six days out. Everything was discussed, and everyone knew where they stood.

Few people gave us a chance. The All Blacks had been on fire in the Championship. We'd lost nine of the past ten games against them, and even that sole victory had only been by two points. New Zealand's win rate at the Westpac, where we'd be playing them, was more than 85 per cent. The best we could hope for, or so we were told, was to avoid a hammering and keep the score respectable. But people who write those things aren't international players, because international players don't think that way. They *can't* think that way. Keeping the score respectable is no aim at all. If that's your mindset, go off and play golf with your mates, have a few beers and a good laugh.

Whether the All Blacks were as confident as everyone else, I don't know. Their assistant coach Ian Foster talked us up: 'They love the collision, they're tough there, they carry hard. They take a lot of pride in their set-piece work and they've got some backs that really enjoy space out wide if we give it to them. They've got a lot of speed.' All of which was true, but what else could he say? He wasn't going to say we were the 23 worst players ever to pull on the green and gold, was he?

Coach Rassie was priming us, telling us to save every ounce of energy in our downtime so we could leave it all out on the pitch. 'I'll massage you if need be,' he said. But he also impressed on us how confrontational we needed to be. 'Make them upset and afraid,' he said. 'Tell them you're going to mess them up, that upsets them. Cleaning a guy out, looking him in the eye and laughing at him – that puts fear into him.'

He told us that the world had fallen into a belief that rugby must be played the way New Zealanders play. 'That's garbage. New Zealanders play that way because it's what suits them, and because they're so successful everyone thinks they have to copy them. Stuff that. Let's stop trying to play like them. Let's start playing like South Africans, as historically that's been a model they've struggled to handle. Strong set phase, strong defence, strong kicking game, strong in the tackle, releasing devastating counterattacks … that's the way South Africans enjoy playing rugby. We don't have powerful outside backs, but we do have devastating outside backs.'

I found a Bible passage which summed up what I felt about this match and how we could win by being true to ourselves rather than trying to play the All Blacks at our own game. It was 1 Samuel 17, verses 38 and 39, the story of David and Goliath. 'Then Saul dressed David in his own tunic. He put a coat of armour on him and a bronze helmet on his head. David fastened on his sword over the tunic and tried walking around, because he was not used to them. "I cannot go in these," he said to Saul, "because I am not used to them." So he took them off.'

There was something very pure about the feeling of putting myself totally on the line. We'd targeted this game right from the start, we had our best team, we'd trained well. We had no excuses. England at Ellis Park had been an important game for me personally and for South African rugby in the round with the symbolism of a black captain. This game didn't carry those resonances, but as a marker of our progress towards the World Cup it was far more crucial. These are the moments, and though I thought every game I played was important, I realised the more my career went on that actually there were very few matches on which everything really did hinge. This was one of them. Ride or die.

And for games like this there was relatively little the coaching staff could do after a certain point. The day before the match, Eben asked Coach Rassie and the others just to give us space and leave us alone; it was down to us, and we needed as few voices as possible. When warming up before the match, we all ran out onto the pitch as one and we ran back to the changing room as one. The stadium was a sea of black shirts, but that only made us even more determined.

Once more it's imperative not to let them get off to a flyer, and once again we do just that. They come out of the blocks like greyhounds. Only four minutes are gone when Beauden Barrett stoops low to pick the ball off his bootlaces and flick it up for his brother Jordie running hard on a crash line. Ten minutes later and they score again, Ben Smith to his namesake Aaron, 12–0. Sixty-nine All Black points since we last scored against them. The crowd think they're witnessing another hiding. God knows what people back home watching on TV think.

But we don't panic. I gather the team under the posts as Beauden Barrett lines up the conversion. It's déjà vu from the first England match, but this time I don't need Duane to do the talking. I just emphasise how well we've trained, how much we need this, how tight and talented this squad is. We've got plenty of time left; we just have to chip away and not panic. I don't want the guys to get scared, go into their shells and be afraid of making mistakes. I want them to keep playing with freedom. We came back against England; we'll do it against these guys too.

And we do. Less than five minutes later Aphiwe crosses near the corner but has the chutzpah to jink the defenders in the in-goal area in order to get closer to the posts, and five minutes after that we score again through Willie. What's significant about that try is not that it puts us ahead with Handre's conversion; it's that it came from an All Black mistake, and a bad one at that. We'd noticed in video analysis that they like to take quick throw-ins, and when Jordie Barrett does so in his own 22 he overcooks the throw and it bounces free. Willie scoops it out of the air and scores, reward for his tenacity, but there had been three more of our guys following up too. That's what it takes to beat the All Blacks: harry them relentlessly, give them no time to settle and no space to breathe, and when the scraps come dive on them like a desert vulture.

Now we're all over them. There's half an hour gone when we set a maul on their five-metre line. Mauls are always an arm wrestle, and if you don't get it moving quickly you have to spin the ball wide once the referee has shouted 'Use it!' for the first time. We set, adjust, start to get the shove on. Malcolm is at the back, and as the maul goes down he dives over on the blindside. There's still time for Ioane to get a score back for them and Handre to knock over a penalty before the break, and we go in 24–17 up.

Second half. We need to score first and put daylight between us and them. If we let them get back into the game, there's no team better at hunting down a lead. We need to score first, and we do score first. Cheslin picks off an Anton Lienert-Brown pass and scorches for the line, somersaulting after he's touched down and screaming his ecstasy to the stands as we rush to mob him. It's only his second Test match, and already he's shown he has that X factor which can make a difference to any team. Handre's conversion puts us 14 points clear, meaning they'll have to score three times to beat us, but there's still plenty of time left for them to do so.

With just under half an hour to go, Ioane scores his second of the match and the gap's back to seven points. Again we have to respond – momentum is everything against the All Blacks. We send it wide: Elton Jantjies with the miss pass, Warren feeding Aphiwe, Aphiwe slamming in a left-foot sidestep which leaves Beauden Barrett for dead and dotting down in the corner with two men clinging onto him. 'The Springboks have brought some razzle-dazzle to Wellington!' exclaims Justin Marshall on commentary. 'Man, that was good!' But Handre can't convert and the gap stays at 12.

The All Blacks ring the changes: four men replaced in one go, two in the pack and two in the backs. That's six of their subs already used before the hour mark, while we've only used three. They're throwing the kitchen sink at us, and it's working; their turn for a close-range maul which ends with a try for the hooker, this time Codie Taylor. Back to seven points. Twenty minutes left.

The crowd are baying. You've had your fun, they seem to be saying; now stand aside and let the natural order of things reassert itself. We swap out our entire front row and me, with

Flo coming on in my place. Still we hang on ... and then we're down to 14 for 10 minutes as Willie's sin-binned for going offside. Any thoughts we might have had of trying to extend the lead again have gone. One man less might not sound much, but boy do you feel it, especially against the All Blacks, especially in defence, and especially in the last quarter of a titanic match.

There's nothing I can do to help now. I scream my support from the touchline and yell whenever I see an All Black unmarked, but my voice is lost in the roar of the crowd. The All Blacks keep coming and coming, dragging our guys this way and that, and it's only a matter of time before Ardie Savea goes over. Beauden Barrett steps up to level the scores at 36–36 – and his kick hits the post and bounces clear! Small margins. Small margins indeed.

Still we defend for our lives. The hooter goes, 80 minutes is up; the match will be over the next time the ball goes dead. Coach Rassie gets up from his seat in the coaches' box and begins to make his way down to pitchside. It's a long way down, and as he descends the stairs he gets glimpses of the play on each landing before taking the next flight down. Still the game goes on, and still, and still ... and when he appears on the sidelines two minutes or more later, it's *still* going on. These are the All Blacks, and they never go down without making you give everything you've got.

They're five metres out. If any team can score from here it's them. Damian McKenzie has the ball. Aphiwe steps in to tackle him, gets enough of McKenzie's arm to dislodge the ball ... and the ball goes forward! The crowd of 35,000 groan in despair: a mass balloon punctured, the last hope gone. Willie picks up the ball and belts it into the stands.

I've never seen players react to a victory like this before, not at any level. Eben's screaming as loud as the entire crowd put together, Handre's on his back with Faf astride him as they yell in each other's faces, Pieter-Steph is in tears: Pieter-Steph, the Terminator himself, the man who absolutely will not stop until the opposition are dead. This is what it means. So few teams ever come here and do what we've done. It's a backhanded compliment to the All Blacks, of course. They're a special team, so we had to be extra-special to beat them. Only our greatest rivals can drive us to these heights.

We never said publicly that we were going to win; we just did it among ourselves. Work hard in silence and let success be your noise. And we'd done it the hard way. They'd had 75 per cent of the possession; we'd made almost four times as many tackles as they had, 235 against 61. But only one stat counted, and those were the points on the board: 36 to us, 34 to them.

And now we knew for sure: we had it in us to win the World Cup. We didn't know that we *would* but we did know that we *could*, and from where we'd been the previous year that was progress bordering on miraculous. The victory over New Zealand gave us belief in that we set the standard there. We looked at each other now and we knew we wanted to be better than that. We knew what we were capable of, so we had to keep on striving to improve and get better each and every single week.

* * *

Massive as that game was, it was still only one match out of six in the Rugby Championship, and we had to get ourselves back up again for the next two. We beat Australia in PE before going up to Loftus Versveld for the finale: the return match against the All Blacks.

The place was a sell-out. Beating them once had been amazing; doing it twice would be seismic. The first half is no repeat of the wild first 40 in Wellington, which is probably just as well for the heart rates of everyone involved: two penalties apiece to make it 6–6 at the break. In the shed, Coach Rassie emphasises how psychologically crucial the next score will be. We need to get out there and stamp our authority immediately, just as we did in Wellington when Cheslin scored within a minute of the restart.

We do just that, working the phases before Jesse straightens the line, cuts between two defenders and outpaces a third to score just three minutes into the second half. Eight minutes later I step into the line at second receiver, bash through Joe Moody and do my best Sonny Bill Williams impression to offload to Damian who runs in unopposed. Handre's conversion makes it 23–6, a lead of 17. Against any other team in the world this would probably be enough, but this is the All Blacks. They were 14 points down in Wellington and only just failed to run us down; and now, regular as clockwork, back they come again, Codie Taylor picking up and going from a poorly-defended ruck and putting Aaron Smith in at the corner. We restore the 17-point margin when Cheslin goes in at the corner just before the hour. Surely now we can put them away?

Not a chance. Beauden Barrett floats an exquisite pass out to the left wing for Ioane to canter over, but Barrett misses the conversion. They come at us in waves, but still we hold on to that 12-point gap. Ten minutes to go. Five, as they camp on our line, the big men making the hard yards again and again until the inevitable happens and Scott Barrett scores under the posts.

Five points now the difference. We can't get out of our half. They're in our faces and up in our 22 the whole time, laying siege to our line. The clock ticks down, but in that situation those minutes feel like hours. With just 70 seconds left Ardie Savea crashes over, and now it's all on Richie Mo'unga: one conversion to win it all.

The clock ticks over to exactly 80 minutes as he drills it between the posts: 32–30 to the All Blacks. It's the first time they've been ahead all game. They've done to us what we did to them: a two-point victory in enemy territory.

We were gutted. To lose any match right at the death is hard to take, especially one that was so close and in which we'd been dominant for such long periods. In the following days I turned the game over in my mind time and again: if only we'd done this, or that, or the other. Just as with the one-point defeat the previous year at Newlands, in many ways it hurt more than the 57–0 loss had done, and for the same reasons: being so close meant we could have won.

We actually played better in this match than we had in Wellington, even though we lost. But with distance came perspective. We had gone toe-to-toe with the best team in the world twice and not given an inch. We'd been within 70 seconds of beating them twice in a row. Most of all, perhaps, we'd restored pride to the Springbok jersey.

And that was because Coach Rassie's attention to detail was phenomenal. Our new fitness coach was a Welshman called Aled Walters – lovely guy outside training sessions, endlessly inventive sadist during them – and he was in constant touch with our franchises so he would always know the state of our fitness and conditioning. The forwards coach Matt Proudfoot examined each forward's skill set in five main areas: scrum, lineout, maul, contesting and maul stop. We were assessed in the round every week, not just our skills and fitness but our mindset too: how we managed stress, how we reacted to setbacks, our resilience, the levels of ownership we took, our leadership qualities … in other words, everything we'd need to win a World Cup.

We talked about the importance of respecting referees. 'What a coach believes of the referee, the players believe of the referee,' Coach Rassie said. 'The moment you as a coach start respecting the referee and looking at how you can help him make the game work, the players do too. It's about the referee feeling comfortable and understanding that you don't look down on him. For that one second you're being nasty to a referee or treating him badly, then the whole team feels that and you lose the Test match because they don't handle the referee well. I had to make a massive mindshift, the other coaches had to make a massive mindshift, and then we had to convince the players to make that mindshift. If we didn't do that and didn't respect the referee, we wouldn't have stood a chance.'

Referees make mistakes the same as players. They do a very difficult job and in the main they do it damn well. They train hard – some of them register higher bleep test results than the players – they're constantly being assessed and reviewed, and they love the game and want to help the players.

At the end of that year, 2018, I sat down and thought of how much I'd developed both as a player and a person since being given the captaincy. I'd come to realise that you won't play well in every game, and that was something I'd had to learn to cope with because as a leader I put myself under huge pressure to perform every week. I was learning to deal with that personal pressure and the captaincy. I still felt as though I was just holding the position temporarily. It was someone else's before and it would be someone else's afterwards. I'd never sought it, but now I had it I tried to use it as well as I could.

Some people saw me as an embodiment of the country's potential, as my story was one of what could happen when people work together across all the lines that have divided South Africa for so long: race, class, generations, gender. Perhaps, too, people projected onto me what they wanted to see about South Africa, its past, present and future, and even about themselves. I didn't mind that. It's the lot of anyone sufficiently in the public eye, and since I couldn't help what people thought of me or about me then there was no point stressing about it.

My role on the pitch had begun to change too under Coach Rassie. From now on I wouldn't score many tries, throw many dummies or win many lineouts. I'd do a lot of the unseen stuff, and if the general public didn't really appreciate all the subtleties in that – and there's no reason why they should have – then my teammates and coaches did, and in purely rugby terms they were the ones I had to please. I'd started to do less running with the ball in hand as Duane and Pieter-Steph would do the hard yards there, and instead I'd do more chasing kicks, clearing rucks, tackling and catching scraps when the wings tapped back. In attack I was going to be on the shoulder of the ball-carrier as much as possible. 'Stay on your feet that last split second in contact,' I'd tell them, 'and I'm there.' Sometimes I'd almost finish the tackle on them myself to ensure that I was first to the breakdown. In defence I wasn't going to be the fetcher, as we had enough of those already – Duane, Malcolm, Kitsie, Flo – but I'd counter-ruck to try and steal turnovers or at the very least slow down their ball long enough to let our defence align itself properly. And I'd defend with my fly-half and not let him make the tackle alone – not that I ever needed to do so with Handre, who may have worn the number 10 on his back and kicked like a dream but still deep down thought he was a flanker and was never happier than when tackling guys 20 kg heavier than him. Lunatic.

I'd visualise dominating the opposition, and if it wasn't playing in my head the way it should have been then I'd keep on until it was. I'd have all that done by the Wednesday before a game, Thursday at the latest – and then when it came to the game itself it would happen exactly the way I'd imagined. I'd make a tackle, hit the ground, make a carry, and each time I'd be like, 'I've been here before.' I hated some of the hard work in training, but if that's what it took to stay in the team then that's what it took, especially as I got older and my body needed longer to recover. And I was extra-careful with things like supplements. Basically, I wouldn't take them; I was too scared there might be banned substances in them, no matter what the label said.

I also made sure to look at other captains to see how they did it, and the obvious place to start was my beloved Liverpool FC. I'd started supporting them because of Steven Gerrard, who had always reminded me of Jean de Villiers (or maybe it's the other way round). I wasn't quite sure why, but I think it must have had something to do with some innate leadership qualities. If you needed a last-minute intercept try, Jean would be the one to get it, just like Steven always seemed to score vital goals when his team most needed them. I learned so much from Jean, not just about empowering teammates but also the importance of stepping up to the plate yourself. Most of leadership isn't saying; it's doing.

The same went for Jordan Henderson. I remember that he'd gone through a tough time, not getting many playing opportunities, and had had to fight for so long for his place in the team. But he'd become one of the most influential leaders, not only in football but in all sport, and the team had gone to new heights under his leadership. He had big challenges ahead and there was a lot of expectation, but he rose to the occasion, and that was encouraging to me because I could see the similarities in our journeys. His resilience inspired me, and that work, that desire, that hunger, paid off; he'd end up being Footballer of the Year in 2020, and he spent much of the early days of the Covid-19 pandemic organising all the other

Premier League captains into helping raise money for Britain's National Health Service. I met him at Melwood, the Liverpool training ground, and I was starstruck. People think that when you're an international sportsman you take all other international sportsmen to be on the same level as you, but that's not true. Jordan gave me one of his jerseys and I couldn't have been more thrilled if I'd been a six-year-old boy. We had a chat, and he was as awesome a human being as he is a player.

I'd never studied captaincy or leadership before I was made skipper, either at the Stormers or the Springboks. I hadn't read books or been on courses or anything like that. Everything I learned, I learned on the job. I took stuff from those around me, and they took stuff from me; more than one person who'd worked with Coach Rassie before he took the Springboks job said that he used to be much more 'my way or the highway', and that his style had softened a bit since then. I wouldn't claim all or even most of the credit for this, but I think I did have some effect on him, and that my softer and more low-key approach rubbed off a bit.

Transformational leadership is not when one person decides what the change will be and pushes it through without discussion or consultation, but when a leader works with other people to identify what needs to be done. Then they all come up with a plan to make the change happen, and they're all inspired to make the change themselves. Transformational leadership involves that change being so huge that each person in the group ends up performing not just better than they did before, but perhaps better than they ever thought they could.

There's an old saying that there's no 'I' in team, but there are four 'I's in the transformational leadership model: inspirational motivation, idealised influence, intellectual stimulation and individualised consideration. Coach Rassie and I used all four of these:

INSPIRATIONAL MOTIVATION

Coach Rassie was adamant right from the start that we could win the World Cup. There's no greater prize in our sport. I can't speak for others, but the prospect of being world champions, and what that could do for our country, was my real driving force. And the fact that I was the first black captain was for many people a sign that everything is possible.

IDEALISED INFLUENCE

Both Coach Rassie and I wanted to lead by example. In his case, it was by being totally transparent with everyone about team selection and the like; in mine, it was working as hard as I could on the pitch. These were the values we wanted to instil in the team.

INTELLECTUAL STIMULATION

We needed to think for ourselves and try out different things. This didn't mean diverting from the game plan, but finding ways to improve it by thinking outside the box. This would reach its peak during the World Cup when two forwards-based indoor sessions, in which we all pitched in and threw out ideas, led to vital scores against Japan and England respectively.

INDIVIDUALISED CONSIDERATION

The number of people in any group is the number of different individual personalities. They all have their strengths and weaknesses, they all respond to situations in different ways, and they all need to be treated as people in their own right rather than just interchangeable parts of the group. I'd go out of my way to talk to everyone and see how they were doing.

Those aside, I realised that most of the rest of what I'd learned about captaincy spelled out, appropriately enough, the word SPRINGBOK:

SELF

I realised early on that I had to look after my own performance first and foremost. Being captain often involves looking outside yourself and considering the needs of other people – your teammates, the coaching staff, the fans, the media, sponsors, match officials, even the opposition. But sometimes you need to be selfish. It's easy to be pulled in several different directions at once, and you have to learn to say 'no', which I always found easier said than done. No rugby team can afford to carry a passenger, no matter how good a leader that person is; and if you're not playing well enough then your leadership is immaterial, as your teammates will know you shouldn't be there. Coach Rassie was really good about this in my early days as Springbok captain, when he saw how much the attention was affecting my form; he took as much of the load off me as possible and told me just to play.

POSITIVITY

A captain has to be upbeat. Teams take their emotional cues from the leaders, and both positivity and negativity radiate downwards and outwards very fast. I'm lucky in that my default nature is upbeat – I'm a glass-half-full person and always look on the optimistic side of any situation – so it comes easy to me to be positive. But there's no point in being positive unless you show it. So I tell the guys: 'You must just enjoy yourselves. You are put here for a reason, because there's something special in you. You must just use that. When you have the opportunity to show what makes you different from everyone else, you must take that opportunity.' I'm always the one on the pitch congratulating teammates when they've won a penalty or secured a turnover; the one who gees people up, gives high-fives and smacks shoulders, and so on. It's not even what you say in those situations, but how you say it. Being positive is about always seeing room for improvement and setting standards rather than limits. I never worry about losing a match; I always think we're going to win. If we lose then we lose, and we can analyse why and see what we can change. But the positive player is excited by a challenge rather than daunted by one.

RESILIENCE

Every leader needs to be able to take the rough with the smooth, because there will inevitably be as much of the former as the latter, and usually much more. Anyone can be a leader when things are going well; few people can be a leader when things are going against them. As Mr Mandela himself said: 'Do not judge me by my success. Judge me by how many times

I fell down and got back up again.' Resilience is not freedom from or the absence of failure, pain or distress; it's experiencing those things and going through them to the other side. There's no resilience needed to travel down a smooth road. I had to be resilient to endure the childhood I had; we as the Springboks had to be resilient to come back from those dreadful defeats by New Zealand and Ireland in 2017. Maybe someone put it best, and most simply, with: 'When you're going through hell, keep going.'

INCLUSIVITY

Being a leader isn't about laying down the law and expecting people to obey without question, especially at the level of international sport when you're dealing with ultra-competitive and ambitious people. There's no point me trying to control everything, to take all that stress on me. I believe in shared leadership, and there are some guys who know stuff I don't know, who are better at some stuff than me; so where I can I let these guys take control in order that we can all grow as people, and everybody has a voice in the team, which is amazing. The coach is not only creating players, but he wants us to be leaders so we can all grow together as a team. I've never been interested in being right for my own sake; I want us to collectively come up with the best ways forward. I emphasise time and again that everybody has a role to play and that we are playing for everybody. It's not just the starting XV, the matchday 23 or the coaching staff who are important here; it's the physios, the chefs, the media managers, the logistics guys, all of them. They all have to feel an integral part of it too, because then their positive attitude will reinforce the general good vibes around the camp. The guys who aren't in the 23 can help do video analysis on our opponents and mimic them in training, both of which are a massive help in the run-up to a big game. One of the things Coach Robbie said about me is that 'Siya's the guy who can sit at any table,' and I always try to bring that into my captaincy, both literally – in a players' canteen I'll always try to sit with different groups on different days – and metaphorically, in making myself open to anyone. Cheslin remembers a time early in his Stormers career when I was out with my friends and he with his in the same place, and I said we should all hang out together. To me that just seems natural, which brings me neatly onto …

NATURAL
There are many different ways to exercise leadership on and off the rugby pitch, and each person must do what comes naturally to them. One way is not necessarily better or worse than another. And everybody has a role to play, and can still contribute to leadership in their own way.

GENUINE
This is advice for life and not just for leadership, but be yourself. If you're not, sooner or later you'll get found out, and people don't respect frauds. I have to be myself. Off the pitch I'm chilled. When I step onto the field it's a bit different. I don't try to be something I'm not. I don't shout and scream when things aren't going our way. I just do what I can on and off the field: lead by example, never ask anyone to do something I

wouldn't do, and so on. When I don't know something, I ask; when I feel someone else will do or say something better, I defer to them. In the long run that gets you respect. No-one's brilliant at everything.

BRAVERY

A leader needs to be brave in three areas – physically, mentally and emotionally (or body, mind and spirit, if you prefer). The physical side is fairly obvious: you have to be courageous to hurl yourself into the path of 110 kg guys running at full pace, or to go clean out a ruck in the knowledge that you'll be hit by those same 110 kg guys trying to knock you off the ball, or to do pretty much everything that 80 minutes of rugby involves. Mentally, you have to be brave in what you aim for; it takes guts to put yourself through all the pressure which comes with being a high-profile sportsman, let alone holding a position like Springbok captain. Emotionally, too, you have to be prepared to go to some dark places and to help your team-mates when they do. Male environments in particular can be deliberately unemotional – guys aren't traditionally good at expressing their feelings – but the stuff we shared about ourselves, our lives, our hopes and fears on the way to the World Cup really helped the team environment.

OBJECTIVE

Objective is both a noun and adjective. As a noun, objectives are crucial for a leader. You can't lead if you don't know where you're going and how you're getting there. Objectives need to be both achievable and measurable. Coach Rassie was very good at this. When he took over he set three objectives: to beat New Zealand away, to win the Rugby Championship and to win the World Cup. Each was a simple either/or proposition, easy to measure, and each followed on from the next. It was no use saying, 'We're going to win the World Cup' without putting intermediate points in there – that would have been measurable but not achievable. As an adjective, objective – the ability to assess things as unbiasedly and dispassionately as possible – is also critical. It's so easy to become blind to the truth of things you're involved with, either because you're too close to and invested in them and/or because you've fallen into routines which you don't bother to change as they've always worked well enough up to now. But a good leader will take a step back now and then and ask themselves, 'Is this all as good as it can be? Is there anything which can be changed to make things go better?' Often you find that there is.

KNOWLEDGE

Within reason, a leader can never have too much knowledge. The more information you have, the better your decisions can be. I'd make it my business to know not just the things which might affect the way my teammates might play – illness, injury, problems at home – but all the things that could affect us from the outside. How does the referee like to engage with the captains? How long does he give at a maul before shouting, 'Use it once'? What are the weather conditions going to be like, and how will that affect our tactics? How do the opposition like to organise their defensive lines? Which opposing player is most temperamental and liable to lose his cool if things don't go his way? And on, and on, and on. You won't need to use most of this knowledge, but you do need to have it – much better to have it and not to use it than not to have it and need it – and you do need to use it wisely.

Almost before I knew it, 2019 came round: World Cup year.

Rachel and I were planning our calendar a couple of days into January. Rachel turned to 2 November, the day of the final, and wrote simply 'Springboks vs …'. She said, 'You're going to win, the country will go crazy, there'll be a bus tour with the trophy, so basically let's write November off as everyone will want a piece of you.'

She knew that our lives would change irrevocably if that happened, a change which would afford us lots of opportunities but also bring new pressures with it. And life wasn't all rainbows and sunshine. We all change, we all go through different seasons, and this happens to everyone, it doesn't matter who you are – president, unemployed, we all go through this. I could still find myself distracted from the path of Christ, and my decisions were affecting those I loved. Rachel put me in touch with Ben Schoeman, an entrepreneur who agreed to act as my Christian mentor. Up to that point, everything I was fighting against was hidden, but when my sin was exposed, I knew I either had to change my life or lose everything. I decided to lose my life and find it in Christ. Right at the start, Ben told me something simple. 'Siya,' he said, 'where you spend your time, that's who you are. You drink a lot, you fool around with women, you go to clubs and strip clubs. You post on social media about your faith in Christ, but you're lying to yourself and everyone else. I don't care how famous you are. I want to know that you're living the right way. When you do bad stuff you're killing yourself slowly and pushing yourself away from God.'

It might sound odd, but actually very few people in my life told me things straight, and those that did were almost all within the confines of established parts of my life, such as my marriage (Rachel) and the Springboks (Coach Rassie). A lot of people said 'yes' all the time because they thought that's what I wanted to hear, because they were impressed or intimidated by fame, or because they wanted something and thought that flattery or agreement was the best way to get it.

Ben gave it to me straight, each and every time. If I was going wrong he'd say, 'This is rubbish' without blinking. He didn't care about offending or upsetting me. He cared about helping me. He said to me, 'You need to stop drinking, because when you drink is when you do dumb things. But don't think of it as stopping drinking forever. Think of it as stopping drinking for a certain period of time, a month or so; but when you get to the end of that month you'll find that it hasn't been so hard, so you can extend it another month, and another, and so on. If that's what it takes to stop then that's what it takes; but it will never stop unless you decide to stop the cycle.'

It was part of something bigger, I realised. I was struggling with a lot of things: temptations, sins, lifestyle choices. I struggled with porn too, like many men. I was in demand as the first black Springbok captain; everyone wanted to know me and have a piece of me. I called myself a follower of Christ, but I wasn't really. Well, I was, but only in the most basic sense. I was getting by, but I hadn't decided to fully commit myself to Jesus Christ and start living according to His way. It was like playing touch once a week and calling myself a rugby player.

While I was really struggling in the midst of my sin, I read a verse in the Bible that really stood out to me. Isaiah 43:2–3 says: 'When you pass through the waters, I will be with you; and when you pass through the rivers, they will not sweep over you. When you walk through the fire, you will not be burned; the flames will not set you ablaze. For I am the Lord your God, the Holy One of Israel, your Saviour.'

When you pass through the waters, I will be with you; and when you pass through the rivers, they will not sweep over you. When you walk through the fire, you will not be burned; the flames will not set you ablaze. For I am the Lord your God, the Holy One of Israel, your Saviour. I read it over and over for days.

Ben asked me to write a mission statement, which would sort out what I wanted to be and help me achieve it. This is what I came up with:

- I want to only trust, love, worship and glorify God with all that I do.
- I choose to love and honour my wife at all times, especially when she's not around. Be a great father to my kids taking guidance from God, for when they leave my household I know they will be prepared to conquer all the worldly challenges coming.

- I want to empower my community by creating opportunities to inspire them out of the circumstances they're in.
- I want all men to see an idea and example of how to be a father.

I changed my whole attitude around. I made sure to open up a space for vulnerability and accountability; to change my ways not just as a player but as a person, as a man, as a leader. I minimised my exposure to situations where I'd be tested when I didn't have to be. If I went to a nightclub, for example, then sooner or later I'd have girls start hitting on me just because I was a Springbok, or there'd be some oke who'd had one beer too many and wanted to show his mates how hard he was by challenging me to a fight. I did enough fighting for a lifetime growing up in Zwide, and I got enough bone-on-bone contact every week in training and games not to feel I needed any more. And everyone's got a cameraphone now, so anything I did would be filmed and on social media within minutes.

All of which meant it was easier all round to have friends over or to go over to their places. We could eat and talk and chill without worrying about who or what's round the corner. Curiously, perhaps, I never found it hard to have alcohol in the house for other people. I didn't regard drink as temptation I needed to turn my head from; I knew it wasn't good for me in any way, so whether it was physically within reach or not made no difference. And if I did have a drink I knew Rachel would find out instantly. Back in the days when I was hiding my drinking I'd stash bottles around the house, and every time she'd find them. She didn't seek them or hunt them out; but when she found them she'd merely reflect to me the true me that I was hiding when I hid those bottles. She'd pray to God that I would stop, and now I had, but the memories were still there. Sometimes, I'd pull a funny face to my sister and she'd say, 'That's what you used to look like when you were drunk.'

Ben challenged me in ways other than just the basics of not drinking and trying to be a good father, husband and person. He encouraged me to ask deep questions of myself and life, because only in asking those questions would I really think about what mattered to me and why. Why am I alive? Why was I born? What are my core values? What is God's picture of success in life? I distilled all this in a personal statement which is included at the end of this book, and that statement sums up the core tenets of my life, the values I hold and how I try to live by them.

But it's interesting what's not there in that statement, and that's the word 'rugby'. That may sound strange, given that the sport has in so many ways defined my life, but rugby's what I do; it's not who I am. I apply my faith to the game, of course. I work as hard as I can during the week, but on Saturday I give the game to God. That's the time to let go and let Him be in control. I do my best and make Him proud; the rest is up to Him. Whether I win or lose, I learn something from Him. I surround myself with Christians – there are many in both franchise and national teams – and they encourage me, build me up, and will always keep me accountable. We have Bible studies as a team, and often pray together. I try to also read the

Word as much as I can when I'm alone, every single night before bed. I always tell my teammates that their talents are God-given. We must always remain humble. It's a great blessing to know that no matter what, nothing can deter God's will – it will always be done. I tell my teammates to always 'train your best and give it your all'; I always ask God to use me. I put it all in His hands. Knowing that He is in control gives me peace. It is important to know your value, to know who you are in Christ.

My spiritual growth didn't only help Rachel and me reconnect; it also helped me become more confident as a captain, too. When we played the Crusaders at Newlands during the 2019 Super Rugby season, we were given a penalty in the last minute while 19–16 down. Jean-Luc du Plessis was our kicker, and I had a simple choice: ask him to kick for the poles and secure three points and the draw, or ask him to kick for the corner where we would get the lineout and a chance to score a try and win the game. The crowd-pleasing option was the second one; every crowd wants to see you go for it, and the passionate Newlands one was no exception. As a newer or younger captain I might have allowed myself to be seduced by the death-or-glory aspect. But this was professional rugby, and results count. A draw was better than a loss, and a reasonably straightforward kick for the poles had a far higher chance of success than a lineout and a maul. We'd lost more games than we'd won up to that stage in the competition, and the Crusaders had only lost one of their dozen games. A share of the points was a good result for us.

So I told Jean-Luc to go for the poles, the crowd groaned, and we secured the draw.

A few of the guys in the shed afterwards took issue with me and said I should have been bolder. But I have to be accountable for my decisions. This wasn't like the Brighton match of 2015, where Japan had a once-in-a-lifetime chance of a famous upset and took it. This was a franchise match where points mattered. I told the guys they had to trust me being in charge, but the only reason I could say that is that I also trusted myself. I had perspective and calm.

The following week, I injured my knee during our 34–22 win over the Highlanders at Newlands. It was 25 May, only a few months before the World Cup was due to start. Injuries were always frustrating, but this one was especially so for two reasons. First, I'd had a really good game, which I needed after those off-field troubles I'd had earlier in the campaign. Second, recovery would be substantially more urgent than usual with the World Cup looming.

It's easy to say afterwards that I always knew I'd make it back in time, but that would be stretching the truth. Certainly those around me always believed. The team doctor wasn't stressed, and Rachel prayed so much for my recovery that she was convinced I'd come through. But maybe it's different being the one in the middle of it all, on the days when my body didn't feel as though it was responding like it should, and when I wanted something so much that the thought of missing out on it was almost a physical pain. I thought of all the times I'd missed big matches and tournaments through injury: Currie Cup semis, Super Rugby semis. There were definitely moments when I wondered whether I'd make it, but I tried to shut out the doubts and just do what I could: follow the rehab protocols to the letter, work hard in the gym to make myself as strong as possible and try to be positive around the team.

I knew that, even if I did make it back, I'd be undercooked in terms of game time and would need to make that up once out in Japan. The guys who'd been fit all the way through the Rugby Championship would be hitting the ground running, but I'd be playing catch-up. We had such strength in depth that I didn't worry about the effect on the team, and nor did I worry about whether or not I'd be worth my place. That was for Coach Rassie to decide, not me; and I knew he wouldn't shirk a hard choice either way.

He was also determined to win the Rugby Championship, even though in World Cup years it's shortened, with each team playing each other only once, not twice as is usual. No team had ever won the Rugby Championship and the World Cup in the same year, and he wanted us to be the first. He was smart about it, too. He named the starting line-ups for all three fixtures in the tournament even before a ball had been kicked, and effectively split the squad so that the guys playing New Zealand in Wellington could arrive early to prepare while the team to play Australia would stay in Joburg. Only a couple of guys would play in both fixtures, and the teams would only change for two scenarios: a player being injured, or a player acting like an entitled jerk. If someone didn't play well or made mistakes, that didn't upset him; he'd want to understand why, and then it would be for the coaches to fix. But if a player got entitled or dropped his workrate or didn't have a positive attitude, that was a different matter.

In other hands it could have been divisive having two teams. But that was the plan, and everyone backed it. The gaps between the players, particularly in the forwards, was so small that it was hard to say who was first choice and who was second. And Australia are never an easy side to beat, so it wasn't a case of 'You guys do your best'; it was 'We trust you to do the job.'

They did that job and they did it well, beating Australia 35–17 and never being behind. Herschel Jantjies scored two tries on his debut and put himself in pole position to be Faf's understudy. Although I wasn't playing, I wanted to be involved in any way I could. I was the water guy at Ellis Park when we played Australia in the opener. Maybe some captains would have been too proud to do that job, or would have wanted to sit in the stands in their suits. Not me. I wanted to be down at pitchside living every moment of it with my guys.

The win had ramifications far beyond just our chances of winning the Rugby Championship. It was a huge lift for the guys already in New Zealand, but at the same time it put pressure on them to perform knowing that the guys competing for their shirts were playing so well. In fact, six of the starting XV against Australia would start the World Cup Final against England just over three months later.

It wasn't just us who had bet all our chips on the All Blacks clash; the All Blacks themselves had done the same, picking 11 rookies against Argentina and only sneaking home 20–16 so they could be at full strength against us. They'd even scheduled the match for Wellington again rather than Auckland, a deliberate decision to take us back to the scene of the previous year's match and rectify what had happened there.

We were all over them in the first half, but Jack Goodhue scored a try from nowhere and they were leading 7–6 at half-time. 'Put yourself in their heads,' Coach Rassie said in the shed. 'They're afraid.' We were playing better than they were, and they knew it. It would be close, we all knew that; one missed tackle, one loose maul, one lapse in concentration could make the difference.

The second half was penalties: three to them, one to us. With three minutes left we were 16–9 down. If it stayed like that we'd get a bonus point for keeping the margin of victory to within seven points, and that bonus point might turn out to be crucial in terms of winning the championship. Coach Rassie tried to get a message to the players on the pitch to settle for that score: don't try to win the match and risk conceding a further score.

But part of empowering players the way he had done for the past year or so was trusting them to make their own decisions on the pitch. So when we won a scrum penalty, Handre drilled the kick into their half, we won the lineout, Willie came round on the long sweep to the blindside to make the extra man and put Cheslin clear on the touchline. Beauden Barrett was tracking across with two All Blacks on the inside, and even Cheslin would have been swallowed up in traffic if he'd stepped inside; so he lofted a kick ahead for Herschel to pluck it out of the air ahead of Aaron Smith and dot down. Handre had the conversion to secure the draw. It was wide on the right and by no means a certainty, not with the match hanging on this and the All Blacks charging to try to disrupt his kick.

Did he nail it? Of course he did. The man could tap dance in a minefield.

The last three matches against New Zealand, we'd scored 82 points, and so had they. We'd won one, lost one and drawn one, and so had they. The margins had been two points, two points and zero points. If they were the best in the world, we weren't far behind. And so much of that came from the fact that Coach Rassie looked for fighters, warriors, dogs. When we were in clutch situations against the All Blacks, nothing in it with two minutes to go, it wasn't down to how good we were at rugby. It was down to how much we wanted it and how much we were prepared to scrap for it. And we were scrappers, believe me.

In the final round of the Championship, we put 46 points on Argentina while, astonishingly, Australia went one better: 47–26 against New Zealand in Perth, the second half against 14 men after Scott Barrett had been sent off just before the break. It was a record-breaking score and a record-equalling margin for Australia against New Zealand, but it made no difference to our position atop the final table, four points clear and the only unbeaten team.

Some people were quick to downplay the achievement: it was a shortened championship and everyone had half an eye on the World Cup. Winning the title this year did not mean everything, they said. But it didn't follow that it meant nothing. We heard it time and again before we set off for Japan: no-one had ever won the Tri Nations/Rugby Championship and the World Cup in the same year. It had never been done, and with that came the unspoken implication: it can never be done. We didn't care. History is there to be made; records are there to be broken.

No-one had done it? Then we'd be the first. Simple as that.

5

SUMMIT

Back from injury, my own build-up to the World Cup was good. I played 53 minutes against Argentina in a one-off Test at Loftus just before we left for Japan, and looked as sharp as I felt. Coach Rassie actually only intended for me to play half an hour, but I was feeling fine so I asked to stay on for a while.

The Gwijo Squad came to the airport to see us off. So much attention was on me, but everyone had their own story, everyone had come different ways to get to where we were now.

We were the first team to arrive in Japan; we would, we vowed, be the last to leave. The reception from the Japanese people was amazing. It wasn't just the fact that there were 15,000 people at those training sessions, or that our faces were all over stores; it was every single person we came into contact with. They were so warm, welcoming and polite, and their manners were next level. The world has a lot to learn from Japan. There were stories of shopkeepers shutting their stores temporarily so they could escort fans to where they wanted to go. I remembered a story about the Japanese team who'd played in the previous year's soccer World Cup in Russia. They'd been 2–0 up against Belgium in the round of 16 before losing 3–2 with the last kick of the match; but they'd still tidied up their changing room and left it absolutely spotless, with a note on the table saying 'Thank you' in Russian.

The heat and humidity were like nothing I'd ever experienced. We had to keep hydrating, and make sure it wasn't just water we were replenishing but electrolytes and carbs too. The first few training sessions, while we got used to it, were absolutely brutal, not least because Aled pushed us so hard. Pieter-Steph lost 5 kg in one session. Aled was merciless, and with good reason. I think it was Muhammad Ali who said: 'The fight is won or lost far away from witnesses – behind the lines, in the gym, and out there on the road, long before I dance under those lights.' These sessions were the ones behind our lines. We knew that they would pay dividends further down the road.

'Don't count the days,' Aled would say. 'Make the days count.' His training was all position-specific and centred around how far we'd run on game days: how many metres we were going to run, how we were going to run them, the kind of impacts we'd be taking en route. It wasn't just one training session for everyone. Take Frans Malherbe and Willie, for example; the demands of their positions were very different, so the training they did was very different too.

Coach Rassie identified five departments in which we needed to be constantly on it, and assigned responsibility for each one to a player. Physicality was Bongi's area, which suited him just fine; Bongi loved that stuff, absolutely loved it, and was never happier than when running around the place smashing people into the middle of next week. Duane was to look after converting pressure in the opposition 22 to points; whether it was three, five or seven, we needed to come away with something every time we were close to their line. Kick chase was Willie and the wings. We'd vary our tactics according not only to the opposition but also field position. In the middle half of the pitch, between our 22 and theirs, we'd sometimes play almost rugby league style, five or six phases and then kick. Kicking wasn't necessarily for territory but momentum, to keep us going forward and the opposition on the back foot; we'd kick high to regather or to defend against them as they came at us and make sure they couldn't get through our defensive wall. Control wouldn't always equal possession.

Dealing with the ref was down to me, and no stone was left unturned. We found out that Jérôme Garcès, for example, liked to be complimented on his fitness, so I'd make sure to say something about what good condition he was in and how he was keeping up with world-class athletes. If we had a problem with how he was refereeing, however, it would be Duane rather than me who'd speak to him. Duane would play bad cop and I'd be good cop. We thought that was easier and more effective than asking me to be both. And Pieter-Steph was in charge of workrate and commitment. He was our not-so-secret weapon. We'd use him not as part of the main defensive shape but in a more roving role, using his fitness and workrate to fly around the park and make a nuisance of himself all 80 minutes long. That made it very hard for opposing teams to analyse him properly. There was a joke going round which summed him up.

Coach Rassie: 'Pieter-Steph, which part of the field do you want to cover?'

Pieter-Steph: 'Ja.'

Put the words 'Japan' and 'rugby' together, of course, and we all thought of the same thing: Brighton, 2015. That defeat had been the most embarrassing moment of my rugby career, and the same went for everybody who'd played that day. Eight of us who'd been involved in that match were now in Japan for this World Cup, and for all eight – Jesse, Beast, Lood, Flo, Pieter-Steph, Eben, Handre and me – the loss burned deep and hard, and we still carried the scars. That hadn't just been our first loss to Japan; it had been the only time we'd ever played them, which meant we'd never beaten them. It was a statistic which rankled and a monkey we needed to get off our back, and the sooner the better; which was why Coach Rassie had organised a warm-up game against them before the tournament proper started.

The Japanese team of 2015 had taken us by surprise. The Japanese team of 2019 emphatically would not, even though they were in every way a better side than they'd been four years before. They were wonderfully coached by former All Black flanker Jamie Joseph, they'd put together some good results – three on the bounce against Fiji, Tonga and the USA recently, a victory against Italy in 2018, a draw against France the year before that – and most of all they played great rugby: fast runners, quick hands, slick moves. They weren't by any means a pushover, especially given home advantage and a passionate crowd, which of course meant that playing them was a bit of a risk. If we lost again, the psychological damage would be immense, perhaps even enough to derail our entire campaign.

But Coach Rassie was adamant it was a risk worth taking. We're a better team than they are, he said, and if we really think we're in with a shout of winning the trophy then we can't be afraid of anyone. There was also another factor in his thinking, though one which he didn't really share with many people. Japan were in a group with Scotland, Ireland, Russia and Samoa, with only two of those five to qualify; and Coach Rassie was convinced Japan would be one of those two. The winner and runner-up of our group would play the runner-up and winner of their group respectively, which meant we had a pretty decent chance of meeting Japan in the quarters if Coach Rassie was right. So he wanted both to get a look at them and to lay down a marker before that match – if it ever took place.

We took Japan to the cleaners in the warm-up, winning 41–7. Job done, monkey lifted, marker laid down. But the match was perhaps most significant for what happened after Mapimpi scored the first of his three tries. He ran to the camera and showed his wristband, on which he'd written NENE R.I.P. in memory of Uyinene Mrwetyana, a UCT student who'd been raped and murdered by a post office worker not long before. Her killing had brought women to the streets all over South Africa in protest against gender-based violence, and the hashtag #AmINext? showed their fear and anger. Rachel had been on the march in Cape Town and encouraged me to use my voice to speak out against GBV because I had witnessed it as a small boy, and she believed that we could use our platforms to make the uncomfortable truths of GBV more visible. But I was so focused on the game that I'd deleted my social media. It was a conflict I'd felt before and would feel again; there are times when I have to be locked into the game and be present, but at the same time I am still part of the greater South African community, so what affects the community affects me too.

Rene, our physio, was in tears afterwards. She'd wanted to say something all week – as one of the few women in our party, Uyinene's murder had affected her really badly – but she'd been concerned not to break our focus. Mapimpi was exemplary in bringing those two worlds together in a powerful and practical way, by both playing well (being present on the field) and still showing the essence of *Ubuntu*: that if one member of our community is not well then we are all not well.

Not long after the match we received some sad news: Chester Williams had died of a heart attack at the age of only 49. He was the fourth member of the 1995 World Cup winning team to die, and for me and other black players he had been a real trailblazer: he'd been the only non-white face in that team, a one-man proof that being a Springbok didn't necessarily hinge on the colour of your skin.

As a tribute, we had his face imprinted in the numbers on our jerseys for our first match of the tournament, against the All Blacks. The match was being held up not just as the pick of the pool matches, but perhaps as the most seismic pool match ever played in the history of the World Cup: two teams who between them had won the tournament five out of the eight times it had been staged. On one level it was true – there had never been such a heavyweight contest so early in the tournament – but on another it was perhaps a little less momentous than it seemed, because whoever lost should still beat the other teams in the group and qualify anyway. Italy, Canada and Namibia rounded off the teams in our group, and though the first were potentially tricky opponents they were also coming off a losing streak in the Six Nations of more than 20 games and counting. Canada and Namibia we knew would pose no real threat.

So we worked hard on analysing the All Blacks. Seek and destroy was their thing; no-one targeted an opposition's weaknesses like they did. From my own positional perspective, their back row – Ardie Savea, Sam Cane and Kieran Read – were as good as any in the tournament, smart and hard in equal measures. In every position on the field, we had to stress them, get in their faces, make them compress in on themselves. They were the best team in the world, but they weren't unbeatable; Australia had put nearly 50 points past them the previous month.

As usual, everything intensified in the week before the match. It wasn't just bragging rights at stake, but the road to the final too; whoever won this would potentially have an easier route through the knockout stages. But Coach Rassie did his best to take the pressure off us. He said we were going to go in hard for it, but the result didn't matter. He just wanted a performance; all he cared about was the workrate and how hard we worked for each other. He said the result was on him, not on anybody else.

'All of us are nervous,' he said. 'I'm nervous that you don't know how physical you must be.' He knew we had the focus, the game plan, the conditioning, the fitness and the passion for the jersey; but he also knew that we'd have to be at our best for 80 minutes, not 70 or 60 – or, as it turned out, for 74.

We start well and are ahead within three minutes, Handre drilling a long-range penalty between the posts. The next 20 minutes are all ours, the best we've played against the All Blacks in a long time: Cheslin taking a mark under massive pressure, Lukhanyo chipping through to make space in midfield, our defenders hunting in packs and forcing Beauden Barrett to clear from behind his own line. We're taking their time and decision making away from them, swarming them, getting in their faces, just like Coach Rassie wanted us to.

But you can never relax against the All Blacks, not for a second, and now they show why. First Richie Mo'unga equalises with a penalty after snaffling a loose pass from Faf, and then they score a try from inside their own half. Sevu Reece slips Mapimpi's tackle and sets off up the touchline. I track back as the ball goes from Reece to Aaron Smith to Ardie Savea, and when neither Willie nor Faf can hold Savea I come in and flatten him. I've run 60 metres to get there, 60 metres which I wouldn't have run when Coach Rassie first came in because at the time I had neither the conditioning nor the mindset. But Savea recycles the ball, Beauden Barrett delays his pass long enough to commit the defence, and George Bridge goes over. Three minutes later it happens again, Anton Lienert-Brown jinking through a couple of poor tackles and finding Scott Barrett on his shoulder to score unopposed. Six minutes ago we were 3–0 up and dominant; now we're 17–3 down. Six minutes – that's all it takes for the game to be more or less over. Only the All Blacks can do that.

Our first task is to get to half-time without shipping any more points, which we do. Coach Rassie emphasises that we need to come out flying in the second half, and we do that too; there are only four minutes gone when Cheslin gathers a Smith box-kick, beats two players and finds himself one on one with Richie Mo'unga, hard up against the right-hand touchline with Mo'unga showing him the outside. Cheslin goes inside, goes outside, takes a couple of steps back in and then out again. It's a foot race for the line, and Cheslin has so much gas, but Mo'unga tracks him, gets his angles right, and takes him down five metres short – one of the best try-saving tackles you'll ever see. Later Cheslin will say that the second step inside cost him, and that he should have just pinned his ears back and gone for it; but these are the split-second heat-of-the-moment decisions that make or break games.

In any case, the ball is still alive. Beauden Barrett cleans up and feeds Lienert-Brown, who dances through a thicket of green shirts before Kitsie takes him to ground still in their 22. They feed it left, but Pieter-Steph – who else? – intercepts it. I make a few metres, then Handre does, then Malcolm, and when it comes back to the right I'm there once more. Willie, Pieter-Steph, Franco Mostert; we keep on coming, pulling their defenders this way and that, looking for the opening. Finally it comes, in a rather bizarre way; Eben takes the ball into contact, and even though there are four All Blacks nearby, not a single one is guarding the base of the ruck. Pieter-Steph picks up and runs over without a finger being laid on him. It's the kind of defensive error a club side would be unhappy with, let alone the All Blacks, but these things don't happen in isolation. It happened because we maintained the pressure and never let them settle. Handre converts, and the gap is back to seven.

I'm pulled off for Flo a few minutes later. The Boks fans in the crowd roar their support as we come storming back. It's end-to-end stuff, both sides going close, and when we're in their territory with a little more than 20 minutes left Handre decides that something's better than nothing and knocks over a drop goal. Now we trail by just four. It's still more our pressure than theirs, but they soak it up expertly. They get a scrum penalty which Mo'unga nails to restore the seven-point gap, and six minutes later we stray offside and Beauden Barrett knocks another one over: 23–13.

Trevor does his calf. He knows it's a bad one, enough to put him out of the rest of the tournament. All that effort, all those sacrifices, and his World Cup has lasted exactly 20 minutes. Kitsie and I try to console him, but what can you say? Cheslin makes another brilliant run deep into their territory, but he's too quick for our support and the All Blacks turn it over. That's our last chance gone, and 23–13 is how it ends.

Coach Rassie was honest with the media afterwards. 'They deserved to win. They scored two tries to one. And the penalty count, I think eleven against us and only two against them. That's a win by them and it showed on the scoreboard. They're a team who know how to ramp up the pressure the moment they're ahead.'

To us in private he was encouraging. 'I can't fault you for your effort. Obviously there's something I messed up somewhere, so we'll go and see why we didn't execute.' The important thing was that we players still believed. We'd gone toe to toe with them; it was just that six minutes and two chances had cost us the game. There'd been nothing wrong with our game plan. Quite the opposite; we'd shown that our game plan was spot on, and we'd created more chances here than we had in any of our previous three games against New Zealand. And Cheslin's performance – 118 metres made and 11 defenders beaten in nine carries – was showing the rest of the world something we'd known for a long time: this guy was very, very special.

For my own part, there were two things I needed to work on. One was match sharpness, as I'd found it hard to live with the pace of the game. I'd always known this would be the case, and that I'd need a few matches back to get into my stride. There was a world of difference between playing Argentina and Japan in warm-up games and the All Blacks in the real thing. The other area in which I hadn't been up to speed was my handling of Garcès. My opposite number Kieran Read had dealt with him much better. The referee was a vital part of any game, and if I couldn't handle him better than the other captain then I had at the very least to make sure I didn't handle him worse. There are five or six grey penalties in every game, and those are the penalties that can win or lose a match. Again, I didn't need to ensure that they all went our way, but I did need to ensure that they didn't all go the opposition's way either.

If we wanted to win the World Cup from here, we'd have to do more than just be the first team to win the Rugby Championship the same year; we'd have to be the first team to win it having lost a pool game. That didn't bother Coach

Rassie either, and he gave the same answer as he had done to the question about the Rugby Championship: 'History is there to break.'

Actually, very little had changed in terms of how we approached the rest of the tournament. Now we knew for sure that we'd have to beat Italy in order to qualify for the quarters; in effect, our knockout phase had started a game earlier than we'd planned. (The same had happened in 2015: we'd lost our first match but won the next three.) There were four big games – Italy and the knockout stages – for us to become world champions, drink from that cup and change our lives forever. If we and New Zealand both kept winning then we'd meet them again in the final, and the international press were saying it would take something pretty extraordinary for that *not* to happen. We joked that we'd have the advantage in that scenario, as they'd have to beat us twice to win the World Cup but we'd only have to beat them once.

In many ways, the purity of the win-or-go-home equation even worked in our favour. As Handre said: 'When the Springboks are getting into that frame of mind when there's no way back, when you've just got to go through every wall that's in front of you, I think that's when we're at our best.' That was how we'd been before our epic victory in Wellington; that was how we'd need to be now. So we hardened our attitudes. *Here for business.* That was now our mantra every time we stepped onto the pitch, be it training or a match. Off the field we were chilled and happy to laugh in each other's company, and of course we loved being out and about in Japan either just finding a place to have coffee or doing community events. But those four white lines which marked out a pitch, any pitch: once we crossed them then we were here for one thing only. We were here for business.

We scored nine tries in our next match against Namibia, one of them mine, and I had a solid 27 minutes off the bench. But the biggest news for us came off the field, or rather on another field, where Japan beat Ireland 19–12. The result shocked a lot of people, but not Coach Rassie. Ireland had been the form team of world rugby, let alone that group, just 12 months ago, and for Japan to beat them was a major achievement. Coach Rassie had always thought Japan would make it through their group, but now they'd beaten Ireland they were arguably favourites to come top of that group, which meant we'd play them in the quarters.

The Italy match was next up, and it was really important not just for the team but for me as well. I hadn't hit top form yet, and we were coming to the sharp end of the tournament. I love being surrounded by other leaders and I have a strong relationship with Handre, so he could see when I was struggling for confidence. He took me for coffee and said, 'Listen, bro, stop stressing. I'll do all the calls I can, so don't worry about it. Just be responsible for yourself.' It was a reminder which I badly needed: that I couldn't be much good to other people if I wasn't feeling good in myself first. It's like those safety demonstrations on planes when they remind you to fasten your own oxygen mask first before helping other people. It sounds selfish, but it's not; it's maximising your own performance to the benefit of those around you, and you think and act most clearly when you're in a good place.

Italy was the first match for which Coach Rassie used the Bomb Squad, a six–two bench split with only two backs. Six–two had been used before, but usually with two back-row replacements for dynamic change in the last 20 rather than a whole new tight five. Now we'd be able to keep the pace and intensity up front for the whole 80 minutes. When a player's fresh, his instincts are sharp and his decisions good, but those drop off when fatigue sets in. The moment the metrics showed that a tight five player's energy was going down, off they came. The coaches didn't wait for them to be exhausted. Aled's training programme meant that the front rows could play 50 minutes at their peak, and then the replacements would come in. It wasn't even a case of rebranding the subs as finishers; it was simply a badge of honour. The first player had given his all; now it was the next guy's duty to keep it up. It was almost like a relay.

There were two reasons why we could enact the Bomb Squad concept here, and they both marked us out as unique among the teams in Japan. First, we had two world-class tight fives with no more than a cigarette paper's difference between them, if that. You could have swapped the starters and finishers around without weakening the team in any way; you could have mixed and matched players between the two sets to the same effect. Sometimes the training sessions were so ferocious that games came as something of a light relief. (And of course all this was very demoralising to the opposition, knowing there'd be no drop off in quality once the bench was emptied.)

Second, we had Frans Steyn. Since one of the two back replacements had to be a scrum-half, the other needed to be as versatile as possible, and Frans was certainly that. He could play anywhere from 10 to 15 inclusive, and indeed had played all those positions – fly-half, centre, wing and full-back – in his 13 years as a Springbok. If Handre had to come off for whatever reason, Frans could step straight in at 10, or Willie could come to 10 with Frans slotting in at 15. The Bomb Squad might have been all about the forwards, but it wouldn't have been possible without Frans.

We were booked in to a hotel in the middle of nowhere before the Italy match. The training pitch was three minutes away; everything else – supermarkets, coffee shops, cinemas – was at least half an hour's drive. There was nothing to do, which was of course why management had chosen it. This was our knockout phase, started one game early. Lose this one and we were out.

We wanted not just to win but to send out a message. So far we'd lost to the All Blacks, beaten Namibia and, with no disrespect, knew we were going to beat Canada in the final pool game. We needed not just a result but a performance against a decent side, and that performance had to involve using the traditionally Springbok trademark: physicality.

Coach Rassie spoke to us about killing teams off. Sometimes we did it through death by a thousand cuts, just whittling away at a team and grinding them down through sheer relentless attrition; but sometimes, like now, we had to go for it from the start. 'Let's physically mess them up,' he said.

That was why he'd chosen Bongi to start, because Bongi was all about physicality. The team came first, and whatever your role was you needed to do it as well as you could. And everyone having a role meant everyone, not just the matchday 23. The guys who made up the rest of the squad had an enormous job. They analysed everything from referee behaviour to maul and breakdown preferences, they played the part of our upcoming opposition in training, and they kept both their own spirits and everybody else's up. As I said, I remember having been one of those squad guys in 2015 and how I'd needed to play a different role. The vibe around these guys was totally different. Of course they wanted to play – the satisfaction of simply having made the squad lasted about as long as the flight out to Japan – but they also knew that helping us prepare as well as possible was vital.

And this worked both ways. Coach Rassie had made sure that the win bonus for lifting the trophy was the same for every player in the squad, no matter who they were (and that included anyone who wasn't there for the whole tournament, such as those who were injured and those who replaced them). It didn't matter whether a player was starting XV, matchday 23 or a wider squad member; didn't matter whether he was Pieter-Steph, who'd end up being player of the tournament, or someone who'd only played against Canada or Namibia. Everyone was equal, and that made a huge difference to team unity. Preaching true equality means acting on it too.

We went at the Italians from the opening whistle. They lost their tighthead Simone Ferrari in the very first minute, tearing his hamstring in the scrum as we hit them hard and fast. Less than 20 minutes later his replacement Marco Riccioni also had to go off, which meant the scrums had to be uncontested as neither of their fit props could play tighthead. It was a blow, as we'd been so superior in the scrum, but it was also a sign of our dominance and the damage we'd done both physically and emotionally. And we could still maul. They couldn't take that away from us. If anything, we channelled all that frustrated scrum energy into every other area of confrontation. We kept on going with relentless, controlled malevolence, putting in bonecruncher tackle after bonecruncher tackle. We were 17–3 up at half-time, and any hope they may have had of a come-back evaporated two minutes into the second half when their prop Andrea Lovotti was red carded for a spear tackle on Duane: adding insult to injury, quite literally, when it came to Italian props. After that we ran riot, scoring five tries in the last half hour to come away 49–3 winners.

I played all 80 minutes and ran 7 km, more than I'd ever run in a game before. I finally felt back in the groove, and so did we all. Something had clicked. If we'd ever doubted ourselves or lacked belief, we didn't anymore. It wasn't just that we'd won; it was *how* we'd won, ruthlessly and imperiously. The most we could hope for from any game at this stage was that other teams would watch it and think, 'We don't fancy playing that lot.' No team watching us would have fancied playing us. We'd laid down a proper marker at last.

Unfortunately we now had to deal with accusations of racism. It started when the Bomb Squad were huddled in a tight circle after the Italy win. Mapimpi was going from player to player congratulating them, and as he approached the Bomb Squad Frans waved him away. A short clip of the incident went viral on social media. Some people looked at it, saw that Frans and the rest of those in the huddle – Flo, RG, Franco, Vincent and Kitsie – were white and accused us of being a racist squad.

But that clip was presented without context, and it hadn't included the moment just beforehand when Frans had also waved Lood de Jager away. It wasn't anything to do with the colour of anyone's skin; it was simply who was in the Bomb Squad and who wasn't. Frans is a good guy and a joker, and this was his way of helping cement the Bomb Squad mentality and group identity.

I could see why the spectre of racism raised its head; this was South Africa, after all, and there had been plenty of times in the past when the squad had suffered serious racial tensions. But not this squad, not with all the hard work around transformation which Coach Rassie had put in and which we'd all bought into. We were shocked to see the public reaction, as it had genuinely never occurred to us that people would interpret what they saw this way.

Rachel and the children came out for the match against Canada. It was so good to see them, such a feeling of peace when they arrived; because this journey was theirs too, and without them I couldn't have done the half of what I have. I would sit in the park with the kids, which helped me stay in the moment and not get ahead of myself. They provided normality so I could decompress when need be, and though it was too hard to go out on the town for date nights when we'd put the kids to bed, we'd just do it in the lobby of whatever hotel we were in instead. The energy not just from my family but from everyone having their families around was so infectious and positive. It wasn't just our team or our squad, but a wider community of everyone we relied on and who'd given up so much for us to be here. We were doing it very much for them, and so in some way they became a microcosm of South Africa itself.

I played another 80 minutes against Canada, which was the easy win everyone had expected, and when the All Blacks' match against Italy was cancelled due to Typhoon Hagibis and Japan beat Scotland to top their group, we knew we'd be playing the hosts in the quarters. They'd won four from four, and they'd been the better side in all those games. Luck hadn't come into it. Sure, we'd beaten them handsomely in the warm-up match, but a World Cup quarter-final was a different beast entirely. We'd underestimate them at our peril.

Coach Rassie was good at finding something in the oppo which we could seize on and make personal. We needed to make the gainline personal, we needed to make the scrum personal. But how could we hate the Japanese? They were such nice people, they were amazing hosts, and no-one ever wants to be the team who knocks out the hosts: it's just rude. How could we make it personal? How could we, just for one week, set ourselves against them?

They changed the WiFi codes in the hotel to Brighton1, Brighton2 and Brighton3, which I found hilarious. There were other things which were probably less intentional, minor problems with training facilities and so on, but we seized on them and made more of them than they were worth, simply so we could rev ourselves up. If that involved blowing those things out of proportion, then so be it. We needed to do whatever it took. The Japanese were amazing hosts and amazing people. They hadn't changed. We just needed to transition them into opponents for 80 minutes.

More than perhaps any other match in the tournament, this was a battle of styles: their speed against our strength, their pace against our power. Whoever could impose their will on the other would win. They wanted to take us to the dancefloor; we wanted to take them to the gutter. Felix Jones, our defence coach, impressed on us how best to bend them to our will: be as physical as possible from whistle to whistle, but then take our time at the set-pieces. Scotland and Ireland had both tried to live with the high Japanese tempo throughout the 80 minutes and come unstuck. We couldn't afford to make the same mistake.

There was a lot of attention around their captain Michael Leitch too, whose picture was everywhere; one poll even had him as the second most recognised person in Japan after Prime Minister Shinzo Abe. He had an interesting backstory: son of a Kiwi father and a Fijian mother, he'd come to Japan on a high school exchange from Christchurch aged 15, found Japan even more of a culture shock than I'd found Grey, had knuckled down and got used to it, learnt Japanese, married a Japanese woman and become captain. He was a dangerous player if not a flashy one: making tackles, carrying into traffic, piling into rucks. He was talismanic for them, and shutting him down would go some way to shutting them down too.

We knew that it was us against the world, that pretty much everyone apart from us and our supporters wanted them to win, and that was fine. They were underdogs, they played brilliant rugby, they were from outside the traditional Tier One rugby powerhouse countries. If I'd been a neutral, I'd have wanted them to win too. They'd captured their

With President Cyril Ramaphosa after he gave us a
motivational speech ahead of the World Cup Final.

I gifted Vincent Mai my 2019 World
Cup Final jersey as a token of my
appreciation for everything that he
has done for me.

My best friend Tanqa and my father
in Japan, both fresh off the plane from
South Africa. This was their first time
ever leaving South Africa.

Together with my family – and the sparkling trophy – in the hotel after the World Cup Final.

On the bus tour around the country to celebrate our World Cup success with the people of South Africa. Here we are in Joburg.

Celebrating in Cape Town with the locals. This was outside the building where Nelson Mandela delivered his freedom speech after being released from prison, and where I met Archbishop Desmond Tutu.

With Rachel in Paris, where we were attending the Midol Rugby Oscars.

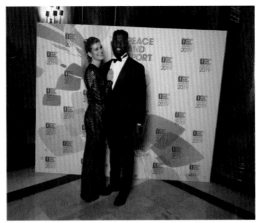

With Rachel in Monaco for the Peace and Sport Awards 2019 – I was so privileged to win the Champion of the Year award.

My acceptance speech at the Peace and Sport Awards, with Didier Drogba on the left.

Champion of the Year award – Peace and Sport.

I met the Liverpool legend Sir Kenny Dalglish when I went to watch a Liverpool match at Anfield for the first time in November 2019.

Alongside Luís Figo at the 2020 Laureus Awards in Berlin, Germany.

With Roger Federer and Rafael Nadal at a fundraiser event for Roger's foundation, the evening before their iconic tennis match in Cape Town, 2020.

We had a fabulous dinner with Gerard Butler and Morgan Brown. We met on a flight back from the USA.

Returning to my old primary school to launch the iSchoolAfrica iPad programme. My dream is to provide more opportunities, as a mentor, for our youth to realise they can be anyone they want to be.

A call with DJ Khaled after I signed for Roc Nation, 2020.

With my brother, Liyema, on holiday in Sabi Sands, 2020.

Rachel and I attended a protest in front of Cape Town's Houses of Parliament in 2020 against gender-based violence.

Working with the Kolisi Foundation, which Rachel and I co-founded during the lockdown in April 2020. The Kolisi Foundation has a vision to change the narratives of inequality in South Africa.

Lining up before the 1st Lions Test in Cape Town, 24 July 2021.

Holding up Robbie Henshaw to save a try in the 2nd Lions Test in
Cape Town, after losing the 1st Test 22–17, was a big moment in the series
for us. We won the 2nd Test 27–9 to tie the series.

Celebrating an incredible series win with Morné Steyn, whose late penalty in the 3rd Test in Cape Town made the game 19–16 and sealed the series 2–1, 7 August 2021.

A special moment as a captain and a player – a Lions series in South Africa only happens once every 12 years.

It's been an incredible journey for this team over the last two years, winning the Rugby Championship and World Cup in 2019 and the Lions Test series in 2021.

country's hearts with the 'one team, one dream' slogan; but every dream has its wake-up moment, and it was our job to provide that.

The stadium is packed and rocking as the Japanese players belt out their anthem. Some of them are already in tears. This is the biggest match in their history – the first time they've ever reached the knockout phases – and the crowd noise is astonishing. The crowd are Japan's not-so-secret weapon, and their team feeds off the atmosphere and electricity. It's a perpetual loop, from players to spectators and back again, and we need to break it. Get far enough ahead on the scoreboard and we'll silence the crowd; silence the crowd and we'll drain belief from the players.

The best way to start doing this is to score early, and we do just that. We're ahead within four minutes. Mapimpi takes a short ball off Faf on the blindside, brushes off Yu Tamura and goes in at the corner.

Five minutes later, the pendulum swings the other way. Beast hammers his opposite number Keita Inagaki, but he lifts him way past the horizontal and dumps him on his shoulder. Beast instantly holds up his hands in apology while the Japanese players make their displeasure known. Referee Wayne Barnes doesn't go to the TMO and shows Beast a yellow.

Beast will later describe it as 'the longest ten minutes of my life'. For those ten minutes we're run ragged, often defending deep in our own 22. They attack so fast and with such quick hands that it's all we can do to contain them. One man down really makes a big difference.

They have a scrum: eight of them against seven of us. I'm off the field so Kitsie can cover for Beast in the front row, and we all know that Japan are going to come for us in this scrum. They get the squeeze on and force us to concede the penalty – and man, the noise! You'd think they'd won the trophy itself rather than simply a penalty. Tamura knocks it over, Beast is back on, we're 5–3 up with a quarter of the match gone – and to be honest if you'd said at the start of those ten minutes that we'd only concede three points we'd have bitten your hand off for it.

Their tails are up now and they're running it from everywhere, the way we knew they would. They're taking us to the dancefloor like it's *Saturday Night Fever*, and we have to weather this. Willie and Pieter-Steph go for the same tackle and collide hard. Willie's hurt, but the six–two split means he has to stay on for as long as possible. He smiles at the doc and seems okay, but a few minutes later he uncharacteristically drops a high ball and winces as he tries to get his left arm moving properly.

Only a few minutes to half-time, and now we start to make some chances of our own. Lukhanyo escapes down the left and has Mapimpi clear on the overlap outside him, but the ball slips from Lukhanyo's hand as he shapes to pass and the ball goes to ground. Right on the stroke of half-time Damian uses his power to batter through some tackles and cross for what looks like our second try, but Barnes rules it out for a double movement. Many of us think it looked fine, and those kind of things can prey on your mind and make you start grumbling.

In the shed at half-time, Duane's having none of it. He tells us in no uncertain terms that if we can't say anything positive then we shouldn't say anything at all, and that the quickest way to feel positive is to make a contribution on the pitch rather than moan at what's going wrong. He's right, of course, as is Coach Rassie when he tells us to double down on our physicality. We have to keep on keeping on, and eventually they'll crumble.

We come out with renewed purpose, determined that this is where we impose our will on the game, this is where we take their soul away. Handre drills over a penalty with just two minutes of the half gone, and then another one six minutes later after Beast wins a scrum penalty and roars with delight. That's more than a score between the teams now, and we're gradually throttling the life out of them. It's not spectacular, but it is relentless.

With 15 minutes to go, we seal it once and for all. Lood secures a lineout on our own ten-metre line and we set the maul with him as the pivot, facing back towards us.

The previous week we'd had a forwards session planned, but then the typhoon came in and it got cancelled. So instead we found a hotel conference room and discussed mauling, all the forwards and the coaches. There were beers for anyone who wanted – a few guys eyed them warily at first, convinced that this was some kind of test! – and for two or three hours we just talked maul tactics, trying different things out, no holds barred and no ideas dismissed out of hand. We knew there'd be a moment where this would be crucial, and that moment is now.

We all know our roles, where we should be and what we should be doing. Malcolm has the ball at the back. Pieter-Steph comes flying in from the rear to add his weight, and we start to move, varying the axis, working points of pressure left and right, never allowing the Japanese to regroup properly and set themselves to stop us.

Stopping a maul is less about technique than commitment. The defenders shouldn't worry so much about where to put their heads; they should just throw themselves in and stop it as hard as they can. The first couple of seconds of a maul are crucial for both sides. If the attackers can set and drive then they're in business; if the defenders can disrupt then the maul is static and the opposing nine has to pass or kick.

We're the ones in business, and how. I see white lines pass beneath my feet as we keep on going: the halfway line, their 10-metre line. My legs are like jelly – it's such hard work pumping them against the resistance of a team desperate to stop you – but I can feel the energy from the guys, hear the grunts of determination and Faf's barked commands from the base. We're moving quicker now. Flashes of red and white in my peripheral vision as Japanese defenders peel off and rush back to try and rejoin, but they can't come in from the side and we're rolling so well now that even when they do lock on they can't slow us down. Another white line: that's their 22, we've gone almost half the length of the pitch, the maul alive and breathing fire like some cartoon monster.

Suddenly, there are three of us bound on to each other – Malcolm the ball carrier, Pieter-Steph and me – with no-one really in front of us. Malcolm bursts free and pops to Faf on his shoulder as the tackle comes in, and Faf hands off the last man to score at the base of the posts. Handre converts to make it 21–3, and they're broken.

The crowd is silent, and I can see some spectators in tears. There are still 15 minutes to go, but we all know they're not coming back from here. Mapimpi scores near the end – his fifth try in two games against Japan – to make it 26–3. We've totally shut them out in the second half.

I drop to my knees when the referee blows the final whistle to give thanks to God. In the stands, our fans are consoling theirs; some are even swapping jerseys. Both teams do laps of the ground afterwards. The Japanese say thank you to their fans for all the support, and they're quite rightly cheered to the echo. They've lit up this tournament and showed beyond doubt that they deserve to be mixing it with the big boys. We also thank the fans, who are of course totally gracious even though we've just ended their fantasy. Interviewed afterwards, one of the Japanese players says simply, 'They beat the hell out of us.'

Now there were just four teams left: England, New Zealand, Wales and us. England and New Zealand would play the first semi, and Wales and us the second one a day later.

The week started badly. Cheslin had injured his ankle against Japan – actually, he'd done it six times in that match alone – and hadn't been able to train on the Monday following the game. One of our squad rules was that if a player couldn't train on Monday then they couldn't be considered for the game the following Saturday. Coach Rassie liked to announce teams early – certainly to the squad, if not to the media – and therefore let everyone know where they stood ahead of time. If someone was playing, he'd have the best part of a week to prepare himself, and he'd definitely play unless he started behaving like a jerk or he got injured. So Cheslin was ruled out and S'bu was told he'd be playing.

As the week wore on, though, Cheslin's recovery came on in leaps and bounds. The physios did their stuff, he and his wife prayed hard, and his daughter laid her hands on his ankle and wished with all her might for her daddy to get better. By Friday he was jinking through everyone in training and back to his usual self. Coach Rassie was tempted to break the squad rule and put Cheslin back into the team; if he couldn't make exceptions for a World Cup semi-final, he reasoned, then when could he? Mzwandile cautioned against it; the collective was the most important thing, he said, and if Coach Rassie lost that trust he'd never get it back, not totally. All the same, Coach Rassie asked Cheslin how he was feeling, and though Cheslin said he felt fine, Coach Rassie got the impression that if asked directly Cheslin would tell him to keep S'bu in the team, because that was what we had all agreed.

Coach Rassie would tell this story himself, and for a good reason: that no-one, not even the head coach, knows everything, and that the learning process never stops.

If there was one team we were – well, not scared of, but certainly concerned about – it was Wales. They'd beaten us four times in a row, a run stretching back four years, and they played the same way we did: physically and with great discipline. Wales weren't a team that we could take into the trenches. They weren't a team that got intimidated and shirked away from physical confrontation. They were a very structured side, and they had great systems. 'Their game plan is to give you the ball, to strangle you,' Coach Rassie said. 'They let you get bored so that you start playing, and then they win.' We'd have to play them at their own game: kick, kick, kick, kick, kick. It didn't matter how ugly we won, just that we won.

The day before the match, we watched the England–New Zealand semi-final. Most people expected New Zealand to win, perhaps even win easily, but England blew them away. The final score of 19–7 scarcely reflected their dominance. If their flying wing Jonny May had been fully fit and outpaced the cover to the corner as he usually would have, if their scrum-half Ben Youngs hadn't had what looked a perfectly good try disallowed, and if they hadn't made a basic lineout mistake five metres from their own line which allowed Ardie Savea to score untouched, it would have been 30-odd to nil, and it wouldn't have flattered them. They beat the All Blacks in every aspect of the game from start to finish, and perhaps even before the start too, forming a reverse arrowhead to face down the haka with Owen Farrell at the base of it, a faint smile playing on his lips as he watched New Zealand go through their war dance. You can tell a lot about a team's chances by their body language before the match begins, and to a man England looked up for it.

So there'd be no Round Two of us against the All Blacks, and the analysts would have to prepare for England instead. But first we had a job to do. Coach Rassie put the two teams up on the board side by side, us and Wales, and went down them one by one. In every position, he said, we were better than them: every single position. A composite XV from the two teams would be all green and gold. We'd watched England physically dominate New Zealand; now we had to do the same to Wales. This would be Wales's third World Cup semi-final, and they'd lost both the other two.

Wales's coach Warren Gatland had talked about getting the emotions right. It wasn't so much about skill or being tactical, but playing right on the edge and wanting it more. Coach Rassie saw it the same way; that's how evenly matched we were. There was mutual respect there too; during the warm-up the two coaches shook hands, gave each other the smallest of hugs, and wished each other well.

The match is exactly what everybody expected: tight, physical, bruising, and a lot of boot to ball. There's aggro too with the tension: Lukhanyo squaring up to Josh Adams, Mapimpi to George North. Discipline, discipline, discipline. This will be won by the team that outlasts the other. It's almost half an hour before we find any real space: S'bu feeds me on the right, I make metres and feed Lukhanyo, who steps inside and offloads to Willie, who in turn sends Faf away, and only a superb tackle by Josh Adams brings him down. Slowly, gradually, we turn the screw, but Wales keep us in sight. It's 9–6 to us at half-time, though they've already had to substitute Tomas Francis and North through injury. It's not a classic to watch, I'm sure, but sometimes that can't be helped. We're well aware that we need to entertain, but more than that, we need to win.

Coach Rassie at half-time tells us to keep doing two things: 'Keep disciplined, and keep dominating them physically.'

We have the wind in the second half, which gives Handre a few more metres with his kicks. Faf squares up to Jake Ball, who's about twice his size, but that's Faf for you: he doesn't care how big they are, he takes them all on anyway. Wales have a penalty to get it back to 9–9. This is proper trench warfare. There's so little in it that a try would make a massive difference … and now it comes, and it's ours, Damian breaking Dan Biggar's tackle and going over with three defenders around him but none capable of holding him. Handre converts, and that's 16–9.

If we think that'll break them, it doesn't. They lay siege to our line, going through the phases, their big men against ours; and when after 20 phases they get a penalty they opt for the scrum rather than a tilt at the poles. Big call. Very big call. But it also makes sense, as there's always space off a scrum when the forwards are packed tightly.

With Faf clambering all over him and the ball at the second rows' feet, eighthman Ross Moriarty does brilliantly to reach into the scrum and pick and flick to Tomos Williams making the extra man by running wide at nine. They work it fast through the hands for Adams to dive in at the corner. Leigh Halfpenny bangs over the conversion from the touchline and it's all-square again. This one is going down to the wire.

This is where all Aled's murderous conditioning sessions count, and against the country of his birth too. This is why he put us through those tortures, for matches like this when one moment can change everything and everyone needs to be thinking clearly. Wales have it on our 22 but can't find a way through, and eventually Rhys Patchell slides a drop goal attempt wide and we have breathing space.

Flo comes on for me. This is exactly the situation the Bomb Squad was designed for: to fix things, to make the crucial difference. And that's exactly what he does. Alun Wyn Jones take the ball into contact, and Flo's the first defender there, a split second ahead of Moriarty and Dillon Lewis coming in from the other side for Wales. In that split second Flo has to decide whether or not to jackal and contest the ball. If he gets it right, we win the turnover; if he gets it wrong, he risks conceding a penalty in a very kickable position. There are six minutes left, so the next score could well be decisive.

What rests on his decision? Everything: the match, the campaign, maybe even the tournament itself. Flo's one of the best jackallers in world rugby, so he has the skills. And this is Coach Rassie's team, where we're encouraged to be positive and go for things like this. Flo clamps onto the ball: feet wide, hands off the floor, body braced against the hits coming in. Alun Wyn Jones, isolated, hangs on. Penalty, green, not releasing. Flo's mobbed as he stands up. I'm surprised he can walk, the number of teammates he's got all over him. These are the margins; Wales have been a split second slower than us to one breakdown. That's all it is.

On the bench next to me, Willie says, 'Handre's going to kick for the corner, we'll win the lineout, get a maul going, win the penalty and he'll kick it over.'

Kick for the corner? Check. Win the lineout? Check. Get a maul going? Check. Win the penalty? Check. Now all Handre has to do is kick it over. It's not an easy kick, not by any means, wide out on the left. But if there's one man I'd put everything on, it's Handre. He takes his time, using every second of the minute he's allowed. It's just process, doing what he's done thousands of times in training: shut out the crowd, shut out the pressure, forget the match situation. Just his foot, the ball and the poles.

There are four minutes left when he drills it clean down the middle.

We have them pinned back, just where we want them to be as the clock runs down. Faf angles a long kick into their 22, we spoil their lineout, get a scrum and win a penalty. That's it; there's no time for them to come back now. Handre doesn't even go for the poles, even though for a kicker of his skill it's more or less a gimme. Why take even the slightest risk that he misses and gives Wales the chance to counter? He taps to himself, leathers it into the crowd and it's all over.

In the post-match interview, I thanked South Africans for their amazing support on social media and gave a shout-out to the people back home. 'Keep sending us your messages and we'll keep doing our best.' And in the changing room after the match, when we were all arms linked before the *Bokke!* cry, I said to the boys, 'Let's do it one more time. And remember, on the trophy it says "South Africa", not the matchday 23. This is for all of us, including Trevor and Jesse.'

And then there were two: England, and us.

It was time to circle the wagons. Our training sessions were on an open pitch with apartment blocks all around. Anybody could be watching us, filming, sending info back to the England camp. They probably weren't, of course, but why take that chance before the biggest game of our lives? So instead of doing different things, we did things differently. The indoor maul session before the Japan match had led to the try which broke their resistance; now we worked on something else which we could use if ever there was a critical moment against England and the match was in the balance. It was a move called, creatively enough, The Move.

We picked the brains of those guys in the squad who played in England. Faf was teammates with Tom Curry at Sale; Schalk and Vincent had spent a long time with Saracens, where Jamie George, Maro Itoje, George Kruis, Owen Farrell, Elliot Daly and the Vunipola brothers played. That kind of inside knowledge – their habits, their weaknesses, what put certain players off and made them uncomfortable – could be invaluable.

The English press were making out that their team had one hand on the trophy already and that all they had to do was turn up to win. Matt Dawson, part of the England team which had won the 2003 World Cup, said that not a single Springbok would make a combined England–South Africa team. John Smit referred to it as 'touching the money', the way you're not supposed to in poker: that the English press and rugby establishment were treating it as a done deal, a fait accompli.

And over and again all we heard about was the kamikaze kids, the English flankers Tom Curry and Sam Underhill; how they'd been the best flankers in the tournament, how they were crazy good for two kids so young, how they'd done a number on the All Blacks and would do the same to us. John Mitchell, England's defence coach, was saying that they were better than David Pocock and Richie McCaw.

Felix came to me. 'You have to sort this out, Siya,' he said. 'There's no other way to put it. All I'm hearing is how amazing they are.' I was like, 'Okay, man. Let's see. Let's see. Sure, they've done it against everyone else. If they do it against us then I'll be the first to shake their hands and give them credit. But until then I back Duane, Pieter-Steph and me every time.'

Willie had suffered a shoulder injury in the quarter-final. The physios took care of his physical rehab, and Coach Rassie took charge of the mental and emotional side. In a team meeting, he put on a video, maybe six or seven minutes long, featuring Willie's greatest moments: the tries he'd scored, the ones he'd created, the times he'd made the extra man in attack, the way he saw what was unfolding in front of him and always kept organising the defence. It was a great booster for Willie, of course, and also for all of us and our faith in him, but perhaps most of all it was a sign of what this squad was about. We didn't let anyone get dragged down. We had each other's back at all times, and like all good armies we left no man behind.

We all knew that this was more than just another match, and perhaps more even than just a World Cup Final. World Cup Finals were sacred to South Africans. We'd played two and won two; of the four countries who'd ever won the trophy, we were the only one not to have also lost a final. When our first training session that week had been terrible – we were tired from the Wales game and too strung up about everything needing to be perfect all week – Coach Rassie called a meeting and told us not to stress about it. 'We need perspective here,' he said. 'We're in a place of privilege. We're not scrabbling around for money, wondering where our next meal is coming from, waking up every morning wondering how we're going to get through to sundown. For this week, it's not just that the eyes of South Africa will be on us; it's that their hearts will be with us too. For this week you're not just yourselves, and you're not even just Springboks. For this week you *are* South Africa. Embrace it.'

You are *South Africa. Embrace it.*

That win in 1995 had told a new nation that the future together was bright. Almost a quarter of a century on, the rainbow had lost its shine for many people. Our country was burning. Attacks on women and foreigners were through the roof, crime was ravaging every part of society, the economy was flatlining, vital services were patchy or non-existent, unemployment was soaring. A win would be so important for our country. And Madiba's words from the inaugural Laureus World Sports Awards in 2000 still burned strong and true. 'Sport has the power to change the world. It has the power to inspire, the power to unite people that little else has. It is more powerful than governments in breaking down racial barriers.'

History on my back and by my side; the weight of expectations and the ghosts of those who've come before. Not just Madiba and Pienaar at Ellis Park but John Smit and Thabo Mbeki at the Stade de France in Paris 12 years later. Mr Mbeki had been Mr Mandela's successor, Tata one of his comrades-in-arms; links through the corridors of power quite as much as on the pitch. Those of the 1995 team who were no more. I'd gone to James Small's funeral a few months before; we had

Chester's picture in our numbers for the All Blacks match. New dreams, old scars.

And now here we were, back at the end of the tournament in the place where it all began for us exactly six weeks before in Yokohama.

There's almost always a tomorrow in professional sport, but not in the World Cup there's not. In the World Cup you have to wait another four years. Only a small number of men have played two finals, and an even smaller number have won two finals. This may be the only chance most of us get, and we have to make the most of it.

'I love the pressure of the big occasions,' Handre said. 'That's why you train, that's why you put in the hours away from the lights. If you imagine being a little boy in the backyard, thinking to yourself, "This kick is for the World Cup Final," and all those scenarios, you've basically been preparing your whole life for it. The side that embraces it and takes all the energy you can get, and uses it in the right way and sends it in the right direction, is probably going to be the side that wins the World Cup. That's the secret to finals rugby.'

I wanted my dad out there to see this; who knows when he and I would ever get the chance again? He'd never been abroad, so he didn't even have a passport, let alone a visa or plane tickets; and it seemed that the world and his wife were trying to get from South Africa to Japan. Rachel and our admin manager Annelee Murray swung into action, calling in every favour they had and quite a lot they didn't, and to this day I'm still not quite sure how they did it; but the upshot was that my dad flew out to see me play in the biggest match of any rugby player's career, and that will always mean more to me than I can say.

On the morning of the final, Rachel took the kids out for a walk while I spent half an hour in Bible study. I did this every day, match or not; it was my time not just to thank the Lord for what He's given me but also to centre myself. On this occasion, and I didn't know this until much later, Rachel came back at a time she thought I'd have finished; but when she walked in the room I was there with my back to the door, clad in only my underpants, with the Bible in one hand while I spoke in tongues. I was in another world, a trance, away with God. She ushered the kids back out and went down to the lobby. I didn't hear them come in and I didn't hear them leave. I was just gone.

'Just go out and play,' Coach Rassie says. 'If you're beaten by a better team then so be it.'

It's my 50th cap, and there's a little ceremony for that. There's also something in the team that 50th and 100th caps are bad luck – we seem to lose as often as we win in the matches when someone has reached that milestone – but today of all days we don't worry about that.

On the Xhosa commentary for the match, Kaunda is exhorting the whole country to come together behind us. 'Stand up, Polokwane! Stand up, Tshwane! Stand up, Mamelodi! Stand up, Gauteng, Soweto! Stand up, Mangaung! Stand up, Kimberley! Stand up, iThekweni, Umlazi! Stand up, Mthatha! Stand up, Butterworth! Stand up, East London, Mdantsane, Port Elizabeth, Zwide! Stand up, Cape Town, Langa and

Gugulethu! Because uGxiya, uGqwashu, child of the soil, is leading us in the biggest rugby match in the history of South Africa.'

We start with a moment's silence for the victims of Typhoon Hagibis. I remember footage of the Canadian guys after their match against Namibia had been called off; they'd gone out into the streets and helped the locals with the clean-up operation, because that was what rugby's also about, giving back to people who've given so much to you.

The previous week, England started flawlessly against the All Blacks: winning the first lineout, working the All Blacks left and right across the pitch, and scoring a try in the first two minutes. How a team starts a match doesn't always determine the course of that match, but it often sets a tone. The tone they set there carried them all the way through the match, and they never gave the All Blacks a sniff.

This time, it's totally different. In the first minute, Courtney Lawes is pinged for not rolling away and we have a penalty. Handre pushes it wide, but England don't take advantage. A minute later, Kyle Sinckler tries to tackle Mapimpi and is knocked out when his head collides with Itoje's elbow. I know instantly that he's unconscious – his arm stays in the air even when he's on the ground – and he's down for several minutes, which you never want to see, but when it's clear he's just unconscious and not otherwise badly injured I gather the team and remind them to focus. The medics are doing their job, and all we can do is wait.

It's a big blow for them; Sinckler's one of their key players, a real powerhouse in the loose but with good hands too, the guy around whom the other runners flow, and to lose him so soon is really bad luck. They bring on Dan Cole, who's probably a stronger scrummager; but Cole is 32, he's now looking at 78 minutes of a World Cup Final, and this is our chance to get into them. Our pack is lighter than theirs, but we don't mind that. That's testament to Aled's conditioning: lean, but without sacrificing strength.

It's almost five minutes since Sinckler's injury before the match begins again. They're rattled, badly rattled. Farrell throws a loose pass in his own dead-ball area which could have bounced the other way and gifted Lukhanyo a try, Cole concedes a scrum penalty, Youngs passes straight into touch and we steal a lineout. Small errors in themselves, but cumulatively they build and mount, let the demons in and sow doubts: *This is not our day, this is not our day*. I see in their eyes that they can't believe this is happening. Ten minutes gone and they haven't even crossed the halfway line yet. Their momentum is stuttering and backwards; ours is constant and forwards.

'When they're under the cosh they start to lose it little by little,' Coach Rassie has said to us in the week. 'Play on that. Lean on them, wear them down, make them turn on each other.'

Willie ghosts through a gap, back on form. Handre feeds me, I feed Mapimpi, and we go back for a penalty. Handre chases his own kick and plucks it from George Ford's grasp. Farrell takes the ball into traffic, I jackal, he holds on, and that's another penalty. This time Handre makes no mistake and we're up and running, three points on the board.

We're all over them, winning scrum penalties almost every time the teams pack down. The penalties aren't just welcome in themselves; they're a sign of our dominance which ripples through both teams, giving us energy and making them doubt. 'Bring it on,' Billy Vunipola said in a press conference earlier in the week; well, that's just what we're doing. We're bringing it, and bringing it, and bringing it.

Now Bongi's down injured and we're a man short as England take us side to side. Cheslin takes down Lawes, who's about twice his size, but England have the penalty and it's 3–3. Bongi and Lood are both off for good, with Malcolm and Franco on; much earlier than we'd have liked but that's the way it is, that's what happens in the white heat of a World Cup Final when the tackles are so hard they can be heard in the stands. We have a scrum penalty and Handre makes it 6–3.

Half an hour gone, and now comes the passage of play which will define the match. England start putting some phases together, looking more cohesive and purposeful than they have all match. Underhill takes it on, then George, then Underhill again. They get closer and closer to our line. Curry has it on the 22. Mako Vunipola, Itoje, Tuilagi, Lawes, Billy Vunipola, Curry again, Lawes again, and now they're just five metres out.

This is it. This is irresistible force versus immovable object. This is The Stand.

'You draw that line in the sand,' Duane would say. 'On this side you defend your family, your country, your people. And you don't let anyone get into that space.' The tryline is no longer just a white line on a grass pitch; it's our border, our frontier, and we guard it with our lives.

Billy Vunipola drives and Franco takes him down. Youngs pops to Underhill on the charge; Beast goes low and Duane high, and together they stop him. England are inches away from our line and the referee signals advantage, meaning they can try anything safe in the knowledge that they can always go back for the penalty. Cole plucks it from the ruck, but Pieter-Steph is there and drives him backwards. The ball pops up to Youngs, who takes it back into traffic, where Pieter-Steph – again! – and Frans are waiting to clatter him. There are backs waiting on the short side and out it goes that way. Ford can't find a way through, and nor can Lawes.

Willie's barking orders, marshalling defenders, checking space. Curry feeds Mako Vunipola, who's double-teamed by Frans and Beast, three props coming together like fighting rhinos. Now Mako's brother Billy tries, and this time it's Malcolm and Franco who drill him. The crowd noise is so loud I can hardly hear myself think: the England fans baying for their boys to score, the Bok fans for us to hold on. Again England go to the short side; Tuilagi feeds Lawes, and Cheslin and Handre pounce on him. The energy is unbelievable. This is why you play the game, for moments like this: two world-class teams at the edge of their limits going hammer and tongs at each other.

Check your line, check your positioning, do whatever it takes. The hell with technique; just throw yourself in there, meet fire with fire. They shall not pass.

Handre calls for reinforcements on the short side and then immediately has to tackle Cole. They're right on our line now, literally right on it; when I set myself like a sprinter waiting for the next contact, my hands are on the whitewash. I'm guarding the left side of the ruck; whoever comes round will be mine. Youngs looks, assessing his options. I watch his eyes, his hands, anything to give me a split-second advantage. It's Billy Vunipola again. *Come at me, Billy. Come at me. Bring it on.* He bursts free from the ruck, and Frans and I hit him as hard as we can, the pain of the impact vanishing beneath the surging adrenalin. Keep him away from the line, that's all that matters.

There's no way through for the big men, so they fire it wide. Daly floats one over the top for Watson, but he's hard up against the touchline and Willie scrags him as he steps back inside. They set the ruck and Farrell plays nine, but when he picks up he's too slow to pass and Willie's on him too. Two key tackles for Willie inside 15 seconds. That's why Coach Rassie stuck with him, and that's the payback for him having done so. Lawes is chopped again. Faf gets in Youngs' face, making him hurry the pass. They go all the way to the left again, trying to set May free, but Cheslin and Handre bring him down.

I see the strangest thing: some of our guys are actually smiling. In the heat of battle, the conflict raging at its most intense, everyone still laser focused on what they need to do, there are guys smiling, because they can feel the change and the shift. We know that England aren't going to get through. No matter how hard England hammer away at us, there's no way through, or round, or over or under. England send it wide to the right now, but they look just that little bit deflated. Daly tries to pass out of Lukhanyo's tackle for Curry, but Curry knocks on and we go back to the original penalty: 20-odd phases, several minutes and a lifetime ago.

Yes, they get three points out of it, but we get much, much more. We get the knowledge that they're not crossing our line today. South Africa have never conceded a try in the two World Cup Finals they've contested so far, and we're not about to start today. There are 50 minutes left and England will have to rely on penalties to win. We look at each other and nod in recognition of what The Stand has meant.

Their penalty makes it 6–6, but we get two more penalties before the break, which Handre knocks over. It's 12–6 at half-time, and we've been clearly the better team.

'No technical stuff from now on,' Coach Rassie says. 'Just physical and mental.' If we want it enough, if we keep putting ourselves on the line, if we get up off the floor quicker than them and blast into contact quicker than they do, then we'll win. Forty minutes away from the biggest prize of all. No side has ever led a World Cup Final at half-time and lost.

When England come back on, George Kruis has replaced Lawes, a sure sign that they want to lock up their scrum better and keep things tight. It makes no difference. Four minutes in we have another scrum penalty, just seconds after Vincent and Kitsie have come on, and Handre makes no mistake. It's 15–6, and we're more than a score ahead.

England ring more changes: Joe Marler on for Mako Vunipola, Henry Slade for Ford. They're spending their chips early, as they have to, and it works. They get a scrum penalty of their own, Farrell kicks it, and we're back to 15–9. Six points means the game's in the balance still. We've been in the ascendancy for so long, but that'll count for nothing if they can turn the tide now. We can't let them back in.

They have another penalty almost immediately, 45 metres out wide to the right. I force myself to remain calm. We weathered storms against Wales and Japan, and we can weather this one too. But the kick slides wide at the last moment and the gap stays at six.

Willie, coming in at first receiver, kicks long with his left foot, forcing Daly to turn. Our cover's up fast on the full-back, and he shanks his clearance kick to give us the lineout. Three points now will put us more than a score ahead. Up in the coaches box Coach Rassie calls for The Move, but we're already on it. This is exactly the situation we talked about: decent field position with the match still in the balance.

From the lineout it goes fast to Damian, and he and the other backs contest the breakdown while the forwards line up en masse just off to the left. Faf fires it out to Duane, and instantly we're in formation round him: the props either side, me behind them, Franco and Eben either side of me and Pieter-Steph at the back. Dan Cole's in position to tackle Duane, but we've formed a maul – the moment a second man from either side commits himself to the action, it's a maul – and so tackling Duane will count as bringing down the maul, which is a penalty offence. But if Cole doesn't tackle – well, England know what we did against Japan, England know how good our maul is. Better to concede three points than risk seven. So Cole tackles Duane and concedes the penalty. That's what he has to do. That's what anyone would do, especially with only a split second to decide.

Handre kicks the penalty, the gap is nine and England have to take risks, which in turn will give us chances.

From the restart, Tuilagi smashes Duane, who's penalised for hanging on. Farrell brings it back to 18–12. Twenty minutes left and still we can't quite put them away, but the effort of staying in touch is exhausting them, while we're still strong.

I'm brought off for Flo. My game is done. *Give it everything and pass it on to the next guy.*

Now it comes. Youngs box kicks from his own 22. Willie catches it but is tackled by Mark Wilson and we have the ruck. On the short side, Lukhanyo is screaming for the ball. He sees the mismatch, forwards against backs: him and Mapimpi up against some of their big men, so there's space to be exploited if only we use it now.

This goes almost unnoticed in what happens next, but it's another small if telling example of what transformation really means. Because Lukhanyo feels he belongs in the team, he feels free to play his natural game. It wasn't so long ago that a black centre would have thought twice about yelling at a white scrum-half to give him the ball: that's what happens in environments where white players are the default and where black players are rarely, if ever, put in positions of tactical responsibility. But Coach Rassie has driven all that out. Lukhanyo sees the opportunity, so he calls for it; Faf hears the call, trusts Lukhanyo's judgement, and gives the pass.

Fast through the hands, Lukhanyo to Malcolm to Mapimpi. Mapimpi leaves Marler, Cole and Kruis struggling in his wake, sees that Daly's still covering across from centre field, and kicks ahead. The ball sits up for Lukhanyo, who glides onto it and gathers cleanly. Daly's almost on him but Lukhanyo's momentum will take him over if he chooses to go for it; but no, he gives the briefest of glances to his left and flicks it to Mapimpi, one of his closest friends, to go over untouched and touch down near the posts. He doesn't wait, he doesn't think about it; he just makes the pass. It's so unselfish. He's almost certain to score himself, a try more or less to win the World Cup, and what does he do? Gives it to his mate. *We do it together.*

As the stadium erupts, Lukhanyo just keeps on jogging into the in-goal area, as though this were a training session rather than the biggest game of his life. Confidence, teamwork, nonchalance, panache: they're all there. It's the first try South Africa have ever scored in a World Cup Final – the 1995 and 2007 vintages might not have conceded any tries, but they didn't score any either – and for that to come from two men of colour in the most diverse and representative side in our history means so much. That's 25–12, and we're still not done quite yet. Sure, England need two converted tries to win, and apart from The Stand in the first half they've never really threatened, but from the bench I still don't feel totally comfortable.

There are two ways you can take the game away from the opposition, points and time, and with every minute that passes I dare to feel just a little more confident, but I know that another score would kill it stone dead no matter how long's left.

Seven minutes to go. England are still trying to find a way through the green wall, but we shut them down every time. Malcolm tackles Slade on their 10-metre line and the ball squirms clear. Lukhanyo pops it up to Pieter-Steph, who feeds Cheslin on the touchline right in front of us on the bench. Even before Cheslin has the ball we're on our feet, because we know what he can do, Cheslin and his magic feet.

Marler's covering across. Cheslin slows, fixes him, goosestep and accelerates away. Farrell's across to cover, trying to show Cheslin the outside, but Farrell's tired and his hip placement's all wrong: he's facing the touchline rather than being square on to Cheslin, practically begging Cheslin to step him. Cheslin doesn't need asking twice. He slams his weight onto his right foot and sidesteps back inside, as quickly and violently as only he can. Farrell gets a hand to him, but it's not enough to slow him down, let alone stop him. Billy Vunipola's coming across too, but Cheslin's too quick for him, and Vunipola gives up the chase even before Cheslin's crossed the line. Cheslin dots the ball down and punches the air. On the bench, we're going crazy. That's it, we know it is.

They're engraving the trophy before the match has even finished. SOUTH AFRICA, it says, just as I'd told the boys the previous week. Not just the matchday 23, not just even all the management and other staff, but the entire country and everyone in it. This is for them.

The hooter goes: 80 minutes up. Herschel fires a pass back to Handre, who boots it high into the crowd, and we go berserk. I run onto the pitch and kneel down next to Cheslin, who's on his haunches trying to take it all in.

World champions. We're world champions. We're world champions.

I'd got to every breakdown before the kamikaze kids apart from one, and that had been because I'd slipped. Curry got a single turnover. Other than that, we didn't give them a sniff.

Put that together with our scrum dominance, and that's where the match was won. Mapimpi and Cheslin's tries came when we were already up and they were chasing the game. As the saying goes: forwards win matches and backs decide by how much. The World Cup Final was a perfect example of that.

TV journalist Elma Smit grabs me. 'You asked me to do it. You asked us to do it. We did it,' I say, and she collapses onto my chest in tears.

I go for the official post-match interview. 'Since I've been alive I have never seen South Africa like this,' I said. 'We really appreciate all the support we've had from back home, people in the taverns, people in the shebeens, people on the farms and homeless people. Thank you so much. We have so many problems in our country, but to have a team like this – we come from different backgrounds, different races, and we came together with one goal. We love you, South Africa, and we can achieve anything if we work together as one.'

I make sure to find all the England boys, congratulating them on a great tournament and commiserating that they fell short at the last.

Now it's our turn. The boys go up one by one to get their medals and wait by the trophy. I ask Coach Rassie to come and lift it with me; we couldn't, wouldn't have done this without him. He's having none of it. This is our moment, he says, not his. I persist, but he's adamant. A lot of the non-playing staff are on the podium with us, and quite rightly, but at this moment of ultimate triumph Coach Rassie prefers to leave the stage to others. If ever you wanted to know the kind of man he is, here it is. Exactly six weeks earlier he'd taken the blame for us losing against the All Blacks; now he's letting us take the credit for winning the World Cup. There's an old saying that 'victory has a thousand fathers and defeat is an orphan'. Coach Rassie is the exact opposite. As a coach, he's the best in the world. As a human being, he's even better.

I get my medal and take hold of the trophy. This is what we've dreamed about for so long. It's only a second or two between me taking hold of the trophy and lifting it, but in that time so much goes through my head, a cinema reel of my life speeded up 100 times but with each frame crystal clear: my grandmother giving me sugar water, the purple boxers I wore for the U12 tournament in Mossel Bay, my first day at Grey, coming on for my Springbok debut after four minutes, proposing to Rachel in the helicopter, the births of my children, driving Liyema and Liphelo back home for our first Christmas together, running out at Ellis Park for the first time as captain, and so much more. Everything that's brought me here, everything and everyone that's made me who and what I am, have all found their place at this moment.

I make sure everyone's ready, and then with the loudest roar I can muster I thrust it skywards as fireworks explode and glitter rains down. Tata is here on the podium with us, and when I lower the trophy again we hold it together. He's wearing a Springbok jersey with the number six on the back, just like Mr Mandela had done 24 years before. This one is all hi-tech fibre rather than cotton, and the cut is rather less forgiving, but the symbolism is the same. Tata and Mr Mandela had been very close, and I feel a closing of the circle, that in some way this is what Madiba would really love to have seen: a team representative of the nation because of genuine transformation rather than just through his own instincts for reconciliation.

Rachel, Nick, Keziah and my dad are on the pitch with me. I pull Rachel close, and though the stadium noise and the adrenalin in me mean I can't really formulate what I want to say to her, I hope she knows: that I wouldn't be who I am, let alone what I am, without her, and that I owe her and love her more than she will ever know. I go over to do an interview with the British ITV network, holding Keziah in one arm and letting Nick grab the microphone and steal the show. Bryan is there, and he's in tears. 'Hopefully Siya will run for President,' he says.

In the press conference afterwards, Coach Rassie explains the mindshift we'd had earlier in the week. He explained that South Africa has a lot of problems, and how talking about rugby shouldn't be one of them. Rather, it should be something that creates hope, not pressure. But hope isn't created through just talking; it's through playing well, watching the game with peers on a Saturday and feeling good, no matter the political differences at play. For those 80 minutes, everyone agrees. As for us as players, to create that hope is a privilege.

He went on to say how important it is to remember our wives and partners, who so often get overlooked in these moments. We are all so grateful to have our families, and to be given the time to train and play. He just wanted to inspire his children and every other child in the country, and he hoped he made them proud. Amid the hunger and poverty, there are so many people in South Africa who just need an opportunity. He wanted the win that day to provide people with hope and make the country better. After all, you can never forget where you've come from, and the people that have stuck with you through life.

We shower, change and go back to the team room in the hotel, through hundreds of delirious supporters, and the party goes on there.

I fall asleep in the team room, and then go up to my room and fall asleep again. I don't worry about missing out on anything. What we've been through the previous nine weeks is something we will never forget and something which can never be taken away from us. That's where the memories and the bonding are, not in the parties afterwards.

As I fall asleep for the second time, three words run through my head over and again.

We did it. We did it. We did it.

We came home two days later, and I'd never seen anything like it. When we landed at Joburg's OR Tambo International I could literally feel the airport shaking. Heaven alone knows what their security was like for the time we were there, as pretty much every security guard seemed to have abandoned their posts to come and greet us. The reception was unbelievable. All three tiers surrounding the arrivals hall were packed, and had been like that for hours; some people had been there almost 12 hours. The noise when I came through with the trophy … It gives me tingles even to think about it now. There was a South African Police Service brass band; there were people singing 'Shosholoza' over and again. There was so much happiness, gratitude, hope and love.

They laid on a tour, and the scale of it was insane. In Cape Town, for instance, it wasn't just the players' bus; there was a bus for SA Rugby Union staff, a bus for the media, three large coaches, five unmarked 4x4s, nine SA Police Service cars, seven metro cop cars, two ambulances and heaven only knows how many motorbike outriders. A stage had been set up on the Grand Parade, and thousands of Capetonians roared as we came out. I took the mic. I hadn't planned what to say; I'd just speak from the heart, as I always did.

'It's really been a tough journey. We have been together for 20 weeks. I think this week has been the most amazing one. Look at us,' I said, gesturing at my teammates behind me on stage. 'We are all different races, from different backgrounds.' I gestured towards the crowd. 'And take a look around at you guys. There are different races, different people of different backgrounds, but look how you have made this special for us. It's time for us South Africans to stop fighting and stop arguing. Let's put South Africa first. We appreciate you.'

It wasn't just a race thing either. One of the things I've always liked about rugby is the way it caters for all shapes and sizes: big solid props, giraffe-like second rows, tiny scrum-halves, flying wings. No other sport, apart perhaps from track and field, offers and encourages such diversity. All these very different people mould their talents to be greater than the sum of their parts, and that is a beautiful story not just for rugby but for life. Everybody needs to work together if you want to be successful. It was also great that our two smallest players, Faf and Cheslin, were also two of the most influential. When we talk about inspiring people, that also includes those kids who might otherwise think they're not big enough to be Springboks, but who'd look at Cheslin and Faf and see that it's not the size of the body but the size of the heart which counts.

We went to Joburg, Durban, East London and PE. We tried to get to as many places as we could, especially the home towns of the guys in the squad: Mdantsane for Mapimpi, King William's Town for Lukhanyo, New Brighton for Mzwandile, and of course Zwide for me. To hold the cup outside the Dan Qeqe stadium, where it had all started for me with Coach Eric and the African Bombers, was almost an out-of-body experience; I imagined my eight-year-old self looking up at this and what that would have meant to me at that time.

For some of the white guys in the team, these were some of the first townships they'd ever been to, and they were stunned at the reception we got. It was full on, all day every day. Even at night there'd be hundreds of supporters outside the team hotel; at every new airport there'd be thousands more waiting. We were exhausted, but the crowds kept our adrenalin high. The noise: so much cheering and whooping, and flags and placards everywhere, and people running alongside, and seas of smartphones turned upwards to us like sunflowers seeking the light as they filmed and filmed and filmed.

By the end of the trophy tour I was finished. Wherever we went we had to give the same energy every time, which was really exhausting. Don't get me wrong – it was an absolute privilege and I wouldn't have missed it for the world. But we were all very conscious that every new place we went to – and there were some we couldn't even reach as there was too much of a crush – was full of people for whom this was their one and only chance to see the trophy and see the squad, and we couldn't short-change them.

There was one moment which stood out above maybe everything else. When we went to Helpmekaar College in Joburg, one of the boys there passed up his boots for Cheslin to sign. The TV cameras focused in on him wiping tears away as I handed them back; this kid, 15 years old, with the school's brown cap on making him look like something out of Victorian London, looking up at us and overcome by it all. If you wanted one image to sum up what this tour was about, here it was.

A few weeks later, Rachel and I were due to go to the BrightRock Players Choice Awards, and we thought it would be nice if we asked this kid to come with us. So we put out the word on social media, and soon enough we had his name: Lebo Mogoma. It turned out that he and his mum had had a rough time one way or another – his dad had died only the previous year – so this really meant a lot to him. I asked him who his favourite player was, and he said it was me (I knew he was a kid of great taste) and Cheslin, because, like Cheslin, Lebo also played on the wing. Cheslin was due to get the Backline Player award that night, but he was back in France with his club Toulouse; so we FaceTimed him to give Lebo a chance to talk to his hero, and then Lebo went up to get the award on Cheslin's behalf. He was so thrilled and it was such a joy to help out in this way.

* * *

I knew our win wouldn't by itself solve anything. The day before the final, South Africa's economic outlook had been downgraded from stable to negative. We won the trophy on a day when, according to averages, 58 people would be murdered, 114 people raped, and 200,000 would go to bed without a roof over their head. People wouldn't stop murdering and raping just because we'd won a trophy. The World Cup wouldn't help all the problems with electricity loadshedding or water scarcity. It wouldn't provide food or shelter or money, or bring back people who'd been killed, or undo the violence against women who've been raped.

But for what it represented – a light in the darkness, a lightning rod for change, a platform for role models and future heroes – yes, our win could do good. It could start a revolution. It could change the world.

6

SOCIETY

The night before the World Cup Final, Rachel and I sat down in the lobby on our date night and made a list of everything we wanted to help change in South Africa. We were determined to tackle the big issues. We started to look at what it would take to make this possible, and we knew we had to get going immediately. I felt that my influence had increased and that I could use this to make a difference. It was great to be in the spotlight, but that wouldn't last forever. I might only have this influence for a limited time, and I needed to use it wisely.

There is one cause which moves me above all, and that's gender-based violence. People think of that being a problem only for a certain section of society, but it's not. It doesn't matter whether you're male or female, black or white, rich or poor. If you're a human being then this affects you. As the old quote goes, the only thing needed for evil to triumph is for good men to do nothing. If you say nothing then you're actually saying something. Silence is picking a side. Silence isn't by itself violence, but silence certainly enables violence. I used to be the quiet guy in the corner who never spoke out. I have been silent too long on things which matter too much. No longer.

I think, for example, of the women in Zwide who were beaten up every day when I was growing up. People ask now: well, why didn't the women say something? To which I say: like what? They couldn't fight back physically. They could have all got together and said that they weren't going to take it anymore, and while they were in a crowd out in the open of course no-one would have dared touch them; but then that night they'd have gone back to their homes and it would all have started again. And also why *should* the women have had to say something? It wasn't their fault.

When I think of gender-based violence, I think first of all of my mother. I have a picture of her looking young, beautiful and most of all unscarred; I never saw her look like that. Never. Because her face changed so much from different men beating her up. That breaks me, you know? When I was five, I remember playing in the street and picking up a couple of her teeth which a man had knocked out. She got robbed of her youth, to be her beautiful self like she was made. By the time she died, she had scars all over her face.

She was one of millions. Sexual violence is through the roof in our country. A woman is murdered every three hours in South Africa, a rate five times the global average. You arrive at a rugby match half an hour before kick-off and stay another half an hour afterwards having a drink with your mates; on average, one woman will have been killed in that time. Women like Tshegofatso Pule, who was found hanging in a field eight months pregnant with a stab wound to her chest, or Uyinene, or any number of others who are as anonymous in death as they were in life. More than 100 women are raped every day, and they're only the ones we know about, as most rapes and sexual assaults aren't reported. For all the desperate cries we hear, there are many, many more that we don't, many more whose suffering is silent but no less agonising for that.

This happens every day, and every day people say that it's awful, and every day it goes on just as before. Now and then a case captures the public attention and sparks protests, just as Uyinene's case did, and politicians speak in sombre tones about how the problem needs to be fixed, and after a while the focus fades, the news agenda moves on to something else, and any urgency towards reform is stalled.

The reality is that as a country and as men, we have demonstrated that instances of violence will not translate into the individual or collective will to stop this. Our problem is not a lack of awareness, and we cannot in good conscience say, 'We didn't know.' We've seen the very worst of violence perpetrated against women and it hasn't caused us to change. Women know this. Without political will, a change in the sensationalism and narratives around the reporting of gender-based violence, and men's greater involvement as allies with women when it comes to gender-based violence, nothing will change.

Various factors are blamed for these insanely high levels of violence: alcohol, drugs, poverty, police forces who don't take these cases seriously, inadequate laws, not enough women in government able to speak for and with other women and to focus on issues affecting women and girls. All these play a part in exacerbating the problem, but one of the deepest causes is the low status women have, and that in turn is down to men.

Men feel entitled to have sex with women as that's how they've always perceived the power relationship between the sexes to be. Polls show that the vast majority of South African men feel that women should obey their husbands; around half feel that a man can never rape his wife as he is always entitled to sex. Many men refer to domestic violence as 'fixing their homes'. This starts early, with the values we instil in our kids. Boys are taught to be tough, strong and unemotional, and this damages them in two ways. First, it prevents them from accessing their own weaknesses, meaning they don't know how to deal with emotionally anxious situations; and second, it sets them up in direct opposition to women, who behave in very different ways. Boys who don't assert their power over girls are shamed by other boys. Weaker girls are picked on because they don't resist; more assertive girls are seen as needing to be put in their place and taken down a peg or two. There's no way a woman, whoever she is, can win here.

Sexual abuse starts early and is a series of points on a scale rather than just one thing. At one end is women being demeaned, called names, objectified as sex objects; next comes sexual harassment and pestering; then sexual assault; then rape; then murder. Not every man goes all the way to the end of that chain, obviously, but no man who's killed a woman has started right at the deep end either. And with each step a man takes, the sense of entitlement towards taking the next step grows. The attack on women starts long before physical violence; it's in our conversations with our fellow men, how we treat women in our own lives, and how we treat and perceive women we don't know. And because so many men feel this and do this, it is socially acceptable, so other men don't call them out on it; indeed, they often positively encourage it.

It's men doing these things, but so far men have not faced the consequences, not really. People always ask, 'Why don't women leave abusive relationships?' but they never ask, 'Why don't men stop beating women up?' We talk about how many women were raped last year, but not how many men raped women. These aren't things which just happen and are done to women by some impersonal force. These are things which men do, and the way we talk about this issue needs to reflect that.

Only women have had to adjust their behaviour. Almost every woman has walked with her keys between her fingers, varied her route, made a fake phone call, arranged for a friend to call her at a certain time, doubled back on herself, pretended to dawdle by a shop window to let a man walking behind her pass, kept to well-lit streets at night as far as possible, been nice to a creepy guy in a bar in case he turns nasty, locked her car doors the moment she's inside the vehicle, asked a cab driver to drop her a little way from her front door, made efforts not to leave her drink unattended, texted friends to say she's home safely, worried in the small hours when a friend hasn't texted to say she's home safely, and so on. Almost every woman has wondered three words which speak a lifetime of fear – am I next?

Fire brigades use the word 'flashover' for the moment a fire in the room becomes a room on fire. Only when society reaches this point, and realises that here we have a problem which is burning us all to cinders, will things change. We as men, we need to first of all own up and say we don't want to be the problem. We want to learn, to listen, to use our voices.

Otherwise it's a vicious circle; it's what young men are exposed to, so it's what they do themselves, and that in turn exposes the next generation to it, and on it goes. We shouldn't demonise men just because they're men. In fact, to be feminist, whether as a male or a female, is to advocate against stereotyping based on gender, and part of that is to believe that men shouldn't be stereotyped as inherently violent. One needs to make a distinction between men and masculinity, with the latter being looked upon as conditioning, some of which – such as aggression – is culturally taught and can consciously be taught differently. To be feminist is to believe in the full humanity of men and dismantle the structures that encourage violence on the basis of gender. Violence is so normalised. I was shown how to put a condom on in sex education, but we never had anyone really teach us about violence against women and girls.

But as a man I've realised there's no way you can call yourself a man if you're lifting a hand to a woman. There's no way you can call yourself a man if you're putting a woman down by your words just to make yourself feel good. But there's not a lot of men standing up, and there needs to be. Especially us rugby players. We're seen as macho men, as hardcore men, and when we stand up and say, 'This is not right' it has a greater effect than from other men. And it's also very necessary that rugby players speak out, because let's be honest here: the male rugby dressing-room culture, along with male sport in general, has much to do to get their house in order when it comes to ingrained attitudes towards women.

Even though I've never hit a woman, I have degraded them. I was part of the problem. I used to go to strip clubs, I treated women badly, so in some ways who am I to speak? I feel guilty, but also I know I have to forgive myself. I can't let that guilt keep me quiet. You can't undo what was done in the past, but you can be responsible for what you do in the present and future. So now I'm learning new things, and I'm unlearning a lot of the old stuff I had learned in terms of how we treat women and even how we speak to women.

Now I choose to respect, protect, support and hear the women in and outside my environment. I haven't always got it right and I've messed up a lot of times, but I've chosen to be better. I try to show respect by doing my share of what has often been seen as women's work – cooking, cleaning, ironing, tidying. When I hear my friends say they're babysitting I reply: 'No, you're being a parent.' I put cooking videos on Instagram. It's not *MasterChef*. It's about encouraging other men to be more involved at home, to chip away at those strict gender roles which construct a mindset that leads to violence. Life has changed. We all have a responsibility. We as men, we're more than just bringing bread home. That's what the wives do these days too. That's what women are asking for in our country, just to be equal. So we have to be good men, and we have to have other good men holding us accountable for our actions.

Even on the field, the coach should say, look, this is not who we are. This is not how we treat women. I have to go around my circle of friends and take people on. I've got to tell them that they can't treat women this way because that is not what I'm about. I've got to make it clear that I can't be mates with anyone who treats women that way. It's easier to tell people you don't know what you think. It's a lot harder to take on people you know. It's always easier to walk on by. It's much easier not to do things. But even little things make a difference if enough people do them, and the only way they do them is if they see other people doing them. Without the women in my life, I wouldn't be where I am today. If I don't stand up and use my voice for women, I'll not only be letting down the women in South Africa, I'll be letting down the people who raised me, my grandmother and my aunt and my mother. All the stuff that I've seen, I don't want to let that go to waste, because it still drives me to make sure that another kid doesn't go through life witnessing their mum or their aunt being abused. I just don't want people to go through that kind of thing.

If we educate our sons, we won't have to protect our daughters, we won't have to teach them how to defend themselves. That's not what my son is learning, so why should my daughter learn how to protect herself? She should be learning how to play a sport or be a doctor. I'm talking about education at home as well as at school. Nobody told me that it was not right when I was younger. When as a boy I saw the abuse in my community and even in my own home, there was no-one around to say, 'This is fundamentally wrong.' I've been hard on my son Nicholas about this; almost too hard on him, perhaps, but I want him to realise how important this is. If every man does that to their sons and for their sons, we can feel safer about our daughters as a community.

We need to show our sons two things. First, that women are their equals and need to be respected and protected rather than attacked. Raising boys to be good men comes down to the smallest of things. It's about being super-mindful and respectful of women and girls in every single way when they interact with them. They've got to look at them, they've got to listen, they've got to speak to them respectfully. Second, we have to show our sons that it's not unmanly to show their feelings; that fear, disappointment and anxiety are totally normal, and that experiencing them doesn't make you less of a man. I try to show Nicholas both, not only in the way I treat Rachel around the house but also how I treat myself; letting him know it's okay to cry, it's okay to ask questions.

It's important for men to be vulnerable, to cry, to tell each other they love each other. I didn't get it when I was young, but I'm making up for lost time. I sat round a fire with my Stormers teammate Chris van Zyl one night. I'd known him for years, but it wasn't until that night that we'd spoken deeply and properly. Now I know what he stands for and he knows what I stand for. When you get to know someone beyond just being a teammate, you draw closer to them in every way. You know what drives that person, why they do what they do; and 'Why?' is always the most important question. In understanding these things, you also hold each other accountable for your actions and theirs.

It has to be men and not just women telling boys these things, and in turn that means that men have got to stick around and be good fathers to their children. Anyone can father a child, but bringing up that child properly is a very different matter. Fathering a child is biology, and too often in our country that comes with abuse too: a man who has sex with a woman because he can rather than because he cares for her and loves her, and when she has a baby he's not around to support her and help raise the child. Indeed, he's probably done exactly the same thing with several different women. And so his children grow up without a responsible father figure in their lives, and in turn they see that women are left alone to do the most important job in the world, raising the next generation, and they think it's okay, and when they grow up they do it too, and on it goes.

I'm proud to be a UN Global Advocate for the Spotlight Initiative aiming to eliminate all violence against women and girls. Women have suffered too much and too long. Let's be the generation of men to break this attack on women.

Transformation also needs to happen in more general terms. We talk about transformation a lot, but transformation has to begin in your heart: the way you see things, how you look at somebody, how you treat people. And this has to start at grassroots level. Kids need to see that these things are possible so they can dream; they need to be given chances and facilities. This is where true equality resides. Transformation is not really transformation if it takes the township to it rather than goes to the township. Kids shouldn't have to leave their community.

If you take the best people out of their communities then those communities don't grow. Role models have to be there and present every day, not just remote and on billboards or TV. If you take all those guys out of townships, who will kids look up to?

Transformation needs to be done at grassroots. Something like 90 per cent of all players in Springbok history have come from two dozen schools.

It's not just a rugby thing; it's about potential in any area of life. There are brain surgeons and rocket scientists and legal geniuses and rock stars and artists and a million others whose talents will never be known because they will never get a chance to develop them, or perhaps not be aware that they even exist. These are the things which need changing. True transformation means that the next Siya Kolisi is at school in Zwide and can compete equally against guys from Grey. If the next Siya still has to get a scholarship to go to Grey, and they transform him there, it's the same system. It's not transformation, it's assimilation.

Yes, I made it, but I only did so because I came through the system. Don't get me wrong; I'm grateful every day, literally every day, for the opportunities Grey gave me, and my friendship with Uncle Vincent, the philanthropist who gave me my chance, is one of the most precious things in my life. But a child shouldn't necessarily have to leave his own culture like I did.

When we set up the Kolisi Foundation, this was our aim: to change narratives of inequality in South Africa. Every act of change is important, no matter how small it is. We approached it with hearts willing to respond, hands ready to serve and heads ready to learn. The slogan for the foundation is 'Remember the One, One By One'. *Remember the one, one by one.* Focus on the one heart, and the one person, and the one life that you are changing. We carry that close to our hearts, as it reminds us that every person matters no matter their situation. We want to help those people in really desperate situations, but we also want to help those with problems that may not be as bad by comparison. The person whose life you touch touches the next person, and on it goes. It's like it says in the Talmud: 'He who saves a life saves the entire world.' We rise by lifting others.

We identified three drivers behind what we wanted to do. The first was being biased to action: showing up, starting somewhere, doing something, living better stories than we tell. The second was collaboration: building relationships and working alongside others to perform better together than we could alone, while adhering to the principles of *Ubuntu*, which recognises that we live in relationships of reciprocity and always need to respect other people. *Ubuntu* is a Zulu word and means 'I am because you are'. It's about lifting everyone up. My grandmother did it for me, I try to do it for other people. It's about treating everyone the same, no matter who they are. It's not about if you need something from them or if you're in a position of power over them. It was drummed into us at school: you get up when an older person enters the room, you show respect, you call the teachers 'sir' and 'ma'am'. And the third was learning: researching and developing best prac-tice in our projects, continually seeking to grow from our mistakes, interrogating the old stories we've been told and starting to tell more nuanced ones.

Before we started the foundation, I thought I knew as much about suffering in South Africa as most people. I know what hunger feels like, for example. I've fallen asleep to the sound of my stomach grumbling. I've seen my grandmother not know what to do except offer kind words and sugar water. If I hadn't made it in rugby, I'd have probably been one of those people receiving stuff from the foundation. But when the Covid-19 pandemic forced me onto the road and I saw how some people were living – man, it hurt. I went out to Limpopo to drop off some food and I was shocked to see people sharing drinking water with animals, kids using that water to wash in and women getting that water for cooking while carrying their baby on their back. One man we saw was so embarrassed at his house that to start with he wouldn't let us in, and when he eventually did I saw why: he had to lift the door off for us to come in, as there wasn't enough room inside to open the door into the room. An ordinary-sized door. Imagine living some-where that small. My heart was broken.

I went to the North West. I was pushing a wheelbarrow full of stuff through the township. There is absolutely nothing happening, and ultimately nothing for kids to enjoy or aspire to. It made me think, what are we doing as a nation? How are we letting this happen? And almost the worst thing was this: often when we went to help at soup kitchens or to drop off food at shelters, the people told us that they were grateful for the coronavirus, as this was the most help that they've ever received. Some of the people I brought food to in Zwide were the same people who'd given me food as a kid. One day, when we were delivering food to a house in Zwide, an old lady came out of the house to receive the food and stunned us with her words. Through her tears and sobs, we managed to hear: 'I never thought I would see this day. I remember you when you were just a kid coming around our houses and asking for food. I remember how we would give the little that we had when we could. Now we are the ones in need and here you are in person to give us food!'

But of course, in general coronavirus has only accentuated and accelerated these inequalities. It spread faster in high-density black settlements where people couldn't socially distance if they tried. It had a far greater effect on people's health there, as health standards were already much lower; what a healthy, well-nourished person can brush off as a few days' illness can be fatal for someone with respiratory issues, diabetes, hypertension, tuberculosis or of course HIV. Crowded and underfunded public hospitals in poor areas were over-whelmed far more quickly than those in richer areas. Schoolkids with internet connections could learn remotely far more easily and effectively than those without.

And that education gap has always been there to see, clear as day. You see it at kids' rugby tournaments, the differences between the teams from townships and those from richer, whiter suburbs. Everything's different. The pitches can be dustbowls or beautifully manicured grass, depending on where the matches are played. The richer teams have better kit and much more support from their parents, because they can afford to take a few hours off work to come and watch;

they're not working two or three jobs just to provide the minimum.

Among the many things the foundation is doing is building rugby fields, because I didn't have a proper one when I was young. We had ten teams and we all played in the same jerseys. After one team had played, you would take the sweaty jerseys off and give them to the next team to wear. I was only 12 then, but I said, one day when I make it I will buy each team jerseys. And now I have. I bought each team a pair of socks, shorts and jerseys with the school name and badge on it. It was amazing, one of my proudest moments. It means a lot to me, as I want to change the narratives for kids' lives in South Africa: to face all the challenges I faced as a kid and help improve the next generation. That's the kind of life I wish for other people in the township, by bringing good teachers and equipment into the township, to give the kids the motivation to wake up and study. I would love to make sure that the kids get the same opportunities as others, and that at school tournaments you can no longer tell who's from where by the quality of their kit or how much food they've brought along with them.

Even the best government in the world can't do everything; we all need to step up, private individuals and corporations alike. When I work with commercial partners, I insist that we offer something of social use. Panasonic, for example, donated more than 100,000 solar-powered lights to poor families living without electricity. OpenView were offering free access to satellite television for poorer communities, providing them not only with entertainment but education too. Kellogg's is feeding my old school, Emsengeni Primary, three times a day for the next five years. They're renovating the playing fields and bathrooms, providing a computer room and a library, and all to ensure that kids with talent for both sport and academia can shine. It's only one school in one township in one province, but imagine that rolled out across the nation. If we keep on pushing on the ground then something's got to give, things have got to happen – people will see that all these things can be done. And it's not an issue confined to South Africa. I look at what the soccer player Marcus Rashford is doing in the UK, forcing the government to extend the provision of free school meals. That's also a Roc Nation thing, the agency which represents Marcus and me among others – you have a voice, you have a platform, so use them.

My dream is for my foundation never to be needed again, and that will only happen through education. Education is the most important thing of all, as only education can open people's eyes to the possibility of a bigger role than simply making money for themselves. Only education can provide a community with sustainable ways to look after itself: to work the land, grow food, sell enough to earn what's needed and keep the rest to eat. Everyone has their aims and goals. It's not a case of be a Springbok or think you've failed. There are plenty of people who work as cashiers in stores and who aspire to move into management. Is that as spectacular as playing rugby in a World Cup Final? No. Is it as important? Yes, easily; more so, in some ways.

In a sense, I'm tired of being celebrated because I suffered and still managed to make it. The individual stories of people triumphing against the odds are inspiring, but it would be even more inspiring if one day those stories weren't so piquant as the odds would have been so greatly shortened. It's great to read these stories and feel moved, but that's not enough unless we look at the conditions which oblige the stories to happen in the first place. All these stories, mine included, are double-edged. On one hand, you don't have to remain in the same place all your life; on the other, it shouldn't only be exceptional talent and/or a huge slice of luck which help lift a child out of poverty. Sheer hard work and positive mindsets can't by themselves guarantee success, and failure to 'make it' isn't a reflection of some character flaw or weakness. Be inspired by those who defy the odds, sure, but also be angered and appalled by the fact that they had to face such odds in the first place.

So rectifying all these inequalities is what's most important to me. I want to be a better person off the pitch than I am a player on it. I know I'm not the world's best rugby player. I'll never be remembered as one of the greatest ever, and I'm fine with that. All I care about is what kind of person I am. What am I doing to make someone's life better? What am I doing to make sure the next Siya doesn't go through the same battles that I did? I must be accessible to people so they know my story. People forget steals and tries, but they don't forget these kind of things. These people who are our fans are often also people who need help, and if we can provide that in any way then it's on us to do so, and do so properly with deeds rather than words. Well said is good; well done is better.

It's a long road, and it won't be done in my lifetime. I don't see rugby as a job. I love doing what I do and I want to inspire as many people as I can, especially those from the same background as me. It's not about the pay cheque. I want to help people as much as I can. You have to know who you're doing it for and why you're doing it. Sports records will be broken, but these things endure. What did I do when I had the chance? What did I do when people listened?

That's my purpose in life, and I use rugby as a platform. It's vital that people are an example for younger kids; show them how you can make it in South Africa so they don't have to look elsewhere for role models, to the US or other countries. It's important not to lose hope. Once that happens, you're in trouble. I try to create hope for kids who are in hopeless situations. I want people who grew up the same way I did, or even worse, to know that it is possible. Someone like me has to create hope by giving back so that kids know there's someone they can relate to, who's been in the same situation as them, and who's fighting to make sure that they don't suffer like I did.

Because this is my fight. You fight until you inspire the next generation, and then they do the same for the generation after them. The more people you get, the more people you will get, and when enough people understand then the whole culture shifts. There'll always be a few who stand against progress and equality; don't give them your time or effort. You have to give your absolute best in everything you do, because you're trying to make a difference in someone else's life. You're going out there and having the hard conversations. You're trying to change people's minds about certain issues.

I believe passionately in South Africa. On any given day it can be both the best and the worst place on earth to live. We live life at a very intense pitch. Other places can seem boring by comparison. As I said at the very start of this book, we are a great people, and we are good people. I believe in a country, and a world, in which we root for each other rather than against each other, in which we celebrate each other's successes rather than rejoice in putting each other down. As Justice Malala wrote in the *Sunday Times* on 11 November 2019, not long after our World Cup triumph: 'In our South Africa we are generous and large-hearted, not mean and ugly in spirit. In our South Africa we love laughter and we lean towards it with our entire beings while, at the same time, rejecting the crippling negativity that many want us to live under. It is a beautiful if flawed country, our South Africa. At its best, it is the country of our dreams: aware of its brutal past, alive to its deeply unequal present, and hopeful for an equitable and just future. It is a country for and of those who know that our past can be vanquished by the choices we make in the present.'

Those choices have never been more critical; for there is no freedom until everyone is free, no safety till everyone is safe, and no equality until everyone is equal.

7

SOLIDARITY

On 23 January 2021, I played in the last-ever match at Newlands. It was a Currie Cup semi-final, we lost to the Sharks, and Covid-19 restrictions meant the stands were empty. In the 131 years since the first match played there, the place had played host and borne witness to some of the greatest moments and matches in the history of South African rugby. The fairytale ending for that last match would have been the Stormers scoring in the last minute to win the Super Rugby Final in front of a capacity crowd. But sport, like life, doesn't often do fairytales.

The Stormers and Western Province squads will move to Cape Town stadium in Green Point, which was built for the 2010 soccer World Cup. But I won't be going with them. That semi-final loss wasn't just the last game at Newlands; it was my last game for Province too, a team I'd been with since academy days. Province had been the team I wanted to play for even when I'd been a schoolboy; Province the only place I'd ever really imagined myself being at. I'd gone there straight from school and ended up playing 118 matches for them, second only to Schalk Burger. I have so many happy memories of the club that I'd hardly know where to begin listing them; not only the matches and the victories but the teammates, the coaches, the laughter, the camaraderie, the sense of togetherness. And the fans, of course; their non-stop cheering, positive chirps and uplifting tone had carried me through many a match.

I'd been there 11 years, but my gratitude for my experiences there will last a lifetime. I'd arrived as a boy, and departed as a man, and that transition would never have been possible without the people of Province who welcomed me in with open arms and wrapped them tightly around me and my loved ones ever since. The things I learned there stretch far beyond the rugby field. The decision to move was without doubt the hardest one I've ever taken. I agonised over it for months, turning it over and over in my head, one moment convinced that it was the right thing for me and my family, the next that it would be the biggest mistake of my life.

So why go? And why move to the Sharks rather than anywhere else, home or abroad?

There were three main reasons. First, I wanted a new challenge. My life has always been about challenges, and in professional terms I've never played more than two or three seasons without some sort of obvious progress: from Stormer to Springbok, from Springbok to starting player, from starting player to skipper, from skipper to world champion. I've always relished the chance to test myself in new roles, varied environments, taking on different responsibilities. A move to the Sharks gave me all that. There's no comfort zone when I move somewhere new. No matter who I am, what I've done and how experienced I am, I'm still the new kid on the block when I start.

Second, I want to win trophies, and the Sharks to me represent the best chance a South African franchise have of doing so. I've only ever won one trophy in my career. Sure, it's the biggest one of all, but that doesn't matter. Trophies are the lifeblood of professional sport, and each one a player wins is not just a cup but everything that goes in getting there. The cup is the destination, but the journey is just as important. Those memories are ones held between that player and his teammates, and they can never be taken away.

And finally, I wanted to stay in South Africa. There are plenty of guys who play abroad – the 23 who played in the 2019 World Cup Final included players who were then or are now based in England, France and Japan – but I never wanted to follow them. That's nothing against their decisions. But I feel very strongly that the captain of a national side should play his domestic rugby in that country, and also my foundation work means that I have to be based in South Africa.

On the day I arrived, the latest academy intake were being inducted. There's a four-sided monument just inside the entrance to King's Park, each side representing one of the cardinal directions, and the new recruits gathered here by the *isivivane*, the pile of stones which symbolises togetherness. They each carried a stone on which they'd written something important to them: a memory, a motivation, a mantra. In laying their stones on the pile, they committed not just to their own personal journey but to that of the collective too. Those stones represent struggles and dreams, hopes and fears.

I saw them, and remembered what it had been like to be that age and at that point in my career, just starting out, with the whole road ahead of me and a world of infinite possibilities. I hoped they'd see in me not just someone who'd walked their own road but was still doing so, still looking for the twists and turns in that road rather than just trudging straight on. I had things to learn, just as they did. There'd been speculation about me taking over the captaincy of the Sharks, but I never wanted that. Lukhanyo was doing a grand job as skipper, and I didn't feel it was my place to usurp that. It made no difference to me being Springbok captain; I could easily do one job without the other, just as Eben had when he'd led the green and gold while playing under my leadership at the Stormers. And in fact not being Sharks captain lets me play with a lot more freedom than would otherwise be the case. I can be a normal player, come in, train, do what I need to do, and then go home and see my family.

But over and above anything on the domestic rugby front loomed a once-in-a-lifetime challenge: the British and Irish Lions.

The last time the British & Irish Lions came to South Africa it was 2009 and I was in high school doing matric. The Lions tour was such a huge thing, and I'd never seen the like of it before; it was next level, in every way. Everyone was so excited to see them, there were crowds gathered wherever they went, and of course there were tens of thousands of British and Irish fans who'd come over to follow them round the country and who turned one side of every stadium into a sea of red. Springbok assistant coach Mzwandile Stick played for the Southern Kings against them in PE and was really struck by how quick and physical they were.

The preparation this time began months before their arrival. The analysts would send us clips and data downloads. This is where you were in the World Cup, they'd say, and this is where you are now. A long way off. A long, long way off. It was a big shock, but I was in the best place to do something about it. When I arrived in Durban, the staff said I wouldn't be playing any time soon; I'd just be doing strength and conditioning until I got to match fitness.

The city was hot and humid, the training brutal. Even early in the morning when we had our first training session the sweat bloomed thick and fast, and when you sucked in the air it felt like a wet towel. Sometimes my hands were so slick with perspiration that it was hard to grip the handle of a weighted sled or the edge of a tractor tyre. The work was hard, and the climate made it harder. I loved it. Early on there, they gave us a running session. I did the run and thought that was it; but no, it was just the first one, and there was another. The coaches said that if anyone failed to make the time on the second run then everyone would go again. I didn't know if I could do it, and I didn't want to let anyone down by finishing outside the cut-off. Fly-half Curwin Bosch just looked at me and said, 'You do not stop.' So I made it, and it almost finished me, but that was what I needed: going through the fire to get back to where I needed to be.

For a long time we didn't know what was happening with the Lions tour because of the Covid situation. One day the rumours were that the tour would be postponed a year, the next that we'd be playing in Europe or even Australia, and the day after that it would happen here as planned but behind closed doors. We didn't really care as long as we got to play. We were prepared to go anywhere. The coaches gave us the best preparation they could, but it was still hard to really get into the groove when there was so much uncertainty.

Eventually, it was confirmed that the tour would go ahead as planned, and we'd have a couple of warm-up matches against Georgia as well. We were all so excited to be back. Some of the guys who played overseas – Cheslin, Handre, Willie – I hadn't seen since the World Cup two years before. We couldn't hug each other when we met up because of Covid protocols, but it was just so good to see everyone. It was pretty much the same team as the one that had won the World Cup. Beast, Flo and Schalk Brits had retired, and Duane and RG were injured, but other than that we were all still there. But we hadn't played together since lifting the trophy, and we missed each other.

That sense of continuity extended to the atmosphere in camp, which wasn't much different to when Coach Rassie had been in charge. Jacques Nienaber, now Springbok head coach, had worked with him for so long that their mindsets were very much aligned and their styles so similar. It was very much evolution rather than revolution; we didn't need to get used to too many different ways of doing things. The biggest change from my point of view was that he wouldn't let me call him

Coach Jacques. 'Just Jacques,' he said. 'Imagine if I called you Player Siya.'

We were rusty against Georgia, but that was only to be expected. The important thing was the effort, and there was plenty of that. Georgia were tough opponents, really physical; they tackled hard and low, every man from 1 to 15, and they were challenging in the maul and the scrum too.

We were supposed to have a second match against them the following weekend, but a Covid outbreak put paid to that. From then on it was isolation, proper isolation. I was in a room on my own. Food was either brought to me, or I'd have to go down at a time when no-one else was there, get it and go back up to my room. I took a Covid test every day. We'd do fitness sessions on Zoom, using only what we had in the room: step-ups onto the bed, push-ups on the floor, using a chair as a makeshift weight and so on. It was frustrating to start with, but soon I realised that fighting it would only make it worse. It was what it was. I had to chill and accept it. Easier said than done, though, when I tested positive myself and had to go to another wing of the hotel. I didn't have much by way of symptoms – a runny nose one day, that was it – but that wasn't the point.

All in all, I spent 17 days in isolation. It was only a week before the first Test, with me having flown on a charter flight from Joburg and undergone heart and lung checks at hospital, that we all trained together for the first time. And it was then that we took a decision: we would accept no excuses. All the problems we had weren't reasons we might lose; they were things we needed to find solutions for.

Yes, our preparation had been severely disrupted. Yes, the Lions had played much more rugby than us; not only just recently, in their franchise matches here, but as part of their own national teams. Since the World Cup they'd had two full Six Nations tournaments plus the Autumn Nations Cup. We'd had that solitary Test against Georgia. And yes, the depth of the squad was going to be tested to show we could deal with the loss of some key players, like Duane. He's an amazing player, the best in the world in his position, and any team would miss him. He's got so much to his game. It's not just that he's so physical and skilled; his rugby brain is out of this world, he reads the game so well and he galvanises everyone around him.

But like we said: solutions, not excuses. We had to make the most of the preparation we'd had rather than worry about what we hadn't done. We couldn't control how the Lions were preparing, so there was no point stressing about that. And we had to fill the gap Duane left rather than moan about how irreplaceable he was.

There was talk of what would happen if I didn't pass the return-to-play protocols, or if Jacques decided I was too much of a gamble to risk after having had Covid. 'We're hoping to get good news,' said Coach Stick, 'but if not we've got great players in our squad and great leaders in our team. If Siya is not fit, we know we've got players who can do that job.' Like I always said, a captain doesn't do things by himself. I'd be nothing without the guys around me, and if someone else needed to step in they'd find the same support as I did.

A few days out from the first Test, it was confirmed that all three Tests would be played at Cape Town Stadium. 'The series has already been significantly disrupted by Covid-19,' said South Africa Rugby CEO Jurie Roux, 'and a return to Gauteng at this time would only increase the risks. We now have two teams in bio-secure environments without any positive cases or anyone in isolation. To now return to the Highveld would expose the series to renewed risk. Everyone wants to see the two squads, at their strongest, play out an unforgettable series over the next three weekends and this decision gives us the best opportunity to see that happen.'

Most people thought that staying in Cape Town would favour the Lions, as it meant they wouldn't have to deal with the problems of playing in the thin air of the Highveld. We were more used to that, so that was another potential advantage gone. But again, since there was nothing we could do about it, we didn't worry about it. If we started thinking that certain locations or stadiums favoured us, then we risked taking our focus away from the game in front of us. If it had grass, white lines and posts at either end, we'd play there.

Two years earlier in Japan we'd felt very much that we were playing to give our country hope. We felt just the same way about this series now. A third wave of Covid, this time the Delta variant, was ravaging our country, hundreds of people were being killed in political clashes and civil unrest, a third of the adult population were unemployed, electricity blackouts were happening ever more frequently, and every day brought new stories of suffering, of people losing jobs, livelihoods, family members, hope itself. It wasn't just that there were no crowds allowed in the stadium; it was that people weren't really allowed to gather anywhere. Braais, pubs, shebeens

– these are the places where South Africans gather to watch the Springboks, but even these were banned or only allowed under very restrictive conditions.

There were some who thought that in such circumstances playing rugby was frivolous, irrelevant, even insulting. We felt the opposite. We felt it was more important than ever. We had the privilege of still being able to play and the chance to make people forget about their problems, if only for 80 minutes. We couldn't solve the country's problems or make the situation better, but even if we could put a smile on people's faces for a short time, that was surely better than nothing. I've always wanted to change things for whoever I could. Even if in this case it might be only one or two people, that would be enough.

This was the biggest thing since the World Cup. Maybe even bigger, in some ways. For South Africa, the Lions series happens only every 12 years, and unlike a World Cup there'd be no easy games; it was going to be hammer and tongs from start to finish. Most of all, it's an honour for very few Springbok players, and even fewer Springbok captains, to win both a World Cup and a Lions series.

Sky Sports had a clip which they played before every Test: a few of us saying a line each, which really summed up what we felt and how much this meant to us. It started with Handre: 'In green and gold we represent something special.'

Pieter-Steph: 'Some of us start with nothing …'

Lukhanyo: '… in places you cannot imagine.'

Me: 'We feel the shadow of history …'

Mapimpi: '… but not its stain.'

Eben: 'Once in a rugby lifetime …'

Bongi: '… we face this challenge …'

Pieter-Steph: '… united together as one.'

Handre: 'We are the world champions.'

Me: 'We are the Springboks.'

The first Test is also Handre's 50th cap, so he comes out alone. Handre's been such a great player for South Africa, and he's such a great person, that he deserves 55,000 people standing for him and showing their appreciation. But there are no crowds permitted, and it's not the same without spectators. If any matches deserve a crowd, *need* a crowd, it's these ones: the passionate Springbok fans and the sea of red formed by tens of thousands of Lions fans, many of whom have saved up for years just to have this trip. Only the Lions can make the Boks at home feel almost like an away game for us.

'The roar that seems to come from the depths of the earth when a Springbok team runs on the field in South Africa?' said Gary Teichmann, who captained the Boks against the Lions in 1997. 'It's different to anything else I've ever heard. It's soulful, emotional, timeless. Leading the team out into that will stay in my memory so long as I draw breath.'

But we don't have that, so we'll have to work around it. We'll bring our own noise: upping the levels of communication, encouraging each other for 80 minutes, celebrating the small stuff. These are the things which will help bring us closer as a team.

I lead the rest of the team out after him, and go from man to man giving handclasps and hugs. When we line up for the anthems, I notice that below our identical jerseys and tracksuit bottoms we're wearing boots of varying colours, all of them bright and vibrant: a perfect metaphor for our rainbow nation.

There are only three minutes gone when Lukhanyo flies up out of the line and absolutely clatters Elliot Daly; the kind of hit which would have knocked the air from a crowd, let alone the player on the receiving end. It's the perfect way to show our intent.

With just over 20 minutes gone, Eben wins a lineout on the Lions 22. I break from the maul and make it to the five-metre line, but I'm isolated at the breakdown and Maro Itoje wins the turnover.

It's our half, not theirs; like a python, we're slowly squeezing the life out of them. Handre and Faf's territorial kicking game is pinpoint and intelligent, forcing the Lions deep and challenging them to get through the green wall. We're on top in the tight and loose alike, and if anything the 12–3 half-time scoreline doesn't quite reflect our dominance.

'Watch for the momentum shift,' Coach Rassie says in the shed. 'They'll get some steam up sometime, and when they do you have to ride it out and shut it down.'

As ever, the first score after the break will be crucial. If it's us then we can go a long way towards putting this to bed; if it's them then they're back in it.

It's them: lineout, driving maul, try from Luke Cowan-Dickie. It's the kind of try we've scored countless times, and it doesn't feel great to have it done to us. Dan Biggar converts, and what had been a comfortable gap is now only two points.

We strike back within two minutes, Lukhanyo kicking through and Willie touching down ... or at least we think we have. Referee Nic Berry's on-field decision is 'try', but it is then ruled out for offside. It was a desperately tight decision, but there's no point complaining. Sometimes those decisions go with you and sometimes they go against you, and you have to treat them just the same.

Four minutes later we score for real. The Lions are committing fewer men at rucks and daring us to go wide, so that's what we do. Mapimpi, hard up against the left touchline, kicks ahead. Pieter-Steph tries to gather, and the ball squirms off him for Faf to touch down. Again it goes upstairs, and when the replay shows that the ball went backwards off Pieter-Steph the try is awarded. Handre can't convert, and the gap is back to seven.

But the Lions are working their way back into the game. From the restart they go through the phases and win a penalty, which Biggar slots for 17–13. A few minutes later they do the same thing with the same result, and then on 63 minutes another penalty puts them ahead for the first time, 19–17.

The match is slipping away, and we can't get a grip on it. The more we try to get back into it, the more indisciplined we become. We only need a single penalty to be back in front, but we just can't get one, at least not within kicking distance; and then with two minutes to go Pieter-Steph strays offside at a maul and Owen Farrell, on as a replacement, knocks it through the poles for 22–17 and the match.

* * *

We knew there'd be a media backlash, and there was. Part of the criticism was levelled at the team for letting a winning position slip, but a fair proportion also came my way personally. People said that I wasn't assertive enough in dealing with the referee, and that I let the Lions skipper Alun Wyn Jones outmanoeuvre me by being more in Berry's face. This made me doubt myself a little, because as the captain I was representing not just my team but my country too, and I didn't want to let them down.

But equally I couldn't bring myself to be what I wasn't. I was brought up to show respect to my elders and to figures in authority, to have manners, to let the other person speak and listen to what they had to say. Whatever the referee said, that was the decision. If he told me to walk away then I walked away. No ifs, no buts. Being a referee is a tough job, and I didn't feel it was my place or my right to make it even tougher. So for me to go crazy, scream and shout and all that – no. That wouldn't have been me. If that made some people think I shouldn't be captain then fine, that was their opinion. But being true to myself and the values I hold, on the pitch and off, was more important.

I spoke to the senior players: Eben, Handre, Lukhanyo. We resolved that we had to be in control of the outcomes. We hadn't been that far off where we'd wanted to be in the match, and in the first half we'd been much the better team. We didn't need to panic or reinvent the wheel. There were certain areas we needed to look at specifically, such as our maul and the way parts of our aerial game had gone wrong in the second half – particularly catching high balls – but in general it was just a question of being that little bit quicker, sharper and more ruthless. And in training we were exactly that. The training sessions between the first and second Tests were some of the best I've ever been involved with: next-level stuff, so slick and committed.

Most of all, we knew we'd been here before. In the World Cup we'd lost the first game to New Zealand, which meant we'd needed to win all our other games. The first Test here was just the same. All that losing meant was that we'd have to win the last two matches. The second Test would be the same as a World Cup semi-final, and the third Test would be the same as the World Cup Final. That was how we looked at it.

A video of Coach Rassie pointing out what he felt were marginal decisions appeared online. He wanted clarity in certain areas, as any director of rugby would. Dialogue between coaches, players and referees is not unusual; referees, coaches and captains usually meet the day before a Test match to discuss anything that needs clarifying, and this kind of post-match video feedback is pretty commonplace. The only thing different about this video was that it had gone online and into the public domain.

Coach Rassie said he'd personally take the heat if need be. 'If this causes that I'm not allowed to be water carrier that's fine, I'll step away. If we're going to get a fine, I'll step away from the management team. If this means the Springboks will get in trouble I'll say I did this personally, because I believe in fairness, the system and two teams having an equal chance of competing in a match.'

The pressure was mounting all week. I tried to tune it out and stick to my routine, reading my Bible and doing my devotions, but some things still got through. If we lost this one, we were done.

On the Friday, just before I was due to do a press conference, I did a quick interview with World Rugby reporter Elma Smit. She asked me what advice I'd give a nine-year-old Siya, and I'd hardly started answering when I began to cry so hard that I couldn't finish what I was saying. It wasn't even that particular question which set me off; I'd been asked far harder or more personal ones. It was just that the pressure had suddenly got too much and I needed to release it.

Handre came up to me. 'Chill, bro,' he said. 'We're good. Relax.'

I found solace in seeing my family, which brought peace to my heart. With them, I could zone in to a place of pure joy and unconditional love. My kids didn't care who was saying what about our performance or my captaincy. They just wanted to hang out with their dad.

The second Test is Kitsie's 50th, so like Handre last week he goes out alone ahead of the rest of us. I walk through the human tunnel of our squad members and staff, slapping hands and keeping myself loose. Today, like all days, is in God's hands. As I run out onto the pitch I yell up at the empty stands, part primal roar before a battle, part the sheer joy of being able to play this game.

We have to stand up for ourselves, not hide away, and within two minutes we're doing just that. Alun Wyn Jones takes exception to Mapimpi's positioning in a ruck and clears him out, and instantly players from both sides pile into the melee.

Eben's at the heart of it, of course, going head to head with Alun Wyn, both of them in each other's faces and smiling like this is no big deal. No backward steps, not today.

Pieter-Steph lasts only 20 minutes before being replaced; he hasn't looked fully fit. It's a big blow, as he's so important to our all-round game, but again we can't afford to dwell on it. Solutions, not excuses. I concentrate on my own game, the only thing I can affect, and I'm feeling good today: making my tackles, hitting my rucks, carrying well into contact. Some days I just feel on it, and this is one of them.

Duhan van der Merwe trips Cheslin and is sent to the bin. A few minutes later Cheslin takes out Conor Murray in the air, sparking another melee full of pushing, shoving and collar-grabbing; Tom Curry and Cheslin go at each other first, with Eben squaring up to Maro Itoje and Willie to Stuart Hogg. It's on a knife edge, as you'd expect. We're fighting to keep the series alive; they're fighting to kill it off. By the end of the match one of us will be disappointed, and I'm determined it won't be us.

Cheslin is also given a yellow. Referee Ben O'Keeffe calls Alun Wyn and me over. 'We've got a yellow card for both teams now. I'm very happy to keep going with yellow cards or even further, so I need you both to control your teams.'

There are a lot of breaks while the TMO is consulted on various things. We don't let it disrupt our rhythm; quite the opposite. We keep ourselves focused on the game plan and the next task. Just as we did in Japan, we use the breaks to our advantage: go hard between the whistles, and take as much recuperation as we can when the ball's not in play.

It's 6–6 as we approach half-time. We can't let them score a try now; seven points just before the break are psychologically huge, and if the Lions get something here when we've done so well in containing them then it'll give them a big boost as they go into the shed. The Lions are on our five-metre line with a free play from a penalty. Murray lifts a deft little kick up near the posts for Robbie Henshaw.

No. No way. He can't score.

Three of us are on Henshaw as he jumps, gathers and tries to touch down. Lukhanyo is low on him, with Damian one side and me the other. I reach round Henshaw's body and get my arm under the ball. I can't let him ground it, or it's a try. We clatter to the deck in a heap, all four of us, and all I care about is keeping my arm there. If I can feel the ball against my arm, then he can't have grounded it.

The Lions reckon they've scored. I don't think they have. It goes to the TMO. They look at the angles again and again. No grounding. We've held him up. The Lions go back for the penalty, which Biggar slots, so it's 9–6 to them at half-time, but given the balance of play so far I'll take that.

Last week we dominated the first half and they dominated after that, winning the second forty by 19 points to 5. Today they've had the upper hand for the opening forty, but still the scores are level.

Momentum. It's all about momentum. We have to do to them what they did to us last week: come out and blow them away in the second half. Forty minutes to save the series. We've waited 12 years for this, and will have to wait another 12 once it's done. This is my only shot at playing the Lions. I have to make the most of it. We have the hunger and the passion, and we want to win not just the game but every single facet of it too: out-scrum them, out-ruck them, out-maul them, out-tackle them, out-kick them and out-run them.

Five minutes into the second half we draw blood, and it's a typical piece of Handre genius. We're going right to left, and he's shaping to pass when he sees the Lions defence slightly misaligned; so in the blink of an eye he checks the pass and kicks instead, a perfect chip for Mapimpi to collect on the angle, cut through Hogg and touch down. That's 11–9 to us, and 17 minutes later we score another one: a monster rolling maul crabbing on the diagonal from their 22 to the five-metre line, Faf breaking and sending the grubber through for Lukhanyo to touch down just inside the dead ball line. Again it goes to the TMO and, as he had downward pressure on the ball with his forearm, the try stands. Handre converts to make it 18–9, more than one score ahead.

The Lions keep fighting, but we're in control now. Handre kicks three more penalties, and each of them knocks a little bit more stuffing out of the opposition. It ends 27–9, and the second half has been a shutout with 21 to us and none to them. That's what Coach Rassie meant about momentum.

'It's been a week and a half,' I told the press. 'The toughest week I've ever faced, with everything happening. We made a lot of mistakes last week, and we put all our focus into controlling what we could in this game. The pressure was huge, even more than the World Cup – for me, I handle pressure by praying, reading, spending time with my family. You can't control everything, but we can on the field. Lineouts, scrums, not giving away penalties, and just going all out for it.'

The only important thing was that we'd taken the series to a decider. Another huge final, two years after the last one. Winner takes all.

The build-up to the third Test was both the same and different. The same was our training, our recovery and our physical prep; the difference was my mindset. I was trying to get myself to the same place as I'd been before the second Test, but I just couldn't do it. I couldn't summon up that anger again, and I didn't know why.

Jacques did. 'You're in a different place now. That's why it's not coming to you.'

'Then how do I get it to come?'

'You don't.'

'I don't?'

'No. It came because you needed it. Now you need something else.'

Cheslin said the same thing. Every game is different, so every preparation has to be different. It's not a one size fits all. So I did the only thing I could do: focused on my processes and gave myself to God.

The third Test is Damian's 50th, so this time he goes out alone. To have three players reach the mark in three successive Tests shows how long this squad's been together and how much experience we have. It's that togetherness, that solidarity, that won us the World Cup; it's that solidarity that will win us this series, I'm sure of it.

The Lions have made a few changes to their team to counter our physicality. Dan Biggar goes off injured early and is replaced by Finn Russell, who has himself only recently come back to full fitness. Russell instantly starts to cause us the kind of problems we haven't yet faced: he plays very flat, right up in traffic, and likes to use the support runners on his inside shoulder with little pop passes back against the direction of play, forcing us to readjust.

They had the better of the first half last week, and the same is true here, only more so. Ken Owens dots down after a rolling maul from the lineout, and the Lions could easily have scored two more, but Curry loses his bind when another rolling maul is only a few metres from our line, and Liam Williams hangs on and takes the contact when he might have released Josh Adams outside him to race for the corner. But this is what happens in top-quality Test matches: players have to make split-second decisions under intense pressure, and what looks easy from up in the stands or on TV is very different at pitch level.

It's 10–6 to the Lions as we approach half-time. I think back to how determined I was not to let them score at the same stage last week, and it's just as vital now. They have a scrum near our line, and Ali Price picks and goes. I'm on him in a flash, and when he doesn't release we have the penalty and can clear our lines.

I've heard some former Lions players say that when the Springboks' Plan A doesn't work, we switch to Plan A. It's funny, but it's also true. We keep doing the same thing over and again, and eventually it comes good.

And it does this time too. With 55 minutes gone, Willie has space on the right with Cheslin outside him. Willie draws his man and pops the pass to Cheslin. Cheslin still has work to do, but this is Cheslin; he could find space in a telephone box. He breaks Williams's tackle, hands off Cowan-Dickie and touches down. It was no more than a half-chance, but when it comes to taking those there's no-one better than Cheslin. He's absolutely ruthless.

That's 13–10. Russell gets it back to 13–13. Morne comes on for Handre, and almost immediately kicks a penalty for 16–13. With six minutes to go Russell levels again: 16–16. Scores level, games level. Almost four hours played over the series and we can't yet be split.

There are just two minutes left when the Lions are pinged for not moving away.

Morne lines up the kick. Twelve years ago he won the 2009 series with a monster kick at Loftus. This isn't as hard, but there's the pressure of the whole series being on the line. I don't know how men like him and Handre do it, I really don't. Morne hasn't played for the Boks for five years, and when Jacques brought him back into the squad there were plenty of raised eyebrows from press and public. And now here he is, placing the ball on the kicking tee; taking his time, going through his routine.

No way. It can't happen again, surely?

He nails it like it's a training kick.

In 2009, when Morne had kicked the winning penalty, Heinrich Brussow was standing behind him. Now I'm standing behind him, and like Heinrich I'm wearing number six. Maybe in 2033 a 49-year-old Morne will come out for the last few minutes to nail the decisive kick again with the number six behind him.

We have to be careful; there's still time for the Lions to come back. They have a scrum as the clock goes red, so they have to keep it alive – but the scrum goes down, referee Mathieu Raynal penalises them for collapsing it, and it's all over. I scream with joy and jump first on Morne and then on Malcolm.

Because of Covid, I have to hand the medals out myself. It's unexpectedly special, to have a brief moment with each of the guys in turn. The medals I put round each man's neck don't just reflect us winning two out of three Test matches; they reflect the whole journey which has led us to this place, the trust in each other and the solidarity of a team that does not accept defeat. I want to be inspirational and aspirational; not just me, but the whole team. I want people to be inspired by our performance, but also to aspire to the values we've tried to show, to choose to respond to setbacks by being better.

The respective squad bubbles and all the restrictions mean that we don't really get to chat to the Lions players all that much. It would be nice to sit around and chew the fat with them a bit more. There's a lovely picture of the Lions team that went to New Zealand four years ago mingling with the All Blacks after their final Test there: a joint team photo but with no order to it, just 46 okes sitting together chatting. We don't get the chance to have anything like that, and it's a shame.

I'm asked after the match what I'd say to kids watching. 'Without this team, I wouldn't be where I am,' I reply. 'To someone who comes from a similar situation, you've got to protect your dreams. Believe in them no matter what your circumstances are.'

It's what I believe and will always believe with all my heart. It doesn't matter what your talent is; if you believe, work hard and grab opportunities and resources that come your way, you can rise, and you will rise.

EPILOGUE

EPILOGUE

In terms of my life as a rugby player, I know I don't have that much time left. I want to go to the next World Cup in 2023, of course. Only one team has ever retained the trophy, New Zealand in 2011 and 2015, and Richie McCaw, who captained those sides, is the only man to have won two trophies as captain. It would be an honour beyond description if we, and I, could do the same. It will be incredibly hard, of course – winning it once is difficult enough – but every player will give their heart and soul in trying to make it happen.

I'll be 32 by then, and can't see myself playing beyond that, certainly not internationally. The burden on my body would be too great. And in any case, rugby is only a short and temporary part of my life. Professional sportsmen and women are unusual in needing to seek new careers at a time in life when many people have established themselves in their own chosen paths, but I've already started to make the transition. As Coach Robbie said to me at my wedding: 'Whatever you do on the field, you've got far bigger things to do off it.'

Rugby's my job, but it's not my calling. The job will be over soon enough, as it is for every professional player, but that will leave me a lot of life left, God willing, and most of all I see myself as a child of God. I find my value in what Christ thinks about me. I've stopped caring about what others think of me or placing value on those opinions. Walking alongside a spiritual mentor, I've been able to discover the truth and saving power of Christ in a whole new way. This new life has given me a peace in my heart I'd never experienced before. As Philippians 4:13 says: 'I can do all things through Christ who strengthens me.' Now that I have given everything to God, nothing else affects me. I now live and play with the freedom of knowing His plan will always happen, and at the end of the day, that's all I care about. I don't have to understand everything in life, and there are so many things I don't, but I know God is in control of it all. My job is to do the best I can and leave the rest in His hands.

I'm still human. I have my moments. I maybe don't say the right thing or do the right thing, or I don't act in the right way. But we all make mistakes, and thank goodness God makes room for that. I love the wisdom of 1 Corinthians 13: 'Love is patient, love is kind. It does not envy, it does not boast, it is not proud. It is not rude, it is not self-seeking, it is not easily angered, it keeps no record of wrongs.'

But I still have to make the decision to follow the good path every day. Jesus doesn't make the decisions for you; He just shows you the choices. And every day I walk that path, my life changes a little more. I've lost a lot of people from my life, not all at once and usually not in some blaze of argument or rancour; they've just slowly faded away. They're not bad people, most of them, not at all. They're just not right for me anymore, nor me for them; the ones who were there in the party days but weren't interested in any more than a superficial friendship, the ones who only wanted to know me because they thought they could get something from me.

My most important role now is as a husband and father. I've been helped in learning how to be a dad through true faith, the love of my wife, and seeking help from outside organisations such as The World Needs A Father, which describes itself as being 'about training communities of men to understand the value of their roles as fathers, and giving them the tools to train other men around them, so that as heaven splashes down in their home, the ripples flow through their community'.

They speak of trying to bring about five main culture shifts which align very much with the spiritual journey Ben has put me on: from a personal orientation to a divine one, from worldly values to morally superior values, from individualism to communal thinking, from self-love to self-sacrificial love, and from reactive parenting to empowering parenting. When I went to their workshops in Stellenbosch, at first people there looked at me like, 'Oh the rugby guy's here,' but they soon saw that I was just like them – a man who wanted to do better in life, to learn from his mistakes, and who wasn't too proud to ask for help. Everyone there had things to discover and wounds to heal from their own childhoods, wounds which were preventing them from being as good at parenting as they could have been: feeling threatened by a child's bad behaviour, losing their temper, that kind of thing. They emphasised that discipline was something to do *with* your child, not *to* them.

I never had that when I was growing up. Discipline was done to me, and with a constant, permanent sheen of violence and aggression which hung over every day. Over the years I've seen so much bad stuff that my heart ended up totally numb. It still affects me in lots of ways. I don't like being shouted at, for example. If you shout at me, I'll just block you out and ignore you (though luckily it doesn't affect me on a rugby pitch, perhaps because that's where I expect violence and shouting to a certain degree. I don't have any problems controlling myself on a rugby pitch, and I've only had one yellow card in my entire career).

For a long time, I'd never talk about any of this; I'd just say sorry and act like it had never happened. Only recently have I started seeing a therapist to try and sort things out in my head, and to become more comfortable in speaking about my feelings and sharing what's on my mind. A real man owns up to his problems rather than pretending they don't exist, and this is doubly important as a father.

It's a long road I have to walk. I don't know where the road is going or if I'll get there, but I do know that walking the road is itself an act of faith and love. It encompasses everything I hope to achieve to make the world a better place. My life beyond rugby will be, I hope, much longer, more purposeful and more meaningful than my life in rugby has been. I have journeyed from Zwide to Yokohama; but the road ahead is the one that will really make a difference.

PERSONAL
STATEMENT

CORE VALUES

1. SPEND TIME WITH GOD

Description: Because I really value my relationship with God as central and core to my life, I want to remain close to Him in prayer and listening to His Word spoken over my life in my inner room. Intimacy and connection are my desire here.

Observable behaviour: Minimum 30 min a day read my Bible; listen to worship music; spend time in prayer.

2. MY MARRIAGE

Description: The most important person in my life, she is the one who will be with me to achieve all that God has in store for us, and she will keep me accountable.

Observable behaviour: One date night a week when I'm in SA; FaceTime calls every day when I'm away; cook once a week with her for the family; read and pray with her; just love her.

3. FATHERHOOD

Description: Want to confirm their identity in Christ, want them to feel unfailing love and support.

Observable behaviour: Show them what love looks like by how I love my wife; be present when I'm with them (put my phone away); prioritise them over work or anything else; they must see and know whose authority we are under (Jesus).

4. COMMUNITY

Description: If we have strong communities which can build income and educational opportunities that can be maintained for generations, we will have a powerful nation.

Observable behaviour: Developing schools; developing sporting facilities; bringing businesses in to educate people on how to run and maintain businesses; starting educational programmes.

5. IMPACTING PEOPLE

Description: I believe God's works will be carried and accomplished by people, so it is important we invest in people.

Observable behaviour: Want to show people what God can do in your life; people should not think twice who I worship when they look at me; give a different option or happiness than a night out; invest in people like my mentors do in me.

MY LIFE MISSION
(my goals for the next 5–7 years)

Problem #1: My career is not ordinary, meaning the span is limited.

Solution: To maximise this opportunity to build financial security for my family that will last us for generations. I'll do this by working hard on and off the field with sponsors and business opportunities.

Problem #2: Disadvantaged and poor communities need hope and inspiration.

Solution: Build one community which can produce products that can bring income and can be passed down to generations to come. They can start teaching other communities.

Problem #3: No South African captain has won the World Cup back to back.

Solution: If it's in God's will to win the World Cup again. Work as hard as I can with God to achieve this. Looking after my body and leading through Christ like before.

ACKNOWLEDGEMENTS

I, Siyamthanda Kolisi, am not a self-made man. I'm a mosaic of the stories of many communities and individuals that have showed me goodwill. Although it's not possible to name all the people that have played a role in who I've become and who I'm becoming, I'd like to mention my Zwide community, Heather Craemer, Hannah Sadiki, Vincent Mai, Eric Songwiqi Mawawa, Tamsanqa Ncwana, Hilton Houghton, Kendra Houghton, Andrew Hayidakis, Emsegeni, Grey High, African Bombers, Eastern Province Rugby, Western Province Rugby, Sharks … and many many more. Thank you.